DUE

CHURCH AND SOCIETY
IN LATE BYZANTIUM

Medieval Institute Publications is a program of
The Medieval Institute, College of Arts and Sciences

 WESTERN MICHIGAN UNIVERSITY

Church and Society in Late Byzantium

Edited by
Dimiter G. Angelov

Studies in Medieval Culture XLIX

Medieval Institute Publications
Western Michigan University
Kalamazoo

Library of Congress Cataloging-in-Publication Data

Church and society in late Byzantium / edited by Dimiter G. Angelov.
   p. cm. -- (Studies in medieval culture ; 56)
 Includes index.
 ISBN 978-1-58044-142-1 (clothbound : alk. paper) -- ISBN
978-1-58044-143-8 (paperbound : alk. paper)
 1. Byzantine Empire--Church history. 2. Christianity and
culture--Byzantine Empire. 3. Church history--Middle Ages, 600-1500. 4.
Byzantine Empire--Civilization. 5. Byzantine
Empire--History--1081-1453. I. Angelov, Dimiter G.
 BX300.C48 2009
 274.95'05--dc22

                              2009000589

      Printed in the United States of America
      1 2 3 4 5 C P 5 4 3 2 1

In memory of

Angeliki E. Laiou

Contents

Abbreviations

BAR	*L'Eucologio Barberini gr. 336*, ed. Stefano Parenti and Elena Velkovska (Rome: C.L.V.-Edizioni Liturgiche, 1995)
BNJ	*Byzantinisch-neugriechische Jahrbücher*
BZ	*Byzantinische Zeitschrift*
Chilandar I	*Actes de Chilandar*, vol. 1, *Des origines à 1319*, ed. Mirjana Živojinović, Vassiliki Kravari, and Christophe Giros (Paris: Lethielleux, 1998)
DMI	Aleksei Dmitrievskii, *Opisanie liturgicheskikh rukopisei khraniashchikhsia v bibliotekakh pravoslavnogo Vostoka*, vol. 2, *Euchologia* (Kiev: Tip. Universiteta sv. Vladimira, 1901; repr. Hildesheim: Olms, 1965)
Docheiariou	*Actes de Docheiariou*, ed. Nicolas Oikonomidès (Paris: Lethielleux, 1984)
DOP	*Dumbarton Oaks Papers*
EEBS	Ἐπετηρὶς Ἑταιρείας Βυζαντινῶν Σπουδῶν
Esphigménou	*Actes d'Esphigménou*, ed. Jacques Lefort (Paris: Lethielleux, 1973)
GOA	*Euchologion sive Rituale Graecorum*, ed. Jacques Goar (Venice, 1730; repr. Graz: Akademische Druck- und Verlagsanstalt, 1960)
IRAIK	*Izvestiia Russkago Arkheologicheskago Instituta v Konstantinopole*

Iviron IV	*Actes d'Iviron*, vol. 4, *De 1328 au début du XVIe siècle*, ed. Jacques Lefort, et al. (Paris: Lethielleux, 1995)
JGR	*Jus Graecoromanum*, ed. Ioannes and Panagiotes Zepos, 8 vols. (Athens: Phexes, 1931; repr. Aalen: Scientia, 1962)
JÖB	*Jahrbuch der Österreichischen Byzantinistik* (until 1968 issued as *Jahrbuch der Österreichischen byzantinischen Gesellschaft*)
Lavra I	*Actes de Lavra*, vol. 1, *Des origines à 1204*, ed. Paul Lemerle et al. (Paris: Lethielleux, 1970)
Lavra II	*Actes de Lavra*, vol. 2, *De 1204 à 1328*, ed. Paul Lemerle et al. (Paris: Lethielleux, 1977)
Lavra III	*Actes de Lavra*, vol. 3, *De 1329 à 1500*, ed. Paul Lemerle et al. (Paris: Lethielleux, 1979)
Lavra IV	*Actes de Lavra*, vol. 4, *Etudes historiques—Actes serbes—Complements et index*, ed. Paul Lemerle et al. (Paris: Lethielleux, 1982)
LIN	Amnon Linder, *Raising Arms: Liturgy in the Struggle to Liberate Jerusalem in the Late Middle Ages*, Cultural Encounters in Late Antiquity and the Middle Ages 2 (Turnhout: Brepols, 2003)
Miklosich-Müller	*Acta et diplomata graeca medii aevi sacra et profana*, ed. Franz Miklosich and Joseph Müller, 6 vols. (Vienna: Gerold, 1860–90)
MOG	*Potrebnik (Trebnik) Metropolita Petra Mogily* (Kiev, 1646; repr. Kiev, 1996)
OCP	*Orientalia Christiana Periodica*
PAL	*Τοῦ ἐν ἁγίοις πατρὸς ἡμῶν Γρηγορίου ἀρχιεπισκόπου Θεσσαλονίκης τοῦ Παλαμᾶ ὁμιλίαι κβ΄*, ed. Sophokles Oikonomos (Athens: Karampines and Vaphas, 1861)
PG	*Patrologiae cursus completus [. . .] series graeca*, ed. J. P. Migne, 161 vols. (Paris: Migne, 1857–66)
PLP	*Prosopographisches Lexikon der Palaiologenzeit*, ed. Erich Trapp, 12 vols. (Vienna: Verlag der Österreichischen Akademie der Wissenschaften, 1976–96)

REB	*Revue des études byzantines*
Rhalles-Potles	Σύνταγμα τῶν θείων καὶ ἱερῶν κανόνων, ed. Georgios Rhalles and Michael Potles, 6 vols. (Athens: typ. G. Chartophylakos, 1852–59)
Vatopédi I	*Actes de Vatopédi*, vol. 1, *Des origines à 1329*, ed. Jacques Bompaire et al. (Paris: Lethielleux, 2001)
Vatopédi II	*Actes de Vatopédi*, vol. 2, *De 1330 à 1376*, ed. Jacques Lefort et al. (Paris: Lethielleux, 2006)
VV	*Vizantiiskii Vremennik*
Xénophon	*Actes de Xénophon*, ed. Denise Papachryssanthou (Paris: Lethielleux, 1986)
ZER	Εὐχολόγιον τὸ μέγα, ed. Spyridon Zervos (Venice, 1862; repr. Athens: Aster, 1980)
ZRVI	*Zbornik radova Vizantološkog Instituta*

Introduction

DIMITER G. ANGELOV

Scholars have long noted that the power and prestige of the Byzantine church were steadily rising in the period of the late empire (1204–1453).[1] The tendency was complex, multifaceted, and sometimes ambivalent. The papers in this volume, presented at the Thirty-ninth and Fortieth International Congresses on Medieval Studies in Kalamazoo, aim to shed light on various aspects of the church's role in late Byzantine society and especially on its relationship with the lay world and the response of individuals to the challenges faced by Orthodoxy. The papers approach the issues of interest from a variety of different angles. The following remarks aim to set the general historical framework, highlight well-known and prominent signs of the church's rising authority, and draw together some of the discussion in individual articles in this volume.

The conquest of Constantinople in 1204 by the armies of the Fourth Crusade ushered in a new period in the history of Byzantium. A Latin empire of Constantinople was established, and large areas of continental Greece as well as the Aegean and Ionian islands fell under the dominion of the Frankish crusaders and the Venetians. Of the three Greek successor states that laid claim to be legitimate heirs to the Byzantine imperial tradition (the states of Nicaea, Trebizond, and Epiros), Nicaea in western Asia Minor proved most successful. In the course of first half of the thirteenth century the Nicaean emperors expanded their domain into the Balkans, in particular Thrace and Macedonia, and in 1261 recaptured Latin-held Constantinople. The hopes for complete reconquest proved illusionary, however. The revived empire after 1261, which was governed by the emperors of the Palaiologan dynasty, never managed to bring together the disparate pieces of the once united Byzantine world, which remained under

1

the rule of rival Greek principalities, Latin powers, and the kingdoms of the Bulgarians and the Serbs. By the early 1300s the Turkish conquests transformed Byzantium into an almost exclusively Balkan state. Late Byzantium was destined to remain much smaller and less resourceful than the empire of previous centuries, and it was fragmented and largely ethnically homogenous.

The church emerged in the post-1204 period as an institution with an enhanced role and authority in society. The patriarchate of Constantinople—reconstituted in exile in Nicaea in 1208 and restored to its traditional seat in the old imperial capital in 1261—held spiritual authority over a larger Christian flock than the tax-paying subjects of any Nicaean or Palaiologan emperor. It was not uncommon for patriarchs of Constantinople to deal with matters of religious practice and church administration in areas well beyond the boundaries of the empire. An uncompromising guardian of Orthodox faith, the late Byzantine church progressively gained in moral ground vis-à-vis imperial authority. Already the Nicaean emperor John III Vatatzes (1221–54) contemplated the possibility of union with the papacy in exchange for political concessions from the West. Emperor Michael VIII Palaiologos (1259–82) used the Nicaean precedent as a model for his own Union of Lyons (1274).[2] Both John III and Michael VIII, however, had to face the stiff, and in the end insurmountable, opposition of churchmen and of a strong anti-Latin public opinion mindful of the events in 1204. The thirteenth century, thus, sowed the seeds of a societal division in Byzantium (especially prominent in the second half of the fourteenth and the first half of the fifteenth centuries) between a political and intellectual elite ready to compromise with the Roman church and even adopt Catholicism, on the one hand, and a popular anti-Latin party supported by most Byzantine churchmen, on the other.[3] The two civil wars (1321–28 and 1341–47) and the concomitant struggles among the Byzantine ruling elite further increased the moral prestige of the church.[4] Armed with mystical theology of Hesychasm, the church was seen as a force of stability at a time of fratricidal internal strife and Turkish incursions.[5]

The judicial powers, institutional strength, and ideological claims of the church were all in the ascendant in the late Byzantine period. The activity of the ecclesiastical courts was, of course, no novelty in itself. A law of Emperor Constantine I (324–37), Byzantium's founding father, confirmed by subsequent legislation permitted plaintiffs in municipal law courts to transfer their disputes to episcopal ones, provided both parties agree to the change of forum.[6] The judicial prerogatives of the episcopal law courts traditionally pertained to matters of asylum, emancipation of slaves, and the advocacy of the rights of the poor and the weak members of society. Yet, as it has been argued, the episcopal courts in late antiquity were engaged mostly in judicial arbitration rather than litigation; the bishop's judgment was based on common sense, customs, and the tenets of Christian religion rather than legal expertise.[7] In the middle Byzantine period, the scope of judicial activity of the church expanded into a new and largely uncharted territory: that of marriage. The chief reason lay in the further Christianization of marriage and in the church's acquisition of an exclusive right to sanction this important social institution. Emperor Leo VI (886–912) legislated that only those marriages which were carried out in the church were to be recognized by public authority.[8] This paved the road to the church's assumption of an exclusive judicial responsibility in matters pertaining to marriage. By the early thirteenth century, we see ecclesiastical courts being involved in various marriage-related issues, such as the legality of marriage, degrees of kinship preventing marriage, divorce, and inheritance.[9] The concomitant development of canon law in the twelfth century (in the form of extensive commentaries by the great canonists John Zonaras, Alexios Aristenos, and Theodore Balsamon) was related to the rising judicial ambitions of the church.

The well-preserved dossiers of judicial decisions of the courts operated by the archbishop of Ohrid, Demetrios Chomatenos (Chomatianos), and the metropolitan of Naupaktos, John Apokaukos, in the early thirteenth century demonstrate how far the reach of churchmen, both priests and bishops, extended into local peasant society.[10] Apokaukos and especially Chomatenos attracted plaintiffs from large areas in Epiros and Macedonia, where the episcopal structure of the Byzantine church was speedily restored after 1204.[11] The church continued to function as a judicial institution in the restored empire of the Palaiologoi, when its importance in this sphere rose further. In 1296 Emperor Andronikos II (1282–1328) introduced a new supreme court of twelve "General Judges of the Romans" that included six churchmen and six laymen. The General Judges were to meet in the imperial palace and their decisions were to be irrevocable.[12] Although the General Judges ceased to operate effectively soon after 1296, this supreme court was permanently re-established from 1329 onward in the form of a college of four General Judges, consisting, again, of an equal number of laymen and ecclesiastics (two each).[13] In addition, local colleges of General Judges began to operate in diverse areas outside Constantinople. Beyond the General Judges, the patriarchal tribunal in Constantinople established

itself as an authoritative court in the late Byzantine Empire. The documents
of the patriarchal register, which survive in great numbers from the middle
and second half of the fourteenth century up until 1402, feature judicial
cases pertaining not only to matters of marriage and inheritance, but also
to disputes over property, money-lending, and commercial contracts.[14]

The fourteenth century witnessed the strengthening of the authority
of the patriarchate of Constantinople. In 1312 the monasteries of Mount
Athos were transferred from the jurisdiction of the emperor to that of the
patriarch.[15] In the first half of the fourteenth century, a novel procedure
of official scrutiny of the miracles of new saints, a quasi-canonization, was
introduced at the patriarchal synod; this gave the patriarchate a degree of
central control over potentially subversive saint cults.[16] As it will be argued,
the landed estates of the patriarchate of Constantinople (that is, the properties of the Great Church of Saint Sophia) enjoyed a privileged status
during the frequent imperial confiscations of monastic landholdings, confiscations usually provoked by acute military needs during the Palaiologan
period.[17] The legal and ceremonial uses of the Donation of Constantine, a
famous forgery regarded as genuine law in late Byzantium, focused, too,
on the privileged status of the patriarch of Constantinople.[18] Beyond the
position of the patriarch of Constantinople and the patriarchate, the Byzantine church raised new and ambitious ideological claims in the period.
These claims were hierocratic in spirit; that is, they advertised the idea of
the superiority of the church over the imperial office. It is, therefore, not
surprising that around the middle of the fourteenth century the coronation promise of the emperors included a new clause, in which they declared themselves to be "faithful and genuine sons and servants of the
church."[19] The Byzantine Empire has often been characterized as caesaro-
papist on account of the control its emperors yielded over ecclesiastical
administration. The papers in this volume demonstrate once again how misleading this characterization is.[20] Doubtless, the entitlement of the imperial
office to confiscate monastic lands points to the continual control of the
emperor over segments of the church. Yet, in many ways, the authority of
the church in late Byzantium mirrored that of the imperial office and the
imperial hierarchy of officials, both at the level of ideology and practice.

The role of the church in any medieval society can be approached at
different levels, as do the papers in this volume. The Byzantine church
was never monolithic in its structure and interests. The composition of
the clergy was diverse—lay and religious, central and provincial (the latter
including parish priests, bishops, and the higher level of metropolitan

bishops)—better off economically, and less resourceful. The vocational, social, and geographical differentiation within the clergy meant that it never
formed a unified interest group. Religious and lay clergy came to logger-
heads when monasteries tried, at the expense of local bishops, to control the
economic resources and spiritual obedience of dependent peasants settled
on monastic lands.[21] Village priests were oftentimes men of humble social
status, even though they were among the most respected members of peasant society, not the least on account of their literacy; the preoccupations
of local priests naturally differed from those of bishops, metropolitans, or
clerical bureaucrats of the patriarchate of Constantinople.[22]

In the constantly changing political landscape of the period churchmen
oftentimes came to face new worldly dilemmas. Endemic warfare in the
fourteenth century—both civil wars and Turkish raids—endangered the
survival of the empire and created the unprecedented prospect of the
church being incorporated into an Islamic state. Beyond operating law
courts and raising claims of a position of leadership, Byzantine churchmen
grappled to find ways of addressing and adapting to the Turkish advance.
In the middle of the fourteenth century, ecclesiastics composed prayers to
boost the morale of their flocks at times of "heathen" incursions and civil
wars. Some of the authors of these prayers were powerful ecclesiastics in
Constantinople, such as Patriarch Kallistos I (1350–53, 1355–63), and in
Asia Minor, such as the metropolitan of Philadelphia, Makarios. The war
prayers of the mid-fourteenth century are comparable to the crusading
liturgy of the late medieval West, even though their content is different, and
they never evolved to become a self-contained mass.[23] Some of the local
bishops in Asia Minor who found themselves amidst Turkish emirates and
the nascent Ottoman Empire were willing to establish contacts and reach
accommodation with the new masters of the area.[24] These bishops acted as
community leaders in accordance with ideals cultivated among ecclesiastics
during the last centuries of Byzantine history. The papers in this volume
contribute to our understanding of how the church was embedded into the
fabric of late Byzantine society and intellectual life, and doubtless raise in
the process questions for future discussion.

NOTES

1. George Ostrogorsky, *History of the Byzantine State*, trans. Joan Hussey (Oxford:
Blackwell, 1956), p. 487; Steven Runciman, *The Great Church in Captivity: A Study in
the Patriarchate of Constantinople from the Eve of the Turkish Conquests to the Greek War*

of Independence (Cambridge: Cambridge University Press, 1968), pp. 64–74; Donald Nicol, *Church and Society in the Last Centuries of Byzantium* (Cambridge: Cambridge University Press, 1979), pp. 28–30; Michael Angold, *Church and Society in Byzantium under the Comneni, 1081–1261* (Cambridge: Cambridge University Press, 1995), pp. 505–63.

2. Angold, *Church and Society*, pp. 522–29. For the political compromise sought by John III Vatatzes during the negotiations of 1234, see John Langdon, "Byzantium in Anatolian Exile: Imperial Viceregency Reaffirmed during Byzantine-Papal Discussion at Nicaea and Nymphaeum, 1234," *Byzantinische Forschungen* 20 (1994): 197–233. On the negotiations of 1250–54, see Joseph Gill, *Byzantium and the Papacy, 1198–1400* (New Brunswick: Rutgers University Press, 1979), pp. 89–96.

3. See the essay by John W. Barker in the present volume.

4. Nicol, *Church and Society*, pp. 28–30.

5. On the Hesychast movement see the excellent study by John Meyendorff, *A Study of Gregory Palamas*, trans. George Lawrence (London: Faith Press, 1964); John Meyendorff, "Mount Athos in the Fourteenth Century: Spiritual and Intellectual Legacy," *DOP* 42 (1988): 157–65.

6. *Codex Theodosianus*, 1.27.1 and 1.27.2 (laws on *episcopalis audientia*), in *Theodosiani libri XVI cum constitutionibus Sirmondianis*, cd. Paul Meyer, Theodor Mommsen, and Paul Krueger, 2 vols. (Berlin: Weidmann, 1905), 1:62–63.

7. See Claudia Rapp, *The Holy Bishops in Late Antiquity: The Nature of Christian Leadership in an Age of Transition* (Berkeley and Los Angeles: University of California Press, 2005), p. 248.

8. Angeliki E. Laiou, *Mariage, amour et parenté à Byzance aux XIe–XIIIe siècles* (Paris: De Boccard, 1992), pp. 9–13; Angold, *Church and Society*, pp. 404–7.

9. Angeliki E. Laiou, "Contribution à l'étude de l'institution familiale en Epire au XIIIème siècle," in Angeliki E. Laiou, *Gender, Society and Economic Life in Byzantium* (Aldershot: Variorum Reprints, 1992), study 5, pp. 275–318; Angold, *Church and Society*, pp. 409–25.

10. See the essay by Angeliki E. Laiou in the present volume.

11. See the essay by Alkmini Stavridou-Zafraka in the present volume.

12. George Pachymeres, *History*, 9.17, in *Georges Pachymérès: Relations historiques*, ed. Albert Failler, 5 vols (Paris: Belles Lettres, 1984–2000), 3:263.

13. Paul Lemerle, "Le Juge général des Grecs et la réforme judiciaire d'Andronic III," in *Mémorial Louis Petit* (Bucharest: Institute français d'études byzantines, 1948), pp. 292–316; Paul Lemerle, "Documents et problèmes nouveaux concernant les Juges généraux," Δελτίον τῆς Χριστιανικῆς Ἀρχαιολογικῆς Ἑταιρείας, 4, no. 4 (1966): 29–44.

14. Paul Lemerle, "Recherches sur les institutions judiciaires à l'époque des Paléologues. II: Le tribunal du patriarchat ou tribunal synodal," in *Mélanges Paul Peeters*, 2

vols, Analecta Bollandiana 68 (Brussels: Société des Bollandistes, 1949–50), 2:318–33, esp. pp. 322–23. Especially busy was the activity of the patriarchal tribunal in the period from 1394 to 1402. For a detailed legalistic discussion of the competence of late Byzantine and post-Byzantine ecclesiastical courts in the application of contract and property law, see Eleutheria S. Papagianne, Ἡ νομολογία τῶν ἐκκλησιαστικῶν δικαστηρίων τῆς βυζαντινῆς καί μεταβυζαντινῆς περιόδου σέ θέματα περιουσιακοῦ δικαίου, vol. 1, Ἐνοχικό δίκαιο, Ἐμπράγματο δίκαιο (Athens: Sakkoula, 1992).

15. Denise Papachryssanthou, ed., *Actes du Prôtaton*, Archives de l'Athos 7 (Paris: Lethielleux, 1975), pp. 249–54, no. 12. Cf. Nicol, *Church and Society*, pp. 19–20.

16. Ruth Macrides, "Saints and Sainthood in the Early Palaiologan Period," in *The Byzantine Saint*, ed. Sergei Hackel (London: Fellowship of St. Alban and St. Sergius, 1981), pp. 83–85.

17. See the essay by Kostis Smyrlis in the present volume.

18. See my essay, "The Donation of Constantine and the Church in Late Byzantium," in the present volume, esp. pp. 107–10, 125.

19. Dimiter G. Angelov, *Imperia Ideology and Political Thought in Byzantium, 1204–1330* (Cambridge: Cambridge University Press, 2007), pp. 351–416. On the oath see ibid., pp. 411–14.

20. Gilbert Dagron has examined the history of the term *caesoropapism* and the intense scholarly discussion it has provoked; see his *Emperor and Priest: The Imperial Office in Byzantium*, trans. Jean Birrell (Cambridge: Cambridge University Press, 2003), pp. 282–312.

21. See the essay by Günter Prinzing in the present volume.

22. See the discussion by Angeliki E. Laiou in the present volume, esp. pp. 43–47.

23. See the essay by Philip Slavin in the present volume.

24. See the essay by Tom Papademetriou in the present volume.

POLITICS, SOCIETY, AND ECONOMY

The Relations between Secular and Religious Authorities in the State of Epiros after 1204

ALKMINI STAVRIDOU-ZAFRAKA

The fall of Constantinople to the Latins on the 13 April 1204 is a turning point in the history of the Byzantine Empire and a central event in the history of the Middle Ages. The empire collapsed, and the Latin empire of Constantinople was established. The leaders of the Fourth Crusade and the Venetians divided Byzantine territories among themselves in accordance with the agreement known as the *Partitio Romaniae*. Baldwin of Flanders was elected emperor of Constantinople and was crowned "emperor of Romania" in the church of Saint Sophia on 16 May 1204. Boniface of Montferrat became king of Thessaloniki, the Venetians claimed Epiros and the Ionian islands, and the rest of the provinces were allotted to the crusaders as fiefs and principalities. Most of these territories had to be conquered from the Greeks, who partly attempted to resist and partly cooperated with the Latins. Relatives of the imperial family who fled from Constantinople founded three independent Greek states on the remnants of the Byzantine Empire: the empire of Trebizond on the Black Sea, the empire of Nicaea in Bithynia in Asia Minor, and the state of Epiros in continental Greece.[1] These states soon became centers of resistance against the Latins, with their main goal being the recovery of Constantinople and the restoration of the empire.

The founder of the state of Epiros was Michael Komnenos Doukas, who set himself up as an autonomous ruler at Arta and strengthened his position in Epiros by diplomatic negotiations and treaties with the Latin emperor Henry of Flanders (1209) and Venice (1210). But he did not keep his word and broke the agreements. Through victorious campaigns Michael

Komnenos Doukas drove away the Venetians from Dyrrhachion (Durazzo) and Kerkyra (Corfu), and captured Larisa in Thessaly and other Latin strongholds. After his assassination in 1214/15 he was succeeded by his half-brother Theodore Doukas, an ambitious and most competent soldier, who conquered most of Epiros and Macedonia at the expense of the Franks, Venetians, and Bulgarians. After a long siege, late in 1224 he recovered Thessaloniki, the second city of the Byzantine Empire, putting an end to the Lombard kingdom.[2] Theodore was proclaimed emperor of the Romans in 1225/26 and crowned emperor in Thessaloniki by the archbishop of Achrida (Ohrid), Demetrios Chomatenos, in 1227.[3]

The consequences of the sack of Constantinople were not only political but ecclesiastical as well. A Latin patriarch, the Venetian Thomas Morosini, was appointed in Constantinople, while the Greek patriarch John Kamateros fled from the city and found refuge in Thrace; after his death in 1206, a Greek patriarch, Michael IV Autoreianos, was elected in Nicaea and crowned Theodore I Laskaris emperor of the Romans. Both the emperor of Nicaea and the patriarch posed as the guardians of Orthodoxy and claimed supervision and influence over the Orthodox world beyond the boundaries of their state in Asia Minor. On the other hand, Pope Innocent III was interested in putting the Greek territories under the protection of the holy see. Greek prelates could be allowed to remain in office, but only by obeying the Latin archbishops. The Latin conquest widened further the breach and deepened the hatred between the Latins and the Greeks.

This paper focuses on the involvement of the Epirote prelates in the anti-Latin policy of the rulers of Epiros, their cooperation—not without reservations—in matters of church and state, even by supporting uncanonical procedures, and the conflict between secular and ecclesiastical authorities over economic issues such as taxation, confiscation of ecclesiastical estates, and monastic revenues. The sources for our investigation are the correspondence and synodal acts of the metropolitan of Naupaktos, John Apokaukos, the archbishop of Ohrid, Demetrios Chomatenos, the metropolitan of Athens, Michael Choniates, the metropolitan of Corfu, George Bardanes, and the patriarchs of Constantinople in Nicaean exile. Use will be made, too, of the charters of Theodore Doukas.

One of the most important tasks of the church in Greece was the defense of the Orthodox faith against the influence of the Roman church. Most of the Greek metropolitans and bishops refused to obey the pope, left their sees, and were replaced by Latins. Michael Choniates, brother of the historian Niketas Choniates, left his metropolis of Athens and found refuge

on the island of Keos; the metropolitan of Thessaloniki Constantine Mesopotamites was also forced into self-imposed exile to Nicaea; he was reinstated only after the reconquest of the city by Theodore Doukas in 1224. A
continuity in ecclesiastical administration was maintained in Naupaktos,
where the learned John Apokaukos had been appointed metropolitan by the
patriarch at Constantinople in 1199–1200. He was the senior bishop of the
church of Epiros and the leading prelate. His correspondence with bishops
and the patriarch in Nicaea, with government officials, with Theodore
Doukas himself and his consort, is one of the main sources on the administration of the state of Epiros.[4] A priority for the rulers of Epiros was to
re-establish the political and ecclesiastical administration in the newly
recovered territories. Former bishops and metropolitans who were still
alive returned to their sees, while vacant sees were filled by new prelates. For
example, at Michael Komnenos Doukas's command metropolitans were
elected in 1212 and 1213 to the sees of Durazzo and Larisa respectively by
a synod convened at Arta under the leadership of John Apokaukos.[5]

The election of metropolitans and archbishops by a provincial synod—
and not by the permanent synod presided by the patriarch—was contrary
to the canon law; thus, these ordinations were considered invalid. Michael
Komnenos Doukas's request for the ratification of these ordinations by
the patriarch remained unanswered. That was due most probably to the
indignation of the patriarch over the audacity of the whole affair and the
violation of the canonical procedure.[6] The same ecclesiastical policy was
continued under Theodore Doukas. At his order Demetrios Chomatenos
was elected archbishop of Ohrid, probably in 1216 or early in 1217,[7] and
George Bardanes metropolitan of Corfu by a synod which convened at Arta
in December 1219. George Bardanes most probably had been elected by the
synod of Ohrid as bishop at Grevena, but had not been ordained; therefore
he is referred as ὑποψήφιος by Apokaukos. His appointment had been
also suggested by Theodore Doukas.[8] This policy worsened the relations
between the states of Epiros and Nicaea, as it was leading to the emergence
of an autonomous church in Epiros. It was only in February 1222 that the
patriarch Manuel I Sarantenos (March 1217–autumn 1222) announced in
his letter to John Apokaukos that the permanent synod ratified the former
two ordinations but not the new ones; he accused Demetrios Chomatenos
of disrespect for the canons and warned the Epirote prelates that no new
uncanonical appointments would be approved in the future.[9]

The appointment of new erudite bishops and metropolitans in the vacant sees was of great importance not only for the spiritual welfare and

moral support of the Greek population and its protection from the Latin doctrine, but also for the ecclesiastical administration of the provinces and the application of civil law. "Neither a town nor a parish should be left without a bishop, even for a short period," declared John Apokaukos in the synodal act for the election of George Bardanes,[10] about whom he continued:

> We have chosen the appropriate and fitting man for this island. For the island is a stopover in the Adriatic Sea where Italian merchants sail often—a people who are contentious in their arguments, hard to persuade, strife-loving, and who are very experienced in sophistic questions and prone to much drivel as they speak in vain about the unleavened (*azyme*) bread and the procession of the Holy Sprit. The great Komnenos [i.e., Theodore Doukas] and our synod appointed him as a battering ram against their hair-splitting constructs, so that he would strike them in the heart and defeat their sophistic arguments with true syllogisms.[11]

In the same act the bishops of the synod made it clear that they had convened not in order to appropriate or usurp the rights of the patriarch but to elect the right person following the prevailing circumstances and political conditions in a spirit of *oikonomia,* that is, with flexibility but not at the expense of dogma.[12] John Apokaukos, in the synodal act in 1219 and in his long letter to the patriarch in 1222, declared that the Epirote bishops acknowledged the spiritual authority of the patriarch, but not his jurisdiction on their state, since the empire had been dismembered and did not exist anymore. The cooperation of the clergy with their ruler, whom they regarded as God's gift and acknowledged as emperor of their regions, Apokaukos said, was justified, because of his campaigns against the Latins, the restoration of Orthodoxy and his service to the people.[13] Yet, the episcopal nominations in Epiros were considered by the patriarch as a threat to the unity of the church.

The anti-Latin policy of the rulers of Epiros was supported especially by two influential metropolitans who had been ordained by the patriarch of Constantinople before 1204: Basil Pediadites of Corfu and John Apokaukos of Naupaktos. Basil Pediadites of Corfu, who perhaps remained on the island even during the short Venetian occupation until his death in the end of 1217, was highly esteemed and praised for his wisdom and his acute theological arguments against the "arrogant Italian priests" (ἱερεῖς ὑψαύχενες Ἰταλῶν). In his answer to the pope's invitation to attend the universal council at the Lateran in 1215, he denied in a sarcastic way its ecumenical character, "since the patriarchal throne was vacant." Pediadites questioned whether it was ever possible for Greek prelates evicted by the pope, such as the metropolitans of Athens and Thessaloniki, and replaced by Latin bishops (whom he called "adulterers") to attend the council.[14]

John Apokaukos was also strongly anti-Latin. In his answer to the patriarch's invitation to Theodore Doukas and himself in 1219 to send a delegation to Nicaea and participate in a council of prelates from the four Orthodox patriarchates (Constantinople, Alexandria, Antioch, and Jerusalem) on Easter Sunday 1220 to discuss the union of the churches,[15] he rejected such an undertaking as a treachery. He made it clear that the proposed negotiations with Rome would only benefit the Latins, who had closed the Greek churches and caused so many troubles and bitterness to the western Greeks. He expressed also his indignation over Theodore I Laskaris's marriage to the daughter of the Latin empress of Constantinople, Yolanda of Courtenay.[16] Some years later, in his letter to the learned bishop of Korone, Athanasios (an Orthodox prelate who remained in the Venetian-held town in the Peloponnese in order to preach the Greek population to follow strictly the Orthodox doctrine), Apokaukos congratulated him for his refusal to swear an oath to the pope and for his adherence to the ecclesiastical canons and tradition despite the insults and sufferings.[17] In a letter consulting a priest from Frankish Patras about the Latin doctrine he said: "None of the Holy Fathers accepts the religion or sacrifice of the Latins."[18]

One of the most serious ecclesiastical problems in Epiros, and especially in the provinces of the archbishopric of Ohrid, was the clergy who had been ordained by the Bulgarian bishops during the Bulgarian conquest of the area by Tsar Kaloyan (1197–1207) and his successor, Boril, in the early thirteenth century, and who remained even after the restoration of Byzantine rule by Michael and Theodore Doukas. It was suggested that the clergy be removed from the Greek churches together with the Bulgarian bishops. The wish and "command" of Theodore Doukas transmitted to the synod of Ohrid was to reach a unanimous and compromised solution. The synod decided in 1217 that the Bulgarian bishops should be deposed, the Greek bishops should be reinstated, and new ones would be elected for the vacant sees. A penance was to be imposed on the lower clergy which would remain in office.[19]

The restoration of the political and ecclesiastical order in the state of Epiros and Theodore's services to the church were praised by the clergy. His intervention in ecclesiastical affairs was highly supported by the church as an unquestionably granted right. John Apokaukos, Demetrios Chomatenos, and George Bardanes hailed Theodore Doukas as savior and protector of the church and as the divine ruler who deserved imperial authority and could claim enthronement to the genuine imperial throne, that of the Queen City, Constantinople.[20] The clergy participated along with the senate, the army, and all the local Christian population in Theodore's proclamation, and it was the autocephalous archbishop of Ohrid, Demetrios Chomatenos, who performed his coronation and anointment in Thessaloniki, most probably on Whit Sunday (29 May 1227). The metropolitan of the city, Constantine Mesopotamites, refused to perform the coronation, because he kept his allegiance to the patriarch and the emperor of Nicaea, and abandoned his see for a second time.[21]

Theodore Doukas's imperial proclamation was considered usurpation of the imperial title and insult to the Byzantine emperor already crowned in Nicaea.[22] The patriarchal synod in Nicaea advised Theodore to lay aside the purple, "because it was not fitting for those who belong to the same race to have two emperors and two patriarchs."[23] Demetrios Chomatenos was accused that by performing the coronation and anointment he appropriated patriarchal rights.[24] He was also said to have undermined the unity of the Orthodox church by promoting a schism for his own interest.[25] There was a suspicion that the church of Epiros might remain independent, and besides the emperor there would be a new patriarchate. Demetrios Chomatenos refuted these accusations one by one in his second letter addressed to the patriarch (end of 1227 or early in 1228).[26] In a long letter to the patriarch, George Bardanes answered further the charges levied against Theodore Doukas for his usurpation of the imperial title and independent ecclesiastical policies, by both of which he was said to have broken his oath of fidelity to Theodore I Laskaris.[27] Thus, a *bellum diplomaticum* was waged between the patriarch and the ecclesiastical authorities of Epiros, in which each party supported the ideological and political reasons why their emperor had the right to claim the *imperium* and the reconquest of Constantinople.

The ideological points of Theodore's imperial authority were supported in the synodal act issued at Arta in February 1227[28] and in the letters which John Apokaukos, Demetrios Chomatenos, and George Bardanes addressed to Patriarch Germanos II (1223–40) immediately after the synod at Arta and the coronation.[29] Scholars have analyzed on numerous occasions the arguments, which included the following ones: Theodore Doukas had been elected by God; he was guided by the divine hand of God and liberated the western provinces from the heretic Latins; he deserved the imperial title because of his bravery and his imperial virtues (piety, justice, care for the welfare of the people, serenity, humility, and sleeplessness); being a descendant of various emperors, he was the rightful heir to the empire of the

Romans; he had been legally proclaimed by the political organs of the empire, that is, the senate, the army, and the people, as well as by bishops and the clergy.[30]

The main argument, however, for the election of an emperor in Epiros was that the true *imperium* (βασιλεία) had vanished together with the sack of Constantinople. Nicaea and Epiros were considered provisional states with two independent and equal emperors, an odd situation due to political turmoil in the world. Their goal and aspiration was the reconquest of Constantinople from the Latins and the restoration of the empire of the Romans. He who would recover Constantinople would sit on the genuine imperial throne of Constantine. Only then would the *renovatio imperii* be accomplished. Thus, the Epirote churchmen remained adherent to the idea of the one and unique Christian Roman Empire.[31]

In her study on the provincial government in Hellas and Peloponnesos in the years immediately before 1204, Judith Herrin made a significant remark: "Ecclesiastical administration was probably the most efficient in the province. . . . Ecclesiastical government had always been based on the lengthy residence of metropolitans in provincial centers . . . whereas governors might change every three years or more frequently, or might be permanently absent. . . . Ecclesiastics embodied an element of continuity in provincial administration."[32] That is true if we take into consideration the case of John Apokaukos, who was metropolitan of Naupaktos in Aetolia, in a region which remained out of the Latin occupation, from 1199 to 1232. Apokaukos was the senior metropolitan of Epiros in a large diocese which extended from the Gulf of Corinth further up the coast to Chimara and Dryinoupolis in the valley of Drin.[33] His support of the rulers of Epiros concerning the ecclesiastical appointments of metropolitans and of the archbishop of Ohrid compromised his allegiance to the patriarchate of Nicaea and his adherence to the canon law. He defended the restoration of ecclesiastical order in Epiros, his authority over his suffragan bishops, and the economic interests of his church. He was preoccupied with the education of the clergy. He did not hesitate to protest against lay officials, even against Theodore Doukas himself, in order to protect his flock and clergy from a heavy taxation and other charges.

In 1226 Apokaukos expressed his annoyance to Emperor Theodore Doukas when the latter suggested a priest for the bishopric of Bela near Ioannina by saying that the imperial order came quite late and that there were other candidates better than the one he was proposing.[34] In another case he urged a bishop of his metropolis to send his proposal with those of two other bishops for the election of a new bishop at Ioannina "before the emperor exercised any pressure on him."[35]

Apokaukos came into a severe conflict with Theodore's brother Constantine Doukas, who had been appointed governor of Akarnania and Aetolia—a conflict that started in 1212 and with some intervals lasted until 1228. In his letter to the metropolitan of Larisa in 1212, he described the tragic situation of the peasants who left their homes and fled to the mountains because of the heavy taxation imposed by Constantine, and because of pirate raids. They lived in fear, he said, to the extent of coming down from the mountains to harvest the fields only during the night.[36] In 1218 Theodore Doukas imposed a tax (πλώϊμον) of 1,000 golden coins (hyperpyra) on the peasants of the metropolis of Naupaktos for the construction and armament of vessels. John Apokaukos reacted by complaining that the crop had been destroyed the previous year by a natural disaster and pirate raids.[37] He tried to meet Theodore at Arta and protest personally, but failed. Instead, he wrote him a letter describing the poverty and despair of the peasants of his metropolis: if their total revenue, he asked rhetorically, amounted to no more than 180 hyperpyra, how then could they pay the sum of 1,000 hyperpyra? He also mentioned that many times he had sent the emperor presents such as gold, textiles, wine, and horses and other animals.[38] Two years later Constantine expelled Apokaukos from the episcopal residence located on the upper part of the city of Naupaktos and enjoying a marvelous view; Apokaukos was obliged to live in a small village cottage, in a courtyard with storage vessels and various animals.[39] Constantine even concocted a false accusation against John Apokaukos, charging him with the attempted murder of the doux of Acheloos.[40]

In one of his letters Apokaukos complained also about the persecutions and tortures of dependent peasants (πάροικοι) and clergymen in the metropolis who could not pay their taxes. They were tied up, hanged upside down, and beaten, as if, he said sarcastically, "starving people could vomit."[41] A young clergyman was tied with a rope around his neck to the tail of a horse and was disgracefully led through the city to prison.[42] Those were, unfortunately, common scenes in Byzantine provinces even before 1204. A similar description of pillories against clergymen was given also by Archbishop Theophylaktos of Ohrid in the late eleventh and the early twelfth century.[43]

In his letters to lay officials as well as to his fellow bishops and metropolitans Apokaukos blamed the secular authorities for their intervention in the ecclesiastical affairs of his metropolis by appointing bishops and abbots without the consent of the metropolitan, by expelling pious priests from their churches and replacing them with illiterate ones,[44] by preventing trials in cases of illegal marriages, and by settling refugees and foreigners in the monasteries in order to appropriate their revenues and deprive the metropolis of them.[45] Constantine Doukas was accused of behaving as a rapacious landholder: he demanded for himself horses and the best furs, geese, and ducks, as well as the best fresh fish from the fishermen of Naupaktos.[46] He even imposed a tax of twenty-four gold coins on those who took the monastic vows and on the families of those who passed away.[47] Theodore Doukas and his two brothers granted dependent peasants, fields, orchards, and olive groves (usually detached from the agricultural domain of the church) to soldiers (στρατιῶται) as *pronoiai*. The metropolitan of Naupaktos characterized as preposterous the fact that many of these soldiers were Latin mercenaries who used Romans as dependent peasants.[48] It was only in May 1228 that the emperor exempted by a chrysobull the metropolis of Naupaktos and its inhabitants from various taxes and charges, particularly those imposed by Constantine Doukas.[49]

In conclusion, the influential prelates of Epiros supported its rulers in their struggle for the recovery of Greek cities and the re-establishment of Byzantine political and ecclesiastical administration. They contributed to the fulfillment of Theodore Doukas's ambition to ascend the imperial throne and accepted his intervention in ecclesiastical affairs, thus coming into strong rivalry with the patriarchate and the emperor of Nicaea. They, however, and especially John Apokaukos, refused to submit to Theodore's demands for taxes and his orders for the election of bishops in his metropolis. Apokaukos also protested against the confiscation of properties and revenues of the church.

Despite the dissolution of the Byzantine Empire in 1204, the church continued to play a significant role in the life of the new Greek states, because, as Ernest Barker aptly remarks, in Byzantium traditionally "the Church was closely knit with the State and intimately integrated in its life."[50]

NOTES

1. Various aspects of the Fourth Crusade have been studied, most recently in *Urbs Capta: The Fourth Crusade and Its Consequences (La IVe Croisade et ses conséquences)*, ed. Angeliki Laiou, Réalités byzantines 10 (Paris: Lethielleux, 2005). For the Greek successor states, see Jacob Philipp Fallmereyer, *Geschichte des Kaisertums von Trapezunt*

(Munich: Weber, 1827), Sergei Karpov, *L'impero di Trebisonda, Venezia, Genova e Roma 1204–1461: Rapporti politici, diplomatici e commerciali* (Rome: Veltro, 1986); Antonios Meliarakes, Ιστορία του Βασιλείου της Νικαίας και του Δεσποτάτου της Ηπείρου *(1204–1261)* (Athens, 1898; repr. Athens: Ionike Trapeza, 1994); Alice Gardner, *The Lascarids of Nicaea: The Story of an Empire in Exile* (London: Methuen, 1912); Michael Angold, *Byzantine Government in Exile: Government and Society under the Lascarids of Nicaea, 1204–1261* (Oxford: Oxford University Press, 1975); Donald Nicol, *The Despotate of Epiros* (Oxford: Blackwell, 1957); Günter Prinzing, "Studien zur Provinz- und Zentralverwaltung im Machtbereich der epirotischen Herrscher Michael I. und Theodoros Dukas," Ηπειρωτικά Χρονικά 24 (1982): 73–120, and 25 (1983): 37–112.

2. For the date, see Jean Longnon, "La reprise de Salonique par les Grecs en 1224," *Actes du VIe Congrès international d'études byzantines*, 2 vols. (Paris: École des hautes études, 1950), 1:141–46; Bernhard Sinogowitz, "Zur Eroberung Thessalonikes im Herbst 1224," *BZ* 45 (1952): 28.

3. For the proclamation see Alkmini Stavridou-Zafraka, "Συμβολή στο ζήτημα της αναγόρευσης του Θεοδώρου Δούκα," in Αφιέρωμα στον Εμμανουήλ Κριαρά (Thessaloniki: Center for Byzantine Studies, 1988), pp. 37–62. For the date of coronation in 1227 instead of 1225, see Elene Bee-Seferli, "Ο χρόνος στέψεως του Θεοδώρου Δούκα ως προσδιορίζεται εξ ανεκδότων γραμμάτων Ιωάννου του Αποκαύκου," *BNJ* 21 (1971–76): 272–79; Alkmini Stavridou-Zafraka, Νίκαια και Ήπειρος τον 13ο αιώνα. Ιδεολογική αντιπαράθεση στην προσπάθειά τους να ανακτήσουν την αυτοκρατορία (Thessaloniki: Ed. Vanias, 1990), pp. 70–71; Günter Prinzing, "Das Kaisertum im Staat von Epeiros: Propagierung, Stabilisierung und Verfall," in Πρακτικά Διεθνούς Συμποσίου για το Δεσποτάτο της Ηπείρου (Αρτα 27–31 Μαΐου 1990) (Athens: Vasilopoulos, 1992), pp. 17–30; Günter Prinzing, "Das byzantinische Kaisertum im Umbruch zwischen regionaler Aufspaltung und erneuter Zentrierung in den Jahren 1204–1282," in *Legitimation und Funktion des Herrschers*, ed. Rolf Gundlach and Hermann Weber (Stuttgart: Steiner, 1992), pp. 129–83, esp. p. 156; François Bredenkamp, *The Byzantine Empire of Thessalonike (1224–1242)* (Thessaloniki: Thessaloniki History Center, 1996), p. 126.

4. Michael Angold, *Church and Society in Byzantium under the Comneni, 1081–1261* (Cambridge: Cambridge University Press, 1995), pp. 197–231. On Apokaukos, see Matthias Wellnhofer, *Johannes Apokaukos, Metropolit von Naupaktos in Aetolien* (Freising: Datterer, 1913); Kosmas Lampropoulos, Ιωάννης Απόκαυκος. Συμβολή στην έρευνα του βίου και του συγγραφικού έργου του (Athens: Basilopoulos, 1988).

5. Vasilii G. Vasil'evskii, "Epirotica saeculi XIII," *VV* 3 (1896): 233–99 (no. 16, p. 268, lines 4–11, no. 17, p. 270, lines 20–26). Cf. Nicol, *Despotate*, pp. 36–39.

6. See Apostolos Karpozilos, *The Ecclesiastical Controversy between the Kingdom of Nicaea and the Principality of Epiros (1217–1233)* (Thessaloniki: Center for Byzantine Studies, 1973), pp. 50–51 and n. 14.

7. For the career and written work of Demetrios Chomatenos see *Demetrii Chomateni Ponemata diaphora*, ed. Günter Prinzing, Corpus Fontium Historiae Byzantinae 38 (Berlin: de Gruyter, 2002), pp. 3*–45*.

8. For George Bardanes see Johannes Hoeck and Raymond-Joseph Loenertz, *Nikolaos-Nektarios von Otranto, Abt von Casole: Beiträge zur Geschichte der ost-westlichen Beziehungen unter Innozenz III. und Friedrich II.* (Ettal: Buch-Kunstverlag, 1965). For his previous election at the bishopric of Grevena see Vasil'evskii, "Epirotica," no. 5, p. 249, lines 4–7, and p. 239, line 31 (a letter of Bardanes to Apokaukos, in which the bishopric of Grevena is referred to as "προμνηστευμένην" and "ἀρραβωνιζομένην"), no. 17, p. 270, lines 26–30 (Apokaukos's letter to the patriarch in 1222): "οὐκ ἂν δὲ καὶ εἰς τοῦ σήμερον Κερκύρων τὴν χειροτονίαν ἐπένευσα, εἰ μὴ τὸν ἄνδρα τοῦτον λόγῳ καὶ βίῳ κατανοήσας κοσμούμενον καὶ παρὰ τοῦ Βουλγαρίας ὑποψήφιον γεγονότα τῆς τῶν Γρεβενῶν ἐκκλησίας τοῦ χοροῦ τῶν Βουλγαρικῶν ἐπισκόπων ἐξενεγκών, τῇ ἡμετέρᾳ συνόδῳ προσήρμοσα." Cf. Alkmini Stavridou-Zafraka, "Τὰ Γρεβενὰ στο πλαίσιο της πολιτικής και εκκλησιαστικής ιστορίας του κράτους της Ηπείρου (α′ μισό του 13ου αι.)," in *Πρακτικά Συνεδρίου: Τὰ Γρεβενά, Ιστορία-Τέχνη-Πολιτισμός*, ed. M. Papanikolaou (Thessaloniki: Parateretes, 2002), pp. 193–202, esp. pp. 196–97.

9. Vasil'evskii, "Epirotica," no. 16, p. 268, line 14–p. 269, line 29; Vitalien Laurent, *Les regestes des actes du Patriarcat de Constantinople*, vol. 1, *Les actes des patriarches*, fasc. IV, *Les regestes de 1208 à 1309* (Paris: Institut français d'études byzantines, 1971), no. 1230.

10. Vasil'evskii, "Epirotica," no. 13, p. 260, lines 18–20. For the responsibilities of bishops see ibid., no. 13, p. 260, line 20–p. 261, line 9; no. 17, p. 277, lines 14–23.

11. Vasil'evskii, "Epirotica," no. 13, p. 262, lines 1–10.

12. Vasil'evskii, "Epirotica," no. 13, p. 261, lines 34–36. For "oikonomia," see Amilkas Alivizatos, *Η Οικονομία κατά το κανονικόν δίκαιον της Ορθοδόξου Εκκλησίας* (Athens: Aster, 1949), p. 68; Günter Prinzing, in *Lexikon des Mittelalters*, 9 vols. (Munich: Artemis, 1977–98), 6:1381.

13. Vasil'evskii, "Epirotica," no. 17, p. 272, lines 28–31; no. 17, p. 274, line 31–p. 275, line 19. Cf. Nicol, *Despotate*, pp. 89–91; Karpozilos, *Controversy*, pp. 64–67; Stavridou-Zafraka, *Νίκαια καὶ Ἤπειρος*, pp. 120–22.

14. Konstantinos Manaphes, "Ἐπιστολὴ Βασιλείου Πεδιαδίτου μητροπολίτου Κερκύρας πρὸς τον πάπαν Ἰννοκέντιον Γ′ καὶ ο χρόνος πατριαρχείας Μιχαὴλ Δ′ Αὐτωρειανού," *EEBS* 42 (1975–76): 429–40, esp. p. 436, lines 65–66. For the letter and the probable journey of Pediadites to Rome see Prinzing, *Demetrii Chomateni Ponemata*, pp. 12* n. 50 and p. 106*. For John Apokaukos's obituary for Basil Pediadites in his letter to Theodore Doukas, see Vasil'evskii, "Epirotica," no. 8, p. 254, lines 1–20. Cf. Nicol, *Despotate*, p. 77.

15. Vasil'evskii, "Epirotica," no. 14, p. 264; Laurent, *Regestes*, no. 1224.

16. Vasil'evskii, "Epirotica," no. 15, p. 266, line 4–p. 267, line 1. Cf. Nicol, *Despotate*, pp. 86–87. Karpozilos, *Controversy*, pp. 54–55; Angold, *Church and Society*, p. 531.

17. Agni Basilikopoulou, "Ἀνέκδοτη γραφή του Ἀπόκαυκου στον ἐπίσκοπο Κορώνης," in Πρακτικά του Β' Διεθνούς Συνεδρίου Πελοποννησιακών Σπουδών, 2 vols. (Athens: Society for Peloponnesian Studies, 1981–82), 2:241–48; Agni Basilikopoulou, "Ἡ ἐπισκοπή Κορώνης στις αρχές του Γ' αιώνα. Ο ἐπίσκοπος Αθανάσιος," Πελοποννησιακά 16 (1985–86): 376–84. Cf. Angold, Church and Society, p. 531.

18. Nikos Bees, "Unedierte Schriftstücke aus dem Kanzlei des Johannes Apokaukos des Metropoliten von Naupaktos (in Aetolien)," BNJ 21 (1971–76): 1–247 (pp. 111–12, no. 55).

19. A full account of the problem is given by Demetrios Chomatenos in his letter to Basil Pediadites (ca. middle or late 1216) and the synodal act: Prinzing, Demetrii Chomateni Ponemata, no. 8, pp. 49–51; no. 146, pp. 35*, 423–28. Nicol, Despotate, p. 85.

20. Vasil'evskii, "Epirotica," no. 25, p. 288, lines 11–14: "πάντα συμπατῆσαι ἐχθρὸν καὶ γῆν πατῆσαι τὴν Κωνσταντίνου καὶ τὴν ἐν τοῖς ἐκεῖσε βασιλείοις αὐλήν· ἀκόλουθον δὲ τῷ πατήματι τούτῳ καὶ ἡ ἐπὶ θρόνου τοῦ βασιλικοῦ κάθισις καὶ ὅσα τῇ καταστάσει ταύτῃ ἑπόμενα." See Bees, "Unedierte Schriftstücke," no. 69, p. 128, lines 70–72; no. 70, p. 129. Cf. Stavridou-Zafraka, Νίκαια καὶ Ἤπειρος, pp. 212–13.

21. Georgii Acropolitae opera, ed. August Heisenberg (Leipzig: Teubner, 1903), rev. ed. Peter Wirth (Stuttgart: Teubner, 1978), p. 33, line 14–p. 34, line 5.

22. Georgii Acropolitae opera, p. 33, lines 14–20: "ὁ δὲ Κομνηνὸς Θεόδωρος . . . μὴ θέλων μένειν ἐν τῇ οἰκείᾳ τάξει ἀλλὰ τὰ τῆς βασιλείας σφετερισάμενος, ἐπειδὴ τῆς Θεσσαλονίκης γέγονεν ἐγκρατὴς . . . πορφυρίδα τε ὑπενδύεται καὶ ἐρυθρὰ περιβάλλεται πέδιλα."

23. Nicephori Blemmydae curriculum vitae et carmina, ed. August Heisenberg (Leipzig: Teubner, 1896), p. 14, lines 17–23 (= Nicephori Blemmydae autobiographia sive curriculum vitae, ed. Joseph Munitiz [Turnhout: Brepols, 1984], p. 14, lines 4–10) (Laurent, Regestes, no. 1239). Cf. Karpozilos, Controversy, p. 77; Stavridou-Zafraka, Νίκαια καὶ Ἤπειρος, pp. 164–65; Prinzing, "Das byzantinische Kaisertum," p. 153.

24. Georgii Acropolitae opera, p. 34, lines 1–5: "ὁ δὲ Βουλγαρίας ἀρχιεπίσκοπος Δημήτριος τὸ βασιλικὸν περιδιδύσκει τοῦτον διάδημα, ὡς ἔφασκεν, αὐτόνομος ὢν καὶ μηδενὶ εὐθύνας ὀφείλων δοῦναι, καὶ διὰ ταῦτα ἐξουσίαν ἔχειν βασιλέας χρίειν οὕς τε ἂν καὶ ὅπου καὶ ὅτε βούλοιτο." Theodore Skoutariotes (= Ανωνύμου Σύνοψις Χρονική), in Μεσαιωνικὴ Βιβλιοθήκη, ed. Konstantinos Sathas, 7 vols. (Venice, 1872–94; repr. Athens: Gregoriades, 1971–72), 7:468, lines 28–30. Nicephori Gregorae Byzantina historia, ed. Ludwig Schopen, 3 vols. (Bonn: Weber, 1829–55), 1:26, lines 14–16: "καὶ πρός γε ἔτι διὰ κουφότητα καὶ ἀφέλειαν τοῦ τηνικαῦτα διέποντος τὴν ἀρχιεπισκοπήν, ἐς τοσοῦτον ἀτοπίας τὸ πρᾶγμα ἐκκεκύλισται." Cf. Prinzing, Demetrii Chomateni Ponemata, pp. 21*–22*.

25. Günter Prinzing, "Die Antigraphe des Patriarchen Germanos II. an Erzbischof Demetrios Chomatenos von Ohrid und die Korrespondenz zum nikäisch-epirotischen

Konflikt, 1212–1233," *Rivista di studi bizantini e slavi: Miscellanea Agostino Pertusi* 3 (1984): 21–64. It was an answer to Chomatenos's letter no. 112 to the patriarch Germanos II after the coronation of Theodore Doukas (after June 1227). See Prinzing in *Demetrii Chomateni Ponemata*, pp. 223*–25*; Stavridou-Zafraka, Νίκαια καὶ Ἤπειρος, pp. 156–58; Karpozilos, *Controversy*, pp. 78–79; Bredenkamp, *Empire*, pp. 135–38.

26. Prinzing, *Demetrii Chomateni Ponemata*, p. 371, no. 114, lines 22–27. Cf. Prinzing, *Ponemata*, pp. 225*–30*; Karpozilos, *Controversy*, pp. 81–86; Stavridou-Zafraka, Νίκαια καὶ Ἤπειρος, pp. 158–84; Ruth Macrides, "Bad Historian or Good Lawyer? Demetrios Chomatenos and Novel 131," *DOP* 46 (1992): 187–96.

27. Raymond-Joseph Loenertz, "Lettre de Georges Bardanès, métropolite de Corcyre au patriarche œcuménique Germain II," *EEBS* 33 (1964): 87–118 (repr. in Raymond-Joseph Loenertz, *Byzantina et Franco-Graeca* [Rome: Edizioni di storia e letteratura, 1970], pp. 467–501). Cf. Karpozilos, *Controversy*, pp. 79–81; Stavridou-Zafraka, Νίκαια καὶ Ἤπειρος, pp. 184–86; Bredenkamp, *Empire*, pp. 138–40.

28. Vasil'evskii, "Epirotica," no. 24, pp. 285–86; no. 26, pp. 288–93 (a letter drafted by Apokaukos on behalf of the synod at Arta addressed to the patriarch Germanos II).

29. Vasil'evski, "Epirotica," no. 26, pp. 288–93 (from Arta); no. 27, pp. 293–95 (from Thessaloniki after the coronation); Bees, "Unedierte Schriftstücke," no. 69, p. 127; Prinzing, *Demetrii Chomateni Ponemata*, no. 114, pp. 370–78; Loenertz, "Lettre de Georges Bardanès," p. 109, lines 161–75. See Stavridou-Zafraka, Νίκαια καὶ Ἤπειρος, pp. 119–45; Karpozilos, *Controversy*, pp. 75–86.

30. See Stavridou-Zafraka, Νίκαια καὶ Ἤπειρος, pp. 119–42, 155–70.

31. See Stavridou-Zafraka, Νίκαια καὶ Ἤπειρος, pp. 119–214; Stavridou-Zafraka, "The Empire of Thessalonike (1224–1242): Political Ideology and Reality," Βυζαντιακά 19 (1999): 211–22; Stavridou-Zafraka, "The Political Ideology of the State of Epiros," in *Urbs Capta* (see n. 1, above), pp. 311–23.

32. Judith Herrin, "The Provincial Government in Hellas and Peloponnesos from 1180 to 1205," *DOP* 29 (1975): 251–84, esp. pp. 258–59. For the relationship of John Apokaukos, George Bardanes, and Demetrios Chomatenos with the local society see Angold, *Church and Society*, pp. 213–62.

33. For the topography of Epiros see Nicol, *Despotate*, pp. 222–26; Peter Soustal and Johannes Koder, *Nikopolis und Kephallenia*, Tabula Imperii Byzantini 3 (Vienna: Verlag der Österreichischen Akademie der Wissenschaften, 1981).

34. Bees, "Unedierte Schriftstücke," no. 84, p. 141, lines 12–15.

35. Bees, "Unedierte Schriftstücke," no. 83, p. 141.

36. Bees, "Unedierte Schriftstücke," no. 68, p. 126, lines 31–42.

37. Bees, "Unedierte Schriftstücke," no. 99, pp. 149–50; no. 107, p. 157, lines 26–55.

38. Sophrone Pétridès, "Jean Apokaukos, lettres et autres documents inédits," *IRAIK* 14 (1909): 69–100 (p. 80, line 26). Cf. ibid., no. 10, p. 82, line 22; no. 11, pp. 84–85 (two letters to a high official of the court).

39. Athanasios Papadopoulos-Kerameus, "Συμβολή εις την ιστορίαν της αρχιεπισκοπής Αχρίδος," in *Sbornik statei posviashchennykh V. I. Lamanskomu*, 2 vols. (St. Petersburg: Tipografia Imperatorskoi akademii nauk, 1907–8), 1:240, no. 6; 1:245, no. 7; Bees, "Unedierte Schriftstücke," no. 27, p. 87, line 72–p. 88, line 121. See Paul Magdalino, "The Literary Perception on Everyday Life in Byzantium: Some General Considerations and the Case of John Apokaukos," *Byzantinoslavica* 48 (1987): 28–38; Alkmini Stavridou-Zafraka, "Η κοινωνία της Ηπείρου στο κράτος του Θεοδώρου Δούκα," in *Πρακτικά Διεθνούς Συμποσίου για το Δεσποτάτο*, pp. 313–33, esp. pp. 325–27. For Apokaukos's policy and the relationship with the local society see Angold, *Church and Society*, pp. 212–31.

40. Bees, "Unedierte Schriftstücke," nos. 30–31, pp. 90–91.

41. Pétridès, "Jean Apokaukos," no. 10, p. 84, lines 15–18.

42. Papadopoulos-Kerameus, "Συμβολή," no. 6, p. 242.

43. *Théophylacte d'Achrida, Lettres: Introduction, texte, traduction et notes*, ed. Paul Gautier (Thessaloniki: Association de recherches byzantines, 1986), no. 45, p. 283.

44. Bees, "Unedierte Schriftstücke," no. 60, pp. 116–17; no. 62, p. 119.

45. Bees, "Unedierte Schriftstücke," no. 27, p. 87, line 87–p. 88, line 100.

46. Bees, "Unedierte Schriftstücke," no. 77, pp. 137–38.

47. Papadopoulos-Kerameus, "Συμβολή," no. 6, pp. 243, 245.

48. Bees, "Unedierte Schriftstücke," no. 71, pp. 131–32.

49. Vasil'evskii, "Epirotica," no. 29, pp. 296–99.

50. Ernest Barker, *Social and Political Thought in Byzantium from Justinian I to the Last Palaeologus: Passages from the Byzantine Writers and Documents* (Oxford: Oxford University Press, 1957), p. 12.

Abbot or Bishop?

The Conflict about the Spiritual Obedience of the Vlach Peasants in the Region of Bothrotos ca. 1220: Case No. 80 of the Legal Works of Demetrios Chomatenos Reconsidered

GÜNTER PRINZING

To Professor Edgar Hösch,
on the occasion of his seventieth birthday

A re-examination of case no. 80 of the legal works of the archbishop of Ohrid, Demetrios Chomatenos—the *Ponemata diaphora* (= *PD*), that is to say *opera varia*—seems an appropriate choice for discussing larger issues related to the position of the church in Byzantine society in the aftermath of 1204, both at a micro and macro level. The choice of a text from the *PD* also gives me the opportunity to inform the reader about the corpus of the *PD*, which was published in 2002 in a critical edition prepared by me for the Berlin series of the *Corpus Fontium Historiae Byzantinae* which replaces Cardinal Pitra's *editio princeps* (1891).[1]

In four steps I would like, first, to give a brief sketch of the history of the city of Ohrid and of the extent and position of the archbishopric of Bulgaria (archbishopric of Ohrid) around the year 1220; second, to provide biographical details about Demetrios Chomatenos; third, to explain the genesis, structure, and significance of the corpus of his *PD*; and fourth and finally, to analyze case no. 80 of the corpus.

1. TERRITORY AND STATUS OF THE ARCHBISHOPRIC OF BULGARIA (OHRID) AROUND 1220

The modern town of Ohrid (in Greek Αχρίς/Achris or Αχρίδα/Achrida)—the settlement that emerged on the location of the ancient and early

25

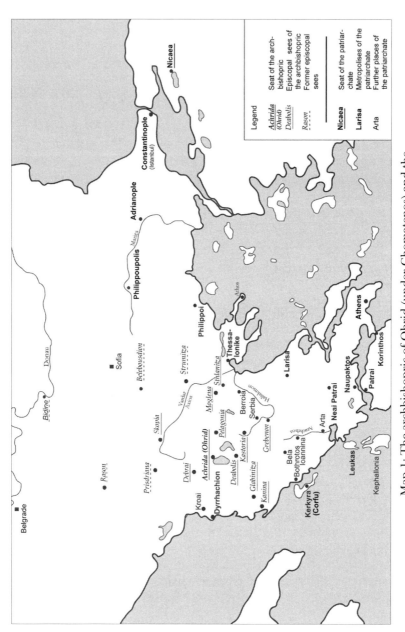

Map 1: The archbishopric of Ohrid (under Chomatenos) and the neighboring metropolises of the patriarch of Constantinople/Nicaea.

Byzantine city and episcopal see of Lychnis (Lychnidos)—lies on the northern shore of Lake Ohrid, in the southwestern part of the present-day
Republic of Macedonia (Former Yugoslav Republic of Macedonia) (see map
1). In the Middle Ages Ohrid was part of Bulgaria from ca. 842 onward.
Returning to Byzantine rule after the conquest of Bulgaria by Emperor Basil
II around 1020, Ohrid became the metropolis of the autocephalous Byzantine archbishopric of Bulgaria (Βουλγαρία), remaining so until 1767, well
into the Ottoman period, which here lasted from ca. 1400 until 1913.[2]

What was the status of the archbishopric of Ohrid and its head around
1200, and what was its territorial extent at that time? From 1020 onward,
the autocephalous archbishopric of Bulgaria was in effect associated with
the patriarchate of Constantinople, although as a completely independent
ecclesiastical province within the framework of the empire. Therefore, as
a rule, the archbishops attended the imperial church synods convened
by the emperor and patriarch, but they went only sporadically to the so-
called permanent synod (*synodos endemousa*) of the patriarchate. It was the
emperor, not the patriarch, who held the right to appoint the archbishop—as a rule a member of the clergy of the church of Saint Sophia
(the Great Church) in Constantinople—from a list of three names submitted by the synod in the same fashion as the emperor designated the
ecumenical patriarch of Constantinople.[3] The position of the two great
autocephalous archbishops of Bulgaria (Ohrid) and Cyprus was potentially
like that of a quasi-patriarch, especially in view of their independence from
the ecumenical patriarch. Nevertheless, before 1204, the archbishops of
Ohrid enjoyed close links with the emperor and the patriarch, and thus
there was no real separation from the patriarchate of Constantinople.[4]

When trying to determine the territorial extent of the archbishopric
and the number of its suffragan sees in the period between 1200 and 1220,
one has to consider that theoretically it still encompassed an immense territory extending from Belgrade on the Danube to central Greece and western
Bulgaria. But, as Michael Angold has already observed, "Demetrios Chomatianos found that large areas of his church were controlled by the Serbs and
Bulgarians, who were creating their own ecclesiastical organizations."[5] On
account of the secession of Bulgaria (from 1185 onward) and Serbia (from
ca. 1195 onward) from the Byzantine Empire, the territorial extent of the
autocephalous church of Ohrid, formerly consisting of over twenty bishoprics, was reduced around 1200 (see map 1) to the bishoprics of Achrida
(Ohrid), Debrai (Debar), Diabolis (Devol), Glabenitza, Grebenon (Grevena),
Kanina, Kastoria, Moglena, Pelagonia (Bitola), Prisdriana (Prizren), Skopia

(Skopje), Strumitza, and Sthlanitza. These thirteen episcopal sees, with the exception of Prisdriana, which fell to Serbia in 1214, also shaped the extent of the archbishopric of Ohrid under Chomatenos.[6]

Apart from the regions subject to the autocephalous archbishopric of Ohrid, the church in the state of Epiros under its ruler Theodore Doukas (1215–30) consisted also of territories subject to the ecumenical patriarch of Constantinople seated in exile in Nicaea: these "patriarchal" territories were formed by the metropolises of Dyrrhachion, Kerkyra (Corfu), Leukas, Neai Patrai, Naupaktos, Larisa, Thessaloniki, and Philippoi, and their respective bishoprics (see map 1). Chomatenos worked closely together with the metropolitans John Apokaukos of Naupaktos (1200–32), Basil Pediadites (d. ca.1218), and George Bardanes of Corfu (1219–40). Hence the most important metropolises for Chomatenos were Naupaktos and Kerkyra (Corfu). Actually, all three individuals were close to Chomatenos personally, as can be seen from his correspondence with them, which has partially survived. Personal closeness bound Chomatenos most of all with John Apokaukos, his mentor and probably best friend.[7]

2. WHO WAS DEMETRIOS CHOMATENOS?

The question of who Demetrios Chomatenos was can be answered only partially, as our knowledge is fragmentary. His parents as well as the year and place of his birth are unknown. He probably came from a family of clerics from the region of Constantinople. He must have been born in the third quarter of the twelfth century and had, as is indicated by the *PD*, a brother, Stephanos, who was certainly not a cleric. It is not known where Stephanos lived and how he procured his living. In addition, according to the *PD*, Chomatenos had a cousin, Constantine, who was probably a high ecclesiastical *archon*, although we do not know where. We know only a little about Chomatenos's education before 1200. He was apparently a pupil for some time of the aforementioned Basil Pediadites, while the latter was still a teacher of rhetoric at St. Paul's church in Constantinople, and he probably acquired basic knowledge of law as a private student of John Kastamonites, metropolitan of Chalcedon from 1191 onward.[8]

The only substantial information about Chomatenos's early career can be gleaned from a letter of Apokaukos written in 1222 and addressed to the patriarch in Nicaea, which tells us that from ca. 1190 to around 1200 Chomatenos held the post of *apokrisiarios* (i.e., *nuntius*) of the archbishops of Ohrid to the patriarchate of Constantinople. Since the office of *apokrisiarios* was exercised by clerics with the rank of deacon, we may readily conclude that Chomatenos was at the time at least twenty-five years old.[9] As *apokri-siarios* he must certainly have learned a great deal about ecclesiastical policy, the patriarchal chancery, and the practical application of canon law.[10] In any event, Chomatenos later became the leading legal expert (*nomotribou-menos*) of his times and one of Byzantium's best canonists.[11] Apokaukos was also employed at the patriarchate from ca. 1186 to 1200, getting to know Chomatenos and becoming his mentor and patron.[12]

The next piece of biographical evidence is found in the first record of the *PD*, which in combination with other sources shows that Chomatenos was the *chartophylax* of the archbishopric of Ohrid since ca. 1215. He probably obtained the post under Archbishop John Kamateros (shortly before 1191[?]–1215) only after the latter returned to Ohrid ca. 1214 from his exile in Nicaea. Kamateros died shortly afterward, and Chomatenos became his successor in 1216, remaining in office until at least mid-1236 (see *PD* no. 106; *terminus ante quem* of his death is 1240). Theodore Doukas, the ruler in Epiros, had appointed Chomatenos archbishop of Ohrid on the recommendation of Metropolitan Apokaukos.[13]

Chomatenos rose to historical prominence twice. First, in 1220 he addressed a famous, but fruitless, synodal letter of protest to Sava of Serbia against the latter's consecration in Nicaea as autocephalous archbishop of Serbia; Chomatenos based his protest on the reasoning that the Serbian bishoprics were all suffragan sees of Ohrid (no. 86 of the *PD*).[14] Second, in his capacity of autocephalous archbishop and on the basis of a special synod held in Arta, Chomatenos crowned Theodore Doukas emperor in Thessaloniki in 1227. As a result, this new Byzantine emperor entered into open rivalry with Emperor John III Vatatzes of Nicaea (1221–54) who, of course, together with Patriarch Germanos II, regarded this coronation as usurpation.[15] An impassioned controversy carried out by the exchange of letters ensued, which grew to become a schism between the Nicaean and the Epirote church that was not resolved until 1233. Chomatenos's involvement in this ecclesiastical controversy was always coordinated with the leading patriarchal metropolitans in Epiros, John Apokaukos and George Bardanes. Only the archbishop of Thessaloniki, Constantine Mesopotamites, protested and left his see, going on a self-imposed exile to Nicaea.[16]

3. GENESIS, STRUCTURE, AND SIGNIFICANCE OF THE *PONEMATA DIAPHORA*

The corpus of the *PD* consists, nominally, of 152 numbered "works," which I call *records*. However, two records (nos. 93 and 97) are missing, another record (no. 145) is only a small fragment (it is perhaps a draft of

no. 20), and yet another record (no.113)—Patriarch Germanos II's reply
letter to Chomatenos—is of "foreign" origin, the only text in the whole
corpus of such origin. Thus, we have to deal in reality with 148 records
written or authorized by Chomatenos, whether acting on his own or in
cooperation with his synod. A special group among the records is the forty
letters addressed to rulers, state and ecclesiastical functionaries, as well as
his brother and his aforementioned cousin.[17] However, the great majority
of the records are non-addressed responses, expert opinions or court decisions formulated partially with and partially without the participation of
the synod.[18] As my study has shown, almost all letters, opinions, and rulings
were recorded and entered into the Ohrid register along with formal elements, such as *inscriptio* and other parts of the protocol (e.g., list of the
participants at a synodal session) as well as the eschatocol which included
the date—in accordance with the practice and rules of the patriarchal chancery in Constantinople.[19]

Unfortunately, the original register no longer exists. Nearly half a century after Chomatenos's death, some unknown individual took special interest in the material found in the Ohrid register and apparently tried to
arrange it systematically in order to make it more accessible to practitioners
of the legal profession. This person was probably John Pediasimos, *chartophylax* of the archbishopric of Ohrid temporarily around 1270/80 and subsequently cleric and writer at Thessaloniki. In order to provide information
about its rich contents, he gave every case a heading and had the records
copied, for the most part, without the aforementioned formal elements. The
material was rearranged in a completely new order into groups of subjects,
which themselves were structured in terms of form, content, and date. In
this way the original archetype of the *PD* came into existence. Even though
this archetype has, regrettably, not survived, it is philologically deducible
and partially reconstructible, in particular through *Monacensis gr.* 62 and
Scorialensis gr. 207 (both sixteenth-century codices), with the Monacensis
being a fuller textual witness to the original text.[20]

The *PD* is a valuable historical source in many respects, but for three
reasons above all. First, from a legal historical viewpoint, the *PD* is one of
the few sources that sheds light on the practical dispensation of justice in
Byzantium. Second, from the viewpoint of ecclesiastical history, the *PD* is
a central source in the Nicaean-Epirote schism and in general on ecclesiastical conditions in southeastern Europe between 1204 and 1236. Third, from
the point of view of social history, the *PD* is a first-rate source on ecclesiasti-

cal and secular life in the provinces and in smaller towns in the western and central Balkans.[21] This latter aspect pertains also to our record no. 80.

4. ANALYSIS OF RECORD NO. 80

4.1. Structure and Content

In the corpus of the *PD* record no. 80 belongs thematically to the group of cases dealing with ecclesiastical discipline and internal ecclesiastical administration.[22] In terms of its form, record no. 80 is a reply letter (*responsum*) which Chomatenos and his synod wrote as an *apophasis* (or *diagnosis*), that is, a ruling in response to an inquiry.[23] Bishop Demetrios of Bothrotos (a suffragan see of Naupaktos, today Butrint in southern Albania; see map 1) had addressed to Chomatenos and his synod an inquiry containing four problems, partially formulated as questions, and wished to obtain helpful and legally binding information. The record cites almost the entire text of the bishop's inquiry, with a brief résumé. Demetrios of Bothrotos is said to have complained that the monastery *tou Choteachobou* situated in his diocese acted unjustly toward him and infringed upon his legal prerogatives. He felt that he could not cope with this injustice alone.[24]

At the beginning of his letter Bishop Demetrios states (§ 2) why he considered it appropriate to appeal not only to the synod of the metropolitan bishop of Naupaktos (his immediate superior), but also to the synod of Ohrid. He alleged that in areas in the West under the spiritual authority of the holy synod of Constantinople only "your holy assembly" (that is to say, the synod of Ohrid) was left to clarify disputed questions. For the synod of Constantinople had been dispersed and dissolved "by the terrible assault of the *Italoi* [that is, the Latins] on *Romania* [that is, Byzantium]." As he was too weak to undertake the arduous journey to Ohrid, Bishop Demetrios was sending a letter of request to Chomatenos (addressed as "archbishop of all Bulgaria") and his synod, asking them to find a solution based on the canons of the four problems submitted by him.[25]

It is necessary to stress here the following important point. As is seen from the reference to the consequences of 1204, the court of Ohrid would hardly have been consulted if the patriarchate had still been in Constantinople. It becomes clear here that in the particular historical circumstances after 1204 Chomatenos was seen as, more or less, a substitute patriarch in the West. He indeed acted as such by providing supreme expert opinion.[26]

The four problems raised by Bishop Demetrios can be paraphrased as follows:

Problem A (§ 3): Dependent peasants (*proskathemenoi*)[27] who were Vlachs (*Blachoi*) by ethnic origin and lived in a village in his bishopric went to mass traditionally in the village church.[28] They made gifts to the church and observed Christian rituals. Then their village came into the possession of the neighboring monastery *tou Choteachobou* that had been established "by patriarchal *stauropegion*."[29] After the death of the village priest, the abbot of the monastery "pulled away" (*heilkysen*) the Vlachs from the village church and made them celebrate mass in the monastic church. Thereupon, as Bishop Demetrios reports, "priests were ordained in the village by me when I was going across the *archontia* authorized by ecclesiastical law . . . ;[30] but the priests did not gain any access to the Vlachs."[31]

Problem B (§ 4): Bishop Demetrios states that he was well aware of the circumstances and knew the rights of his parishioners. It was lawful for the Vlachs to gather in the village church where they and their parents had assembled earlier. This was so because, firstly, laypersons of every family or clan (*genos*) were subject to the spiritual power of the local bishop, and, secondly, because it was unbecoming to allow women into the monastic sanctuary under the pretext, for instance, that they should listen to hymns and not miss mass. The abbot, however, objected to the bishop by counter-arguing that it was lawful to allow the Vlachs into the monastery because the village was under the authority of the monastery and the Vlachs had had the custom of attending mass in the monastic church for fifteen years.

Problem C (§ 5): Similar was the situation of the dependent Vlach peasants in the village of Choteachobon (hence the name of the monastery), whose lands had been placed under the authority of the aforementioned monastery. In the past they had attended the village church and were thus part of the bishop's flock. However, the abbot and his predecessors made the dependent peasants settled on monastic land attend mass and be baptized in the monastic church; these peasants no longer paid any *kanonikon* (that is, in Michael Angold's words, an ecclesiastical tax "paid by both the clergy and the laity") to the bishop and were removed from the episcopal dispensation of justice.[32]

The abbot denied the possibility for making any amends by putting forward, again, as an argument the period of time that had elapsed. Bishop Demetrios counterargued that the peasants ought to assemble in the village church or in a newly erected chapel on the monastic land. It was there that they ought to receive from their bishop documents concerning sacred church rituals and pay the usual ecclesiastical levies in his diocese. According to the bishop, neither the elapsed period of time nor any holy canon prevented him from seeking rectification of the situation; therefore, he was inquiring whether the abbot's arguments were correct or his episcopal jurisdiction had been harmed unjustly.

Problem D (§ 6): In another village in the *archontia* of Choteachobon, Tzermenikon, a predecessor of Bishop Demetrios had erected a church dedicated to St. Nicholas by *stauropegion*, meaning in this case an episcopal one.[33] However, a local *archon* by the name of Taronas who lived in the village did not wish to set foot in the episcopal "domain" (*meros*). Therefore, he erected a new church dedicated to St. Nicholas, quite close to the old one, but with the status of patriarchal *stauropegion*. Demetrios now wished to know how the archbishop viewed these facts and circumstances.

Before I discuss individual points in the case in greater detail, I would like to give a brief résumé of the synodal finding under Chomatenos (§§ 7–16). Apart from references to imperial laws and ecclesiastical canons typical for Chomatenos, the synodal finding is also substantiated with detailed quotations from two decrees of the patriarchal synod dating to 1176 and 27 November 1191 under Patriarchs Michael III *tou Anchialou* and George II Xiphilinos, respectively.[34] The decision of Chomatenos and the Ohrid synod ruled that the bishop had suffered injustice in four respects. First, the patriarch's prerogative extended solely to the church erected by patriarchal *stauropegion*. All other churches, including those churches that were "somehow" (*hoposoun*) supposed to be subject to that stauropegial church, were subject to the local bishop's jurisdiction. The episcopal church was entitled to receive from these churches the customary annual harvest levy (*karpophoria*). Second, it was ruled that the Vlachs should gather for mass in their traditional village church; the priests officiating there were subject to the bishop of Bothrotos. Third, the abbot of the monastery *tou Choteachobou* was to be excommunicated if he continued to instruct the bishop's parishioners to come to the monastic church on account of its status as patriarchal *stauropegion* and if he continued to conduct marriages, baptisms, and other rituals concerning laypersons. For in this way he would be undermining both episcopal power and proper monastic life. Fourth, Taronas was determined to have built the new church in the village of Tzermenikon with the dishonest intention of encroaching on the bishop's prerogatives. Therefore, in accordance with the decree by Patriarch George II Xiphilinos (as quoted in the record), the patriarchal *stauropegion* was judged to be fraudulent and invalid. Thenceforward this church was to be part of the diocese of the bishop.

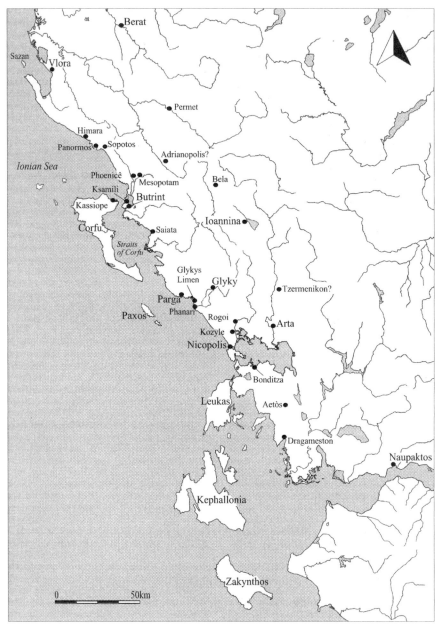

Map 2: The region of Bothrotos (Butrint). Courtesy
of Dr. William Bowden and the Butrint Foundation.

4.2. Dating and Analysis of the Content

4.2.1. Dating. Let me now turn to the dating and the contents of the case. Although it is undated, it can be narrowed down to the known term in office of Bishop Demetrios (end of 1218 to at least 1229).[35] Its position within the structure of the *PD* fits into the period 1220–30.[36] We would certainly have been able to date the case more precisely if we knew the response by Metropolitan John Apokaukos of Naupaktos to the inquiry which Bishop Demetrios addressed to him at the same time as his letter to Chomatenos. However, regrettably, Apokaukos's response has not survived with his letters, which have recently been examined in excellent and detailed studies by Kosmas Lampropoulos and Alkmini Stavridou-Zafraka.[37]

4.2.2. Aspects of the ecclesiastical and state structure in the state of Epiros. More important than the question of dating is the circumstance mentioned above that Bishop Demetrios submitted his query to two senior bishops. Such double inquiry is unknown elsewhere in the *PD*, and so far as I know, is not found in comparable source material of the period. This case is unique and throws light on the special feature of the ecclesiastical structure in the state of Epiros, namely the co-operation of the two distinct ecclesiastical jurisdictions there: that of the autocephalous archbishopric of Ohrid, on the one hand, and that of the "patriarchal" region consisting of the metropolises mentioned above, on the other.[38]

An examination of the microstructure of the bishopric of Bothrotos needs to take into account the recent research by Peter Soustal, Richard Hodges, and others on the topography and the remains of the late Greco-Roman and medieval town of Bothrotos in southern Albania (see map 2).[39] The urban area is rich in ruins and has been well researched archaeologically.[40] The site of the so-called Great Basilica, which was probably also Demetrios's episcopal church, has been identified.[41] Medieval place names in the diocese of Bothrotos are known only from our record no. 80, a proof of *PD*'s value as a source on historical geography. However, the locations of the village of Choteachobon, the monastery *tou Choteachobou*, and the village of Tzermenikon (not to be confused with Tzermernikon lying ca. thirty kilometers southwest of the city of Ioannina; see map 2) have not been established due to the lack of any identifiable remains.[42]

According to our record, during the 1220s the village of Choteachobon was the center of an *archontia*, a term which probably designated the smallest unit of civil administration in the state of Epiros.[43] Apart from Choteachobon, this civil district (located, just like Bothrotos, in the theme of Bagenitia) included at least two other villages: the unknown village with the Vlachs (village NN on map 3) which apparently came into the possession of the monastery fifteen years earlier (and thus soon after 1204) and the village of Tzermenikon with the *archon* Taronas. The monastery *tou Choteachobou* along with its landed properties and dependent peasants in the village of Choteachobon was probably also located in this *archontia* (see map 3). Thus, there were two types of landowners in the *archontia*: first, independent landowners such as the *archon* Taronas and peasant freeholders; and second, dependent peasants such as the Vlachs living at various locations on the monastery's extensive landed properties.

Whether *archontiai*, such as this one, were subject to an *archon* ("governor" or official administrator),[44] as the term suggests, is unclear. According to our text, Taronas was not "the" *archon*, but just an *archon* in Tzermenikon, and thus we do not know whether he exercised any state function. Whether there were other *archontes* apart from him is also an open question. Any precise information about the "indigenous" *archon* Taronas is lacking. The details given in our record—in combination with further sources traced by Paul Magdalino—allow us to conclude only that he was one of several aristocratic holders of this family name (probably of Armenian origin) in the area of Epiros and Thessaly.[45] He was wealthy enough to be able to fund the construction of the stauropegial church of St. Nicholas.[46] The context of the record suggests that as a large landowner in Tzermenikon Taronas was endeavoring to keep his property (probably with dependent peasants living on his land) outside of the control of the local bishop. This is the only possible explanation why he is said to have had ulterior motives when privately founding the new church of St. Nicholas under a fraudulent patriarchal *stauropegion*. The motives of the abbot were not dissimilar. We know that the abbot had put pressure on his tenant Vlach peasants to attend the monastic church in the manner described (literally "pulling them away"). Although they lived outside the monastic grounds, close to the village, whose church belonged to the bishopric of Bothrotos, they were now forced to pay levies to their landlord, the abbot, to which their bishop was actually entitled and were under the ecclesiastical jurisdiction of the abbot instead of the bishop.

The economic claims of the abbot of the monastery *tou Choteachobou* and the *archon* Taronas present us with a conflict typical of its times between a local bishop and large landowners within the bishopric, both secular and monastic. Emil Herman, John Thomas, and Michael Angold have already traced such clashes, which would normally break out when large landowners deprived bishops of regular ecclesiastical levies from tenant peasants.[47] The privileged status of patriarchal *stauropegion* was invoked to support the exemptions of a monastery or a church erected by a landowner from the bishop's jurisdiction. The abbot of the monastery *tou Choteachobou* and the *archon* Taronas both use this line of argumentation. The abbot's reference to a "custom" according to which the Vlachs attended the monastic church for fifteen years could point to the date of the monastery's *stauropegion*: the abbot had probably acquired it in the period 1208–12, when the state of Epiros was beginning to form and contacts with the ecumenical patriarchate in Nicaea had become possible.

Chomatenos, like all archbishops of Ohrid before and after him, never dared usurp a patriarchal *stauropegion*, even though he acted as a substitute patriarch in the West and was seen as such. Chomatenos advocated the protection of the rights of local bishops—and thus also the rights of parish churches and their priests—in order to strengthen their position against expanding large landowners, both lay and monastic, who attempted to circumvent the dues owed to the local bishop. Therefore, Chomatenos and his synod ruled that the Vlachs of the unknown village and the other dependent peasants of the village of Choteachobon should owe obedience to their local bishop and not the abbot.

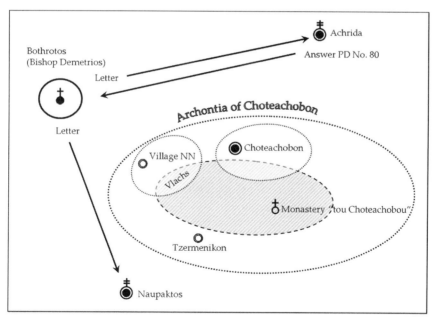

Map 3: A diagram representing case no. 80
of Demetrios Chomatenos's *Ponemata diaphora*.

NOTES

I would like to thank John M. Deasy, Mainz, for his painstaking translation of my paper and Dimiter G. Angelov for his various thoughtful suggestions.

1. *Demetrii Chomateni Ponemata diaphora*, ed. Günter Prinzing, Corpus Fontium Historiae Byzantinae 38 (Berlin: de Gruyter, 2002). *Analecta sacra et classica Spicilegio Solesmensi parata*, ed. Joannes Baptista Pitra, vol. 6, *Juris ecclesiastici Graecorum selecta paralipomena* (Rome: Roger et Chernowitz, 1891; repr. Farnborough: Gregg, 1967), pp. 1–618 (text). Cf. also "Synopticon," ibid., pp. 785–827.

2. See Günter Prinzing, "Ohrid," in *Lexikon des Mittelalters*, 9 vols. (Munich: Artemis, 1977–98), 6:1376–80; Günter Prinzing, "Achrida," in *Lexikon für Theologie und Kirche*, ed. Walter Kasper, 11 vols., 3rd ed. (Freiburg: Herder, 1993–2001), 1:115; Alexander Kazhdan, "Ohrid," in *The Oxford Dictionary of Byzantium*, ed. Alexander P. Kazhdan, 3 vols. (New York: Oxford University Press, 1991), 3:1514; Günter Prinzing, "A Quasi Patriarch in the State of Epiros: The Autocephalous Archbishop of 'Boulgaria' (Ohrid) Demetrios Chomatenos," *ZRVI* 41 (2004): 165–82 (pp. 167–68).

3. See Hans-Georg Beck, *Kirche und theologische Literatur im byzantinischen Reich* (Munich: Beck, 1959), p. 68.

4. See Prinzing, *Chomateni Ponemata*, pp. 14*–16*, and Prinzing, "A Quasi Patriarch in Epiros," p. 168.

5. Michael Angold, *Church and Society in Byzantium under the Comneni, 1081–1261* (Cambridge: Cambridge University Press, 1995), p. 240.

6. See Prinzing, *Chomateni Ponemata*, pp. 29*–30* and 206*, and Prinzing, "A Quasi Patriarch in Epiros," pp. 168–69.

7. Angold, *Church and Society*, pp. 218, 231, 240; Prinzing, *Chomateni Ponemata*, pp. 17* and 39*–40*; Prinzing, "A Quasi Patriarch in Epiros," p. 180.

8. See Prinzing, *Chomateni Ponemata*, pp. 3*–5* and 9*–10* (with n. 41); Prinzing, "A Quasi Patriarch in Epiros," pp. 170–72.

9. Vasilii G. Vasil'evskii, "Epirotica saeculi XIII," *VV* 3 (1897): 223–99 (p. 272, no. 17). About the *apokrisiarioi*, who were for the most part deacons, cf. H. M. Biedermann, "Apokrisiar," in *Lexikon des Mittelalters*, 1:758–59. With regard to the minimum age of deacons, see Beck, *Kirche und theologische Literatur*, p. 79.

10. Prinzing, *Chomateni Ponemata*, pp. 5*–10*, and Prinzing, "A Quasi Patriarch in Epiros," pp. 171–73.

11. Ruth Macrides, "Chomatenos, Demetrios," in *The Oxford Dictionary of Byzantium*, 1:426; Angold, *Church and Society*, pp. 240–62 and 419–25; Prinzing, "A Quasi Patriarch in Epiros," pp. 171 and 179; Costas Constantinides, "Ἀπὸ τὴν πνευματικὴ ζωὴ τοῦ κράτους τῆς Ἠπείρου (1204–ca. 1340)," in *Medieval Epiros: Proceedings of a Symposium* (Ioannina 17–19 September 1999), ed. Costas Constantinides (Ioannina: University of Ioannina, 2001), pp. 232–56 (pp. 240–41).

12. Angold, *Church and Society*, pp. 214 and 218, and Prinzing, *Chomateni Ponemata*, p. 5*.

13. See Prinzing, *Chomateni Ponemata*, pp. 10*–15* (NB: the information that Archbishop Kamateros assumed his office at Ohrid at least about four years before 1195 is obtained from the art historical evidence mentioned on p. 11* n. 45; the date of assumption of his office is erroneously given on p. 8*), 217*, 303*, and 19–26 (text of no. 1); Prinzing, "A Quasi Patriarch in Epiros," pp. 172–73.

14. See John Meyendorff, "St. Sava, Ohrid and the Serbian Church," *St. Vladimir's Theological Quarterly* 35 (1991): 209–21 (pp. 215–16); Gerhard Podskalsky, "Two Archbishops of Achrida (Ohrid) and Their Significance for Macedonia's Secular and Church History: Theophalyktos and Demetrios Chomatenos," in *Byzantine Macedonia: Identity, Image and History; Papers from the Melbourne Conference July 1995*, ed. John Burke and Roger Scott (Melbourne: Australian Association for Byzantine Studies, 2000), pp. 139–48 (pp. 146–47), Prinzing, *Chomateni Ponemata*, pp. 18*–19*, 26*, 179*–82*, and 296–302 (text), and Prinzing, "A Quasi Patriarch in Epiros," pp. 166 and 173–74, and most recently Alkmini Stavridou-Zafraka, "The Political Ideology of the State of Epiros," in *Urbs Capta: The Fourth Crusade and Its Consequences (La IVe Croisade et ses conséquences)*, ed. Angeliki Laiou, Réalités byzantines 10 (Paris: Lethielleux, 2005), pp. 311–23 (p. 322).

15. See Angold, *Church and Society*, pp. 539 and 542; Prinzing, *Chomateni Ponemata*, pp. 20*–22*, Prinzing, "A Quasi Patriarch in Epiros," p. 174, and Elias Giarenes, "Πτυχές τῆς ἰδεολογικῆς θέσης Νίκαιας καί Ἠπείρου. Ὁ ρόλος τοῦ χρίσματος," in *Medieval Epiros* (see n. 11, above), pp. 99–121.

16. Prinzing, *Chomateni Ponemata*, pp. 22*–27* and 223*–30*, Prinzing, "A Quasi Patriarch in Epiros," pp. 174–76.

17. Günter Prinzing, "Zu den persönlich adressierten Schreiben im Aktencorpus des Ohrider Erzbischofs Chomatenos," in *Byzantina Europaea: Księga jubileuszowa ofiarowana Professori Waldemari Ceranowi*, ed. M. Kokoszko and M. J. Leszka (Łódź: Wydawnictwo Uniwersytetu Łódzkiego, 2007), pp. 469–92.

18. Non-addressed responses are replies which feature no recipient or personal addressee, in contrast to responses directed at a specific recipient in the form of a letter.

19. After the provisional comments by Angold, *Church and Society*, p. 241, see now Prinzing, *Chomateni Ponemata*, pp. 269*–306* and 351*–52* (on p. 352* read "no. 114" instead of "no. 146"). With regard to the special feature of the Chomatenos records in comparison with the records of the patriarchal chancery see Prinzing, "A Quasi Patriarch in Epiros," pp. 178–79.

20. See Prinzing, *Chomateni Ponemata*, pp. 40*–41*, 306*–7*, 309*–13* (description of the Monacensis), 322*–24* (description of the Scorialensis), and 351*–52*; Prinzing, "A Quasi Patriarch in Epiros," p. 178, and (about Pediasimos) most recently Costas Constantinides, "Ἀπὸ τὴν πνευματικὴ ζωὴ τοῦ κράτους τῆς Ἠπείρου," pp. 241–42.

21. See Prinzing, "A Quasi Patriarch in Epiros," p. 166.

22. See Prinzing, *Chomateni Ponemata*, pp. 297*–98* (groups 8 and 18).

23. See Prinzing, *Chomateni Ponemata*, pp. 164*–67* (summary of no. 80, but see also below, nn. 30 and 31; for additions to the bibliography given in the summary, see below, nn. 28 and 47), 277*, 288*, 299*, 301*. For the text, see pp. 266–73. For the nearly synonymous terms *apophasis* (= *sententia*) and *diagnosis*, see pp. 273*, 277*, and 487 (the index).

24. Prinzing, *Chomateni Ponemata*, p. 267, line 19–p. 269, line 93 (= § 2–§ 6).

25. Prinzing, *Chomateni Ponemata*, p. 267, lines 19–20 (address), and 25–29 (text); cf. Prinzing, "A Quasi Patriarch in Epiros," p. 177.

26. See Prinzing, "A Quasi Patriarch in Epiros," pp. 173–80, and Prinzing, *Chomateni Ponemata*, p. 277* n. 35.

27. With regard to the term see Mark Bartusis, "Proskathemenos," in *The Oxford Dictionary of Byzantium*, 3:1738. Though it is not entirely clear if the *proskathemenoi* mentioned here were in fact dependent tenants (or peasants), for my part I am inclined to assume that this was the case.

28. On the Vlachs see Alexander Kazhdan, "Vlachs," in *The Oxford Dictionary of Byzantium*, 3:2183–84; and most recently Djordje Bubalo, "Vlaho episkop ili vlahoepiskop," *ZRVI* 39 (2001/2): 197–220 (p. 216 n. 84), referring to record no. 80. Vlach (Aromunian) people still live in several regions of southern and middle Albania until the present, as is shown by Thede Karl, *Ethnizität und räumliche Verteilung der Aromunen in Südosteuropa* (Münster: Institut für Geographie der Westfälischen Wilhelms-Universität, 1999), p. 30 (map 6).

29. On *stauropegion* see Angold, *Church and Society*, p. 149: "The act of foundation of a monastery required the bishop's prayer or *stauropegion*, as it was called, presumably because at the same time he implanted the cross . . . it symbolised that the new foundation came under his authority. By Balsamon's time [second half of the twelfth century, G.P.] it was becoming increasingly common for the act of foundation to come under patriarchal auspices or *stauropegion*." Cf. also Beck, *Kirche und theologische Literatur*, p. 129, and Alexander Kazhdan and Alice-Mary Talbot, "Stauropegion," in *The Oxford Dictionary of Byzantium*, 3:1946–47.

30. The following phrase, apparently an inserted comment, appears here (Prinzing, *Chomateni Ponemata*, p. 268, lines 47–48): "It is usual to call unjust the one who 'carries an ox on his tongue'." The proverbial expression refers to a person who keeps silence, since he lets his mouth be stuffed full (e.g., by bribery). In other words, Bishop Demetrios remarks that it would be unjust to accept silently the violation of his ecclesiastical rights by his opponent. The passage, I think, has been wrongly translated in *Fontes Historiae Daco-Romanae*, vol. 4, *Scriptores et acta imperii byzantini saeculorum IV–XV*, ed. Haralambie Mihăescu et al. (Bucharest: Academia Scientiarum Dacoromaniae, 1972), p. 85, since here the word *ekdikon* (p. 268, line 47) does not seem to designate an ecclesiastical official (*ekdikos*), as the Romanian translation puts it, but simply an "unjust" person (in accordance with the basic meaning of the word).

31. For the quote see Prinzing, *Chomateni Ponemata*, p. 268, lines 45–49. Cf. also the summary, p. 165*. In part it should be corrected. Read from line 19 onwards instead of "Daraufhin weihte er, der Bischof, Priester für das besagte Dorf; doch als

sich diese aufgrund kirchlichen Rechtsanspruches [gegen den der Abt verstoßen hatte] in der Archontie aufhielten, wurden sie von den Vlachen nicht zugelassen," now "Daraufhin weihte er, der Bischof, Priester für das besagte Dorf, als er sich aufgrund kirchlichen Rechtsanspruches in der Archontie aufhielt, doch wurden sie von den Vlachen nicht zugelassen."

32. For this tax see Angold, *Church and Society,* p. 61; Aristeides Papadakis, "Kanonikon," in *The Oxford Dictionary of Byzantium,* 2:1102–3. See also below, n. 47.

33. Cf. above, n. 29.

34. See Venance Grumel, *Les regestes des actes du patriarcat de Constantinople,* vol. 1, *Les actes des patriarches,* fasc. 2 and 3, *Les regestes de 715 à 1206,* 2nd rev. ed. by Jean Darrouzès (Paris: Institut français d'études byzantines, 1989), no. 1179 (referring to the decree by George II Xiphilinos, in which the decree by Michael III is inserted).

35. See Prinzing, *Chomateni Ponemata,* p. 167* (with n. 66).

36. See Prinzing, *Chomateni Ponemata,* pp. 297*, 299*, 301*–2*, and 305*.

37. Kosmas Lampropoulos, *Ioannes Apokaukos: A Contribution to the Study of His Life and Work* (Athens: Vasilopoulos, 1988), and Alkmini Stavridou-Zafraka, "Η χρονολόγηση επιστολών και εγγράφων του Ιωάννου Αποκαύκου," *Egnatia* 4 (1993–94): 143–68.

38. Ivan Snegarov, *Istoriia na Ohridskata arhiepiskopiia (ot osnovavaneto i do zavladiavaneto na Balkanskiia poluostrov ot turtsite,* 2 vols. (Sofia, 1924; repr. Sofia: Akademichno izdatelstvo M. Drinov, 1995), 1:194, already hinted at this fact.

39. Peter Soustal (with the collaboration of Johannes Koder), *Nikopolis und Kephallenia,* Tabula Imperii Byzantini 3 (Vienna: Verlag der Österreichischen Akademie der Wissenschaften, 1981), and Peter Soustal, "The Historical Sources for Butrint in the Middle Ages," in Richard Hodges, William Bowden, and Kosta Lako (with contributions by Richard Andrews et al.), *Byzantine Butrint: Excavations and Surveys 1994–1999* (Oxford: Oxbow, 2004), pp. 20–26.

40. See Soustal, *Nikopolis und Kephallenia,* pp. 58–63, 84–87, and 132–34; Timothy Gregory, "Bouthroton," in *The Oxford Dictionary of Byzantium,* 1:318–319.

41. See now William Bowden and John Mitchell, "The Christian Topography of Butrint," in *Byzantine Butrint* (see n. 39, above), pp. 104–25 (pp. 106–11), and Richard Hodges, "Byzantine Butrint: Concluding Remarks," ibid., pp. 321–26.

42. See Soustal, *Nikopolis und Kephallenia,* pp. 133 and 274, and Soustal, "The Historical Sources," p. 23.

43. See Günter Prinzing, "Studien zur Provinz- und Zentralverwaltung im Machtbereich der epirotischen Herrscher Michael I. und Theodoros Dukas (Teil II)," *Epeirotika Chronika* 25 (1983): 37–112 (pp. 88–93).

44. See Jadran Ferluga, "Archon," in *Lexikon des Mittelalters,* 1:911; Alexander Kazhdan, "Archon," in *The Oxford Dictionary of Byzantium,* 1:160; Constantine Hatzidimitriou, "The Decline of Imperial Authority in Southwest Central Greece and the Role of *Archontes* and Bishops in the Failure of Byzantine Resistance and Reconquest 1180–1297 A.D." (PhD dissertation, Columbia University, 1988), p. 7.

45. Paul Magdalino, "Between Romaniae: Thessaly and Epirus in the Later Middle Ages," in *Latins and Greeks in the Eastern Mediterranean after 1204*, ed. Benjamin Arbel, Bernard Hamilton, and David Jacoby (London: Cass, 1989), pp. 86–110 (pp. 94–102; treats our record on pp. 94, 100–102, with n. 52) and esp. p. 94: "Taronas in Arta, Naupaktos, Avlona and Thessaly in the early thirteenth century."

46. Donald Nicol, "Refugees, Mixed Population and Local Patriotism in Epiros and Western Macedonia after the Fourth Crusade," *Studies in Late Byzantine History and Prosopography* (London: Variorum Reprints, 1986), study 4, p. 6 n. 15, noticed that "this church of St. Nicholas τοῦ Ταρωνᾶ," erected in Tzermenikon, "is also referred to, as a 'patriarchal monastery', by John Apokaukos, ed. Athanasios Papadapoulos-Kerameus, *Συνοδικὰ γράμματα τοῦ Ἀποκαύκου, Βυζαντίς*, 1 (1909), no. 10, p. 27" (recte: 28). That statement, however, is clearly wrong, since the record of Apokaukos just mentioned refers to a monastery *tou en hagiois patros hemon Nikolaou tou Tarona* in Arta, which can not be identified with the church at Tzermenikon (though it may be possible, that the founder of the monastery church in Arta is the same Taronas as our Taronas in Tzermenikon). With regard to the record of Apokaukos see also Lampropoulos, *Ioannes Apokaukos*, p. 291 (no. 30).

47. Emil Herman, "Die kirchlichen Einkünfte des byzantinischen Niederklerus," *Orientalia Christiana Periodica* 8 (1942): 378–442 (pp. 409–10); John Thomas, *Private Religious Foundations in the Byzantine Empire* (Washington, D.C.: Dumbarton Oaks, 1987), pp. 238–43, esp. 241–42; Angold, *Church and Society*, pp. 339–42. Cf. also recently W. Becket Soule, "The Stauropegial Monastery," *Orientalia Christiana Periodica* 66 (2000): 147–67 (p. 153). The authors all comment on the present case.

Priests and Bishops in the Byzantine Countryside, Thirteenth to Fourteenth Centuries

ANGELIKI E. LAIOU

The Byzantine countryside has been the subject of numerous studies. It has been discussed from the point of view of the fisc, which
collected from peasants and villages its major revenues in the form of tax;
social relations and the significant changes that they underwent over time
have been much debated; its demography has been established, on the basis
of sources of varying accuracy; archaeology has been used to determine
patterns of settlement and land exploitation.[1] One important desideratum
is the study of spiritual life in the countryside, and the role of priests and
bishops, the clergy generally, in rural society. The late Božidar Ferjančić has
written on the parish clergy in late Byzantium, both in the cities and in the
countryside.[2] His valuable study is an important contribution to this topic.
My own paper has a different focus, namely, the role of priests and bishops
in the life of the inhabitants of the countryside. It is limited chronologically
to the thirteenth and fourteenth centuries, a period in which the documentation is abundant; and it is limited geographically to Macedonia, Epiros,
and Thessaly.

The village priest is a common figure in our documentation. It is not
certain that every village had a priest, and some of the very small ones
perhaps did not. On the other hand, there are villages with more than one
priest. Gomatou, in Macedonia, with a population of 562 souls in 130
households in 1300–1301 had three priests; in 1321, the population was
of similar size (537 people, 150 households), and there were two priests.[3]
The first thing that may be stated about village priests is that their social-
juridical status was, generally speaking, not different from that of the other

villagers. When the inhabitants of a village were *paroikoi*, that is, peasants who paid their taxes and rent to a landlord, and whom we usually call "dependent" peasants, the priests too shared the same status. They were, in that sense, totally integrated into village society, a fact which has been observed for this period by Ferjančić, and by Michel Kaplan for the period from the eighth to the eleventh century.[4] In terms of economic resources, they are on the high end of village society. However, in the vast majority of cases they are not outliers, that is, they do not lie outside the normal distribution of wealth in the village. Ferjančić has also pointed out that alongside the wealthy priests one finds very poor ones. Their recorded resources—vineyards, animals, and other goods—are similar to those of their fellow villagers. Both the priests and their households worked in agricultural activities like the other peasants.[5]

Occasionally we find people who do not fit that mold at all. Such is the priest Modenos, who had a peasant holding of 3,000 *modioi* (300 hectares, or 750 acres), property of a size that no other Byzantine peasant is ever known to have held, and larger than the lands of many *pronoia*-holders. Sometime before 1281, he requested and received an imperial chrysobull guaranteeing him that he would hold this land without any of the obligations of a *paroikos*, or indeed any fiscal obligations, in hereditary manner.[6] Modenos obtained the same privilege for his son-in-law, another priest named Vorkenos who, it is stated, "has until now been free of any charges owed by *paroikoi* and free of any obligations toward the fisc" (ektos pases paroikias kai pantos demosiakou telous eleutheros). In 1281, the next emperor, Andronikos II, granted the same privileges to another son-in-law of the priest, a certain Porianites. One is able to follow the fate of this piece of land down to 1321, at which point much of it had passed to the monastery of Chilandar, either through sale or through donation.

So here we have an extraordinary case of a priest, who by all indications lives in the countryside, who not only has very extensive landed property but also receives broad privileges from two successive emperors. It is a curious situation, made especially so by the insistence of Modenos and his sons-in-law to be explicitly confirmed in their status, "outside of all obligations of a *paroikos*," something which suggests that at some point they may have been *paroikoi*; but the matter is obscure. Certainly, when we meet them, the priest and his descendants themselves owned *paroikoi* in the village of Zdravikion.

Such extraordinary cases aside, the priest was, normally, a member of the village, with the same rights and obligations as the other peasants. He was, however, part of the village elite: the *prokritoi*, or *ekkritoi*, or *protogeroi*, the most respected villagers, the privileged interlocutors of the authorities, probably the mediators in everyday disputes. It should be noted here that our documentation is neither consistent nor always accurate. Sometimes the priests are specifically mentioned as one category of village society and take precedence over the rest: thus, in one of the documents regarding the village of Kometissa, in a matter of establishing the proper boundaries between the properties of the monasteries of Chilandar and Vatopedi, we find mention of "all the inhabitants of Kometissa: priests, elders (*gerontes*), householders (*oikodespotai*) and the rest of the people."[7] Two priests are mentioned ahead of the other villagers in the document, and their signatures appear first, followed by an *anagnoste*s (lector), who is the most important elder of the village (*protogeros*) and who wrote up the deed in very misspelled Greek. Thus, the priests here are distinguished from the *gerontes*. But in another, earlier, document, which is also an *in situ* investigation of a dispute between two monasteries, we find mention only of the *gerontes* of Kometissa, who are thus presented as a group. The list is headed by Michael tou Androne, priest, and Demetrios, son of the priest Vasileios.[8] Here, then, the priest is not separated from the *gerontes*, but appears as part of the group and heads the list, which is a fairly common, although not universal, occurrence.[9] The decision regarding yet another land dispute, fraught with problems, mentions the *protogeroi* and *chresimoteroi anthropoi* (the most serviceable men) of Kometissa, without distinguishing the priests.[10] In other cases, it must be admitted, the *gerontes* who act as witnesses do not include priests.[11] In such cases, as when one or two *gerontes* sign an act as individuals, and the men are not acting as a group, the transaction is unproblematic.[12]

As members of the village elite, priests are sometimes given the honorific title *kyr* or *kyros*, as are other members of this group.[13] The role in which they are most visible, given the nature of our documentation, is that of reputable witnesses to acts of land sale, or to the establishment of the boundaries of a village or of landed possessions. More, it seems that when a property transfer is problematic, the presence of the priests and/or the other village elders was necessary, as an additional guarantee of the transaction. The examples of priests acting as witnesses to land transfers are numerous, and certainly there is no question of listing them all here.[14] I will mention only one case that brings home the role of priests and other members of the clergy in important transactions.

In 1271, a number of peasants sold plots of land to Nikolaos Komnenos Angelos Maliasenos and his wife, and by extension to their heirs and to the nunnery of Nea Petra, which these two members of the aristocracy had established. One of the acts was redacted, and payment was made, in the presence of "the best men" (*hoi kreittones*) of the village of Dryanouvaina; the "best men" are described as priests, monks, and laymen, in that order.[15] Also present was their "*archiereus* (bishop) and *protosynkellos* of Demetrias, Michael." This was the most important piece of land that changed hands in the recorded transactions. The sale was, furthermore, attended by an extraordinary piece of business. All the inhabitants of the village of Dryanouvaina, acting as a community, promised that they would be, and would remain, responsible for the taxes owed to the fisc on this piece of property.[16] It is also to be noted that the sale of the land was not quite clean legally speaking: the price paid by the couple was far inferior to the "just price," as may be readily seen by the fact that the estimated tax on it was disproportionately high with regard to the sale price.[17] It may well be that this set of circumstances made it necessary for all the notables of the village, headed by the priests, to witness the act. If this is the case, then we have a situation in which the priests of the village, in their capacity as notables, are called (required?) to witness a transaction that is important to the entire village and which may also have about it more than a whiff of illegality. Of course, the presence of the bishop plays the same role; what is more, the bishop also wrote up, in his own hand, the promise of the village inhabitants to defray the tax on this piece of land. Unfortunately, the register in which the acts are recorded does not bear the signatures or the signs of the witnesses or of the villagers who signed the promissory note, and thus we cannot know how the priests appear, that is, whether in fact they head the list of signatories.[18]

It is in any case clear that the priests were among the most respected men in the village; their presence gave weight to testimony and to transactions, and perhaps, along with that of the other notables, bound the inhabitants of the village to whatever was being decided. We may imagine that the priests played the same role in internal property disputes between villagers; certainly, they are among the most frequently recorded witnesses to transactions among villagers. Furthermore, it appears that in some cases, which may be exceptional, priests imposed canonical punishment for major crimes such as murder.[19]

The priests were also the most literate people among the common folk of the countryside. Literacy is not always easy to establish, even when the documentation is more tractable to such questions than what we have here. For example, how does one establish basic literacy? Being able to write one's name rather than simply make the sign of the cross is a first guide to the most basic type of literacy.[20] Quite often, our documents give clear evidence of who can or cannot write: those who can sign their name, and those who cannot make a sign.[21] Unfortunately, many documents are copies and some of them do not include signatures or even mention who wrote his name and who made a sign. Other documents are perfectly good originals, but mention local experts, priests among them, who did not sign; or they mention the witnesses, but we do not have their signatures. Finally, there are cases where one person appears in several documents, but only in one is it mentioned that he signed his name, while in the others there is no clue as to his literacy.[22] So, no meaningful statistics are possible. What I think is possible to establish is that among the village notables no one who is not a priest or a cleric signs his name, while a number of priests do.[23] Sometimes we find priests who simply make the sign of the cross.[24]

In this period which, according to Nicolas Oikonomides, saw the highest levels of literacy in Byzantine history, our village priests had a varying level of success: they were, as a group, more literate than the laymen whom they shepherded, but among them were some who could not even sign their name.[25]

Such are the indications we have of the role of the priests in village society. A great deal escapes us still, but may be uncovered with more sustained effort. What is clear is that the priests were part and parcel of village society; they lived in the villages, they originated from these villages, according to all evidence, as the property-holding patterns show, and sometimes their sons became priests after them.[26] They were part of the social hierarchy that provided structure to the village, and they doubtless commanded some moral authority.

Of course, there were various grades of priests in the rural environment.[27] The exceptional case of the large holdings of Basil Modenos has already been mentioned. The priest Moschos, village chief of Ano Pologou, was another person of influence. We do not know how wealthy he was, but we do know that he had power, which he exercised harshly, intimidating (*piezon*) the local inhabitants. He is called an *exarchon* of the village, and a *dynastes*, probably in the general sense of the word, that is, an unjust powerful person.[28]

Even within the same family priests could hold differential power, authority, and economic stature. There were, in Arta or the area around it,[29] two brothers who brought a plea against the widow of their eldest brother, Ioannes. One of the two, Niketas, was a priest (*presbyteros, hiereus*). The dead brother, Ioannes, had also been a priest, and he was *chartophylax* of the bishopric and *tavellion* (notary). The two younger brothers were under the authority of Ioannes because, as they explain, he was the firstborn. But they also say that they worked the land because he was a *tavellion* and spent all his time studying the scriptures, while they worked in agricultural labor and on his passing were bilked by his widow. The priest Niketas does not seem too well informed about his rights; he knew only that in cases of intestate succession the siblings shared the inheritance equally. The resolution of the case is of no interest here. What is interesting is that being a priest did not, by itself, place one in a privileged economic position; that although there were two priests in this family, one was in a much more powerful position than the others by virtue of his seniority, his learning (or at least his studying), and the office he held; and that, finally, this family had all of the problems of other peasant families, and the priest Niketas was hoodwinked: to get justice he had to appeal to his bishop, who eventually referred the case to the metropolitan of Naupaktos, John Apokaukos.

The bishop, indeed, was a dominant figure in the countryside, in the lives of both the peasants and the members of the aristocracy, although the latter disposed of other avenues of appeal as well. We find bishops intervening on behalf of the people under their authority. Thus, for example, John Apokaukos tried to plead for a reduction of taxes levied on the *paroikoi* of his church, which he considered excessively large.[30] In 1307, the bishop of Kanina sought to protect the see's *paroikoi* as well as the other inhabitants of the region of Berat and Kanina from the exactions of imperial officials.[31]

The bishop's presence and authority in the lives of the inhabitants of the countryside was multifaceted, but the extent to which the authority was exercised and the presence felt, as well as the mechanisms that followed, depended on secular issues of dominance as well. The bishop as landlord had all the same rights and drew all the same benefits as secular landlords. It is possible that his interference in the lives of villagers was more extensive because of his spiritual authority, and because of the fact that there were certain aspects of family life, divorce for example, that only he could control. Hence the fascinating case of a peasant couple, Irene and Constantine, from the village of Govlastou, a dependency of the metropolis of Naupaktos. Irene hated her husband bitterly and refused to have sex with him. The metropolitan's representatives, the *epitropoi*, shut the couple up in a little room so that Constantine could force his wife to have sex; she, however, bit and scratched the poor man, thus confirming her hatred. Eventually, the metropolitan, Apokaukos, had to grant them a divorce; but the point here is that the bishop's representatives acted as mediators, to use a polite phrase, in this most personal of matters.[32]

In anything to do with marriage, divorce, and impediments to marriage the church had virtually sole authority, unless the case involved persons of such eminence that the state authorities became involved. The church here means the bishop in the first instance. Certainly, no priest could deal with such issues, although one may assume that priests were consulted, and perhaps tried to mediate, before things reached the point where formal recourse was sought or formal representations were made. The same may be said about property disputes arising from questions of succession, inheritance, and dowry. The hand of no priest is visible in our documentation, although again efforts at mediation at an early stage may be assumed; but the hand of the bishop most certainly is visible. Cases of adultery were judged by episcopal courts; so was the crime of murder.

What follows is for the most part based on the dossiers of Demetrios Chomatenos (traditionally known also as Chomatianos), archbishop of Ohrid, and John Apokaukos, metropolitan of Naupaktos, and therefore applies to western Macedonia, Epiros, Thessaly, and Corfu in the first quarter of the thirteenth century. Some of the conclusions reached here are probably applicable to other areas and times in the late Byzantine period. Some may not be: both the gentlemen mentioned above were jurists of learning and eminence, and it is possible that the number of appeals, for example, from provincial episcopal courts, or requests to them to judge cases in the first instance, was higher than in the case of other prelates.

Both Apokaukos and, to a lesser degree, Chomatenos, recognized that the local bishop was, all other things being equal, the most competent person to judge a dispute. The bishop's competence was thought to arise from the fact that he was close to the people and the events, and could launch the necessary inquiries into circumstances and motives. In answering queries sent to him by bishops, or in hearing cases on appeal, Apokaukos would quite often express his own opinion but add something to the effect that the bishop, who was more closely acquainted with the specific issues and circumstances, must exercise his own judgment on the basis of the facts and the law, human and divine.[33] In one case, a priest from a village near Ioannina appeared in Naupaktos before the assembled court, composed of bishops and some highly placed laymen, seeking a divorce for his daughter because her husband would not stay put and farm, as the priest was doing. The bishop of Ioannina was perhaps present at this meeting; in any case, he testified to the truth of the priest's statement. The bishop agreed to, or perhaps suggested that he be charged with, talking to the young man, ordering him to return home and farm, and issuing a divorce if his representations were not heeded or if the man did not appear.[34] Since the choice of occupation is hardly legal grounds for divorce, this case really was one where the bishop alone should not have made the decision.

In other cases, the metropolitan and his synod passed judgment as a court of appeals when one of the parties was not satisfied with the decision of the local bishop. Such was the case of Theodore Diavatenos from Ioannina, who first asked for the opinion and judgment of Bardanes, metropolitan of Corfu, and then appealed to Apokaukos. But even in such a case Apokaukos takes pains to say that his decision was made with the agreement of "the local bishop."[35]

Demetrios Chomatenos, too, was willing to have the local bishops decide some cases. However, being a much stricter jurist than Apokaukos, in the end he allowed the bishops much less latitude. The bishop of Pelagonia sent him a question regarding a woman, the daughter of a deacon, who was seeking a divorce because her husband slept with her "as men do with each other." Chomatenos told the bishop to make some further inquiries to ascertain the facts, and then to issue a divorce.[36] In his response to the bishop of Anaktoropolis, who was asking about the punishment to be meted out to a deacon and a lector guilty of murder, Chomatenos replies that they must be deposed from their ecclesiastical office and then adds: "This is what we say on the basis of what you told us. You will know what to do with people who have sinned in this way" (ἀλλ' ἡμεῖς μὲν ταῦτα πρὸς ἅπερ παρὰ τῆς σῆς ἐμάθομεν ἱερότητος, σὺ δὲ οἶδας, ὃ ποιήσεις ἐπὶ τοῖς οὕτω πταίσασιν).[37] The bishop of Ioannina sent Chomatenos a case regarding concubinage somewhere in the countryside of his diocese and asked to be informed as to the pertinent laws and canons. Chomatenos apprised the bishop of all the appropriate legislation and told him of the decision that should be taken in their light. He added that the bishop should read his response, saying, "you will then decide this wisely, and render a just and sagacious judgment."[38]

The bishop's knowledge of local conditions was of primary importance in determining the facts in disputes or in criminal matters. In the major crime of murder, Chomatenos judged the cases sent on appeal to him as head of the church with an eye on two things: first, preserving the monopoly of the church to punish with ecclesiastical punishment (epitimia) any murderer who sought asylum by confessing voluntarily and seeking the church's judgment; and second, imposing the proper ecclesiastical punishment, for which he sought the expert opinion of the local bishop.

To those ends he heard the cases of the people who came to him and decided on the *epitimia*. Then he would write to the local bishop asking him to ascertain the truth of the facts as stated. If what Chomatenos had heard was true, then the bishop should impose, or oversee, the *epitimia* that had already been decided upon. If not, the bishop should impose *epitimia* himself, guided by the canons.

Finally, the bishop was useful in one other capacity. He was to proclaim in church a letter by Chomatenos saying that no secular authority should subject to civil punishments someone who had already been judged by the church, on pain of excommunication.[39]

Occasionally, Chomatenos had to swallow, in silence or otherwise, episcopal decisions with which he disagreed. Niketas Theologites, a deacon of the bishopric of Servia, brought to Chomatenos a fairly complex property dispute on which the "local judges"—it must be the bishop himself—had been unable to reach a decision. The case, as described by the deacon, included a statement regarding a divorce issued by the bishop sometime earlier not on legal grounds but on the basis of implacable hatred between the spouses.[40] Implacable hatred was certainly not recognized by the civil courts as grounds for divorce; nevertheless, both Chomatenos and Apokaukos had issued divorces on just these grounds, which is really a way of saying that the marriage had irretrievably broken down.[41] In the most interesting, and rather complex, case the bishop of Prizren had many years earlier acceded to a truly illegal type of divorce: one issued on no visible legal grounds, pronounced before the bishop and the girl's parents and relatives, and registered in a document onto which the husband and the girl's parents had appended their signs. The document was an agreement, confirmed by oath, that neither side would claim the other as a spouse. The agreement was further confirmed by the presence of "trustworthy (*axiopistoi*) witnesses" and the signature of the bishop. Chomatenos called this a "local foreign [barbarous?] custom," but nevertheless in the end accepted its validity, doubtless because to do otherwise would cause major disruption; but he justified his opinion by stating that sometimes one must accept local foreign customs, especially when they had been given authority by a bishop.[42] In the case of the divorce described by Niketas Theologites, Chomatenos would have been treading on thin ground. Fortunately, the case was governed by a different law, and so Chomatenos could bypass that aspect of the case completely.

He was, however, not a man to cross. Dragomir, a village priest from Neachovou near Skopje, complained that he had been unjustly implicated in a murder case, and not only had he been deposed by the bishop of Skopje and had his property confiscated, but on top of it he was excommunicated. Having many times pleaded to have the excommunication lifted, he received a negative reply from the bishop, who claimed that it was a matter for the synod to decide. Chomatenos wrote a very severe letter to the bishop, reprimanding him for his handling of the case as well as for his lack of humanity. He furthermore "reminded" the bishop of all the pertinent canons, quoting one of them. In his final statement, he stressed the fact that the bishop was bound by the sacred canons, and that he considered it very important for bishops to make sure that they imposed punishment on no one without lawful judgment. He concluded, "it is up to you both to accept our opinion and to decide matters as the holy canons dictate." The bishop would be severely criticized if he was seen to act unjustly, was the final ominous statement of Chomatenos.[43]

When a bishop dared to reverse a legal opinion of Chomatenos, the archbishop brought the whole weight of his legal learning, his rhetoric, and his scorn to bear on the poor man. Chomatenos had decided a rather complex case involving matrimonial property. Then, for reasons of his own, Emperor Theodore Doukas sent this decision to the local bishops, to have it "tested locally" (*dokimasthenai kata topon*). The bishop of Verroia reversed Chomatenos's decision as if, says our man, it had been one brought from a barbarous land to Roman territory; barbarians, he continued, hold their own will as law. So Chomatenos wrote a long letter to Theodore Doukas citing the pertinent legislation exhaustively and making mincemeat out of the poor bishop of Verroia and his ignorance of the law.[44] The emperor, he concluded, should look closely at the legal reasoning of the two decisions, the proper and the false, and make up his own mind.

Actually, Chomatenos was not far wrong. The learning of bishops, in the law at least, varied greatly. Chomatenos praised the bishop of Kastoria, who held the first position in the hierarchy of the church under Chomatenos's authority, for being a "fighter for justice" (*dikaiosynes agonistes*), full of all kinds of wisdom and knowledgeable in canon law. The occasion for this good grade was Chomatenos's perusal of a decision of this bishop on the matter of the alienation of the property of underage orphans. The archbishop found the disposition of the case excellent, and fully in accordance with the laws.[45] The issue involved civil legislation which, while not of immense complexity, was not simple either. So the bishop of Kastoria must have been quite knowledgeable to have received praise from such an accomplished jurist as Chomatenos. In another instance, however, one is surprised by the fact that bishops claimed incompetence to judge very simple cases and sent them up to Chomatenos or Apokaukos. The dissolution of a marriage contracted before puberty—the legal age—really is open and shut, and yet the bishop of Dryinoupolis appears to have been unable to give judgment in just such a case.[46] Nor should it be so difficult to decide whether a woman whose husband had left her seven years earlier and married another (!) was entitled to a divorce. The impression one gets is not only that the learning of provincial bishops at this time and in these areas varied considerably, but also that they were subject to pressure, especially from highly placed persons. Their own motives and actions were not always pure, as may be seen by the presence of the bishop of Demetrias in the case of the peasants who sold their lands to the Maliasenoi.[47]

On the other hand, it appears that the bishops really wielded considerable power in the countryside and sometimes took decisions on their own initiative: in the case of the "foreign custom" of divorce by consent, the bishop was clearly allowing local custom to get the better of the law. Apokaukos, writing on the occasion of the elevation of the *chartophylax* of Athens Bardanes to the episcopate of Corfu, notes that "no city, no town, no habitation nay not even a single household should be without a bishop."[48] The secular, everyday lives of people in the countryside were profoundly affected by the actions and decisions of the local bishops. One hopes that their spiritual lives were also affected, and positively. But that is a matter for another study.

NOTES

1. For the recent bibliography, see Angeliki E. Laiou, "The Byzantine Village (5th–14th century)," in *Les villages dans l'Empire byzantin (IVe–XVe siècle)*, ed. Jacques Lefort, Cécile Morrisson, and Jean-Pierre Sodini (Paris: Lethielleux, 2005), pp. 31–54.

2. Božidar Ferjančić, "Ogled o parohijskom sveshtenstvu u poznoj Vizantiji," *ZRVI* 22 (1983): 59–117.

3. Angeliki E. Laiou-Thomadakis, *Peasant Society in the Late Byzantine Empire: A Social and Demographic Study* (Princeton: Princeton University Press, 1977), pp. 124–25.

4. Michel Kaplan, *Les hommes et la terre à Byzance du VIe au XIe siècle* (Paris: Publications de la Sorbonne, 1992), pp. 230–31.

5. For anecdotal evidence of the fact see Nikos Bees, "Unedierte Schriftstücke aus der Kanzlei des Johannes Apokaukos des Metropoliten von Naupaktos (in Aetolien)," *BNJ* 21 (1971–76): 1–247 (p. 57, no. 1), where it is unequivocally stated that a priest from a village outside Ioannina engaged in agricultural labor, as did all his family. He obtained a divorce for his daughter because her husband refused to farm and led an unsettled and wayward life of petty crime.

6. *Chilandar* I, no. 26; cf. *Chilandar* I, no. 27; PLP, 19219. Cf. Ferjančić, "Ogled," pp. 83–84. On Zdravikion, see Mirjana Živojinović, "Hilandarski metoh Zdravik i njegovi raniji posednitsi," *ZRVI* 20 (1981): 85–98, and the introduction to *Chilandar* I, p. 67.

7. *Vatopédi* I, no. 26 (1297). Similarly in 1338, we find mention of all the inhabitants of Kometissa, "hiereis kai gerontes kai ho loipos laos"; among the villagers, the priests sign first. The case is again a delimitation between the properties of Chilandar and Vatopedi: Louis Petit, ed., *Actes de Chilandar*, vol. 1, *Actes grecs* (*VV* 17, appendix 1), no. 128. Cf. an unusually important act of sale in 1271, which is witnessed (and signed, but since this is a cartulary the signatures are not included) by the *kreittones* of Dryanouvaina, *hieromenon, monazonton kai laikon*: Miklosich-Müller, 4:398. On this, see here p. 46

8. *Chilandar* I, no. 1b (a little after 1253).

9. E.g., in the act of sale of some land by Voulkanos to the priest Kyriakos, the document is drawn up in the presence of trustworthy witnesses (*enopion axiopiston martyron*): Ioannes tou Valampa; Demetrios tou Gaitani; Constantine Lekomatis, George the priest, son of the priest Demetrios; and Constantine Symeon, priest, *protopapas*, and cleric of the bishopric of Hierissos. All the names are wildly misspelled, as is the entire document: *Vatopédi* I, no. 34 (1302). In 1297 (*Vatopédi* I, no. 27), a number of villagers testify on a boundary dispute: the first-mentioned among the *gerontes* is a priest. In 1339 (Petit, *Chilandar*, no. 130), when a property is being delimited, the man establishing the boundaries relies on the testimony of "local people who know the boundaries," starting with the priests of the village. Cf. Petit, *Chilandar*, nos. 157, 88, 119, etc.; *Le Codex B du monastère St.-Jean-Prodrome (Serrès)*, ed. Lisa Bénou (Paris: Association Pierre Belon, 1998), no. 127 (dispute between the monasteries of Prodromos and Iviron). However, when a *protogeros* is mentioned and named, he is a layman.

10. *Chilandar* I, no. 11 (1288).

11. *Vatopédi* I, no. 43. act 6 (1308–12). The document itself does not pretend to list all of the *gerontes*; it speaks of the "heuriskomenon geronton tou topou ekeinou," which can variously mean "the elders of that place," or "the elders of that place who happened to be there."

12. A very important case, involving the monasteries of Chilandar, Lavra, and Xeropotamou, the notables of one village, are mentioned as "hieromenon kai alloion geronton," but when names are mentioned the priests are not listed first: *Chilandar* I, no. 9 (1274).

13. In this period, the term *kyr* (or *kyros*), denoting deference, is frequent in documents involving private individuals; it is much rarer in imperial documents: see Demetrios Kyritses, "The Byzantine Aristocracy in the Thirteenth and Early Fourteenth Centuries" (PhD dissertation, Harvard University, 1997), p. 12.

14. E.g., when Basil Modenos and his wife sell 950 *modioi* to Chilandar, a priest of the village is among the witnesses (Petit, *Chilandar*, no. 53); similarly, in 1321, one of the Modenos in-laws sells another piece of land to the monastery, with the agreement of a large number of relatives; the priest of the *kome* of Zdravikion, *kyros* Constantine Chlierenos, is among the witnesses: Petit, *Chilandar*, no. 59.

15. Miklosich-Müller, 4:398.

16. Miklosich-Müller, 4:391–93.

17. The sale price was 12 *hyperpyra*. If this had been the true (fiscal) value of the land, the tax on it would have been 0.5 *hyperpyra* per year; but the tax the villagers promised to pay was 2.33 *hyperpyra*; it follows that the fiscal price of the land, which in this case would be equivalent to the just price, was more than four times higher (i.e., 55.2 *hyperpyra*) than the sale price.

18. Similarly, the other acts of sale may well have been witnessed by the priests and other notables, but there is no clear mention of the witnesses: see Miklosich-Müller, 4:410–11. The act of the inhabitants of Dryanouvaina is preceded by a statement that, since it was a copy, it was not necessary to reproduce the signatures or signs of the people involved (p. 391). In other cartularies, however, the signatures (or signs) of the principals as well as those of witnesses were copied: see Nicolas Oikonomides, "Literacy in Thirteenth-Century Byzantium: An Example from Western Asia Minor," in *To Hellenikon: Studies in Honor of Speros Vryonis, Jr.*, ed. John S. Langdon et al., 2 vols. (New Rochelle, N.Y.: Caratzas, 1993), 1:254.

19. This happened to one Zoe Petzikopoulina from the theme of Kolonia: *Demetrii Chomateni Ponemata diaphora*, ed. Günter Prinzing (Berlin: de Gruyter, 2002), no. 129. (hereafter Chomatenos). She had had one of her servants mutilated, an act that led to his death. When she appealed to Chomatenos, he found mitigating circumstances in the fact that she was a woman and that she lived in a remote part of the country.

20. On literacy among the monks of Mount Athos, see Nicolas Oikonomides, "Mount Athos: Levels of Literacy," *DOP* 42 (1988): 167–78, where some of the problems of establishing literacy are discussed.

21. I cannot follow Oikonomides, "Literacy," p. 257, in the statement that when a priest has someone else sign for him he is, nevertheless, literate, or in the assumption that village priests would know how to write; this seems to preempt the question.

22. Such is the case of the priest Theodore Kormos, or Kromos, *Vatopédi* I, no. 43, act 22 répété.

23. *Vatopédi* I, nos. 28, 34, 37: in document no. 34 (1302), the priest is mentioned as "se, ton kyron paneulabestaton papan Kyriakon"; Bénou, *Le Codex B*,

no. 44; *Vatopédi* I, no. 26: a Michael *protogeros* also signs; he is a lector (*anagnostes*) and the scribe who wrote this document.

24. Bénou, *Le Codex B*, no. 95 (1329); *Vatopédi* I, no. 43, act V.

25. Oikonomides, "Literacy," pp. 259–62, finds that in the thirteenth century, in the village of Mantaia in western Asia Minor, as well as in the city of Smyrna, all the priests signed their name, and concludes that thirteenth-century Byzantine society had "a completely literate church," which does not necessarily follow.

26. On families of priests see, for example, Chomatenos, nos. 63, 98; on marriages between families of priests, deacons and lectors: ibid., nos. 66, 53.

27. On this, see also Ferjančić, "Ogled," pp. 83–105.

28. Chomatenos, no. 94.

29. The document says the two brothers came to John Apokaukos from Arta; but they were farmers, as the document shows: Athanasios Papadopoulos-Kerameus, "Synodika grammata Ioannou tou Apokaukou, Metropolitou Naupaktou," *Vyzantis* 1 (1909): 3–31 (pp. 28–30, no. 11).

30. Sophrone Pétridès, "Jean Apokaukos, lettres et autres documents inédits," *IRAIK* 14 (1909): 69–100, nos. 9 and 10; cf. Bees, "Unedierte Schriftstücke," no. 53. See also Alkmini Stavridou-Zafraka in the present volume, esp. pp. 18–19.

31. Paul Alexander, "A Chrysobull of the Emperor Andronicus II Palaeologus in Favor of the See of Kanina in Albania," *Byzantion* 15 (1940–41): 167–207 (pp. 180–83).

32. Bees, "Unedierte Schriftstücke," no. 7; cf. Angeliki E. Laiou, "Contribution à l'étude de l'institution familiale en Epire au XIIIème siècle," in Angeliki E. Laiou, *Gender, Society and Economic Life in Byzantium* (Aldershot: Variorum Reprints, 1992), study 5, pp. 310–11.

33. See, for example, Bees, "Unedierte Schriftstücke," no. 39 (response to the bishop of Velas); no. 97 (to the bishop of Ioannina); nos. 21, 22, 28 (to the bishop of Velas). No such statement appears in Papadopoulos-Kerameus, "Synodika grammata," no. 11, where the case had been referred to Apokaukos by the bishop of Ioannina.

34. Bees, "Unedierte Schriftstücke," no. 1.

35. Athanasios Papadopoulos-Kerameus, "Kanonikai praxeis Georgiou Vardane kai Ioannou Apokaukou," *Ekklesiastikos Pharos* 4 (1909): 62–67.

36. Chomatenos, no. 17; cf. ibid., no 15, to the bishop of Servia, regarding a marriage before the age of puberty: the bishop should ascertain the facts and grant the divorce.

37. Chomatenos, no. 75.

38. Chomatenos, no. 27.

39. Chomatenos, nos. 116, 120, 131. Two of the three are murder cases. On murder, see Ruth Macrides, "Killing, Asylum and the Law," *Speculum* 63 (1988): 509–88 (repr. in her *Kinship and Justice in Byzantium, 11th–15th Centuries* [Aldershot: Ashgate, 1999], study 10).

40. Chomatenos, no. 21.

41. See Laiou, "Contribution à l'étude," pp. 309–17.

42. Chomatenos, no. 153.

43. Chomatenos, no. 76.

44. Chomatenos, no. 26.

45. Chomatenos, no. 85.

46. See Bees, "Unedierte Schriftstücke," no. 28.

47. See above, p. 46.

48. Vasilii G. Vasil'evskii, "Epirotica saeculi XIII," *VV* 3 (1896): 223–99 (p. 260).

The State, the Land, and Private Property

Confiscating Monastic and Church Properties in the Palaiologan Period

KOSTIS SMYRLIS

The Byzantine state's control over land and taxes and the emperor's relations with his subjects have both received considerable attention by scholars seeking to define the political system of Byzantium under the Palaiologoi. The most powerful and coherent theory concerning these questions remains to this day the one proposed more than fifty years ago by George Ostrogorsky. Although Ostogorsky's terminology is today out of fashion and many of his ideas have been questioned, his main argument is still largely accepted: during the Palaiologan period, central authority kept growing weaker as lay and ecclesiastical magnates became stronger and richer.[1] Most recently, Angeliki Laiou has interpreted the questioning of the emperor's prerogatives in taxation matters, taking place at the beginning of the fourteenth century, as evidence of a weak state whose rights were being contested by the church and other privileged groups.[2] Another recent article, by Demetrios Kyritses, concerning this time the control of the empire's land by the state, has reached conclusions that apparently contradict the aforementioned views. According to Kyritses, in the late period the state owned most of the land, which it distributed among the magnates and soldiers, under various conditions. The recognition of full ownership rights on large estates was exceptional, awarded to some privileged institutions or individuals, and did not offer any guaranty against confiscation at times of crisis. As a consequence, the traditional legal notion of full ownership became largely obsolete.[3] The remarks of Kyritses seem to confirm, in particular for the late period, the ideas of Alexander Kazhdan, who has insisted on the state's "supreme ownership" of the land, manifest in its freedom to confiscate properties. Using examples from the tenth and eleventh centuries, Kazhdan has warned against confusing Byzantine law, which was inherited almost unchanged from the Roman Empire, with actual practice in the Middle Ages. Without denying the existence of private property in accordance with Roman law, Kazhdan has insisted on the establishment, in the middle Byzantine period, of a practice according to which the emperor could arbitrarily confiscate the land of his subjects.[4]

What I would like to do here is re-examine the question of the growing weakness of the late Byzantine state by focusing on the emperor's prerogatives over the land of his subjects—one of the areas where the power of central authority can best be measured. The notion of property in late Byzantium, which is closely related to the first question, will also be considered. I propose to discuss these issues by studying the expropriation of monastic and church lands by the state in the Palaiologan period; the property of monasteries, especially, is relatively well documented thanks to the preservation of several monastic archives. I would like to investigate the conditions under which these confiscations took place, their frequency and importance, their nature (whether they concerned land or revenues), and the end results—whether the lands were eventually restored to their owners or the latter were compensated. All these may be called the real circumstances. I will also explore the theory that developed around this issue: the justification of these measures in imperial propaganda and the claims regarding the emperor's rights, on the one hand, and the opposition by those affected, on the other.

From 1259 to the Battle of Marica in 1371

Most of the evidence regarding the confiscation of property in the Palaiologan period comes from the archives of the Athonite monasteries. This fact explains why most cases considered below concern monastic lands; it also accounts for the prominence of Chalkidiki and eastern Macedonia, the areas where most of the Athonites' estates were situated. However, the few examples coming from other regions leave no doubt as to the widespread nature of this practice, at least with regard to monastic property. In this paper, I will distinguish between the period before and after the large-scale confiscations that followed the Battle of Marica in 1371.

The first attested case of confiscation concerns some unspecified properties of Vatopedi monastery taken by the state probably before 1259. We know this from a *prostagma* of 1265 by which Emperor Michael VIII, no doubt at Vatopedi's request, donated to the latter the monastery of Koromista, to the north of Mount Pangaion. According to this act, the emperor donated Koromista in order to alleviate the difficulties caused to Vatopedi by the earlier confiscation of its properties. The *prostagma* in question is particularly interesting since, unlike the rest of our documents, it contains a relatively long explanation of the reasons behind the confiscation: it was done because the state was in need of money and of other resources for the common good, that is, to finance the military effort aimed at expanding the borders of Byzantium and at chasing away the enemies that had enslaved its lands.[5] The enemies in question have been identified as the Latins. As is well known, the Nicaean imperial government needed to mobilize significant resources to achieve victory at Pelagonia in 1259 and to recapture Constantinople from the Latins in 1261.[6] It is worth noting here that, although in the *prostagma* the cession of Koromista to Vatopedi is closely related to the confiscation, it is not considered as compensation, in the strict sense. It is rather presented as a donation freely made by an emperor caring for the well-being of the monks. Also notable is the fact that the imperial donation did not entail any alienation of state land but only the transfer of monastic property from one monastery to another.

In the period leading up to the conquest of Macedonia by the Serbian king Stefan IV Dušan in 1345, we know of a few more Athonite houses that saw their properties confiscated. The monastery of Chilandar lost two properties it had acquired thanks to the patronage of the rulers of Serbia. The first was the monastery of St. Paraskeue and its lands, near Skopje, which were lost in 1259 when the region came under the control of the Byzantines; Chilandar recovered St. Paraskeue after 1282, when Skopje became Serbian again.[7] The second was the village of Kastri, in the lower Strymon, which was ceded to *pronoiarioi* after 1277. Following the improvement of Serbo-Byzantine relations, the monastery regained Kastri in 1300, when, at the request of King Stefan Uroš II Milutin, Emperor Andronikos II restored the village to Chilandar.[8] The estates of the Athonite monasteries of Xenophon, Docheiariou, and Esphigmenou fell repeatedly victim to expropriations by the state. About 1279, Xenophon's land of Neakitou, of 300 *modioi*, in Longos, Chalkidiki, was given to the *kastrophylax* Doukopoulos; the monastery managed to recuperate the land before 1300, thanks to a donation by Doukopoulos that was sanctioned by an imperial *prostagma*.[9] During a rather complicated affair that lasted from the beginning of the fourteenth century (ca. 1300–1304) until 1337, lands of at least 1,500 *modioi* were taken from

Docheiariou's estates of Diabolokampos and Rosaion, in Kalamaria.[10] They were ceded by the state to different persons, no doubt *pronoiarioi*, including some Barbarenoi soldiers. The monastery regained its lands thanks to the patronage of a certain *vestiarios* Manuel, who, having received these lands by the emperor in full property, then ceded them to Docheiariou.[11] In 1344, the monks declared that this confiscation had been done unjustly (ἀδίκως καὶ παραλόγως).[12] Before 1338, Xenophon suffered another confiscation: some abandoned properties (*exaleimmata*) from its estate of Psalidophourna, in Longos, were ceded first to *prosalentai* (that is, rowers of the imperial navy) and then to soldiers from Thessaloniki. These last soldiers donated the lands to the monastery, their donation being sanctioned by a chryso-bull.[13] Before the Serbian conquest of 1345, Esphigmenou saw half of its village of Portarea, in Kassandra, and two-thirds of the village of Krousovo, in the lower Strymon, being ceded to certain individuals. These properties were restored to the monastery by Dušan.[14] Similar events are known to us from outside Athos and Macedonia. Lands in Arcadia, belonging to the monastery of Brontochion in Mistra, were assigned to soldiers before 1320, at which date the monks received in compensation another land of 600 *modioi*.[15] Before the Serbian conquest of Thessaly, the monastery of Zablantia lost its homonymous village, which was ceded to soldiers; Dušan gave it back to the monks.[16]

From the period of the renewed Byzantine control of western Chalkidiki, which began in 1350 and probably lasted until 1357[17], we know of a number of confiscations that hit the estates of Docheiariou in that area. Before 1355, the village of Atoubla and 1,000 *modioi* from Rosaion had been ceded to *pronoiarioi*.[18] In 1355, we also learn that following a *horismos* of Emperor John VI Kantakouzenos, who briefly controlled Thessaloniki and its region in 1350, half of the lands of Docheiariou in Diabolokampos, Hermeleia, and Amygdaleai had been ceded to different persons.[19] These confiscations, which affected most of Docheiariou's properties in the area held by the Byzantines, may reflect a more general measure that hit other monasteries as well.[20] A document from the Athonite monastery of the Great Lavra seems to lend support to this view. It is an imperial *prostagma* of December 1350 confirming the handing over (*paradosis*) of a number of properties that formed the *pronoia* of a certain Demetrios Kokalas. Among the properties given to Kokalas were the half parts of the estates that the Thessalonican monastery of Hypomimneskon and the Athonite house of St. Panteleemon possessed in the village of St. Mamas.[21] We may thus conjecture that in 1350 the Byzantines, in their effort to fight back the Serbs,[22] had taken and ceded to *pronoiarioi* the half parts of the *metochia* found in the region. This measure may have affected all monasteries. At least in the case of Docheiariou, it seems that the lands taken were gradually being restored to the monastery by the state, as soon as the *pronoiarioi* holding them died. Finally, in 1355, Emperor John V Palaiologos, recognizing the ancient rights of Docheiariou, ordered the restoration of all the lands taken by Kantakouzenos.[23]

A remarkable case concerning land belonging to the patriarchate of Consantinople comes from the same period. This case is known to us by a decision of the patriarchal synod. In November 1367, John V asked the patriarch if he could let him have the villages of Oikonomeion and Pasparas in Thrace, which were a property of the Great Church, so that he could install soldiers. The emperor asked to keep them for one year; if the project worked out, he would keep the villages, compensating the patriarchate with properties of equal revenue; if not, the emperor would restore Oikonomeion and Pasparas to the church. The patriarch replied that he did not have the right to alienate these properties and that according to the canons he was simply the guardian of the estates of the church, being the master of the revenues alone. The synod, which the patriarch convened for this purpose, fully backed his position. When the representatives of the emperor asked for the properties to be rented out to the state against an annual rent (*morte*), the synod said that the canons forbade the leasing of church properties to the powerful, even to the emperor.[24] In the end, the patriarch said that if the emperor wanted to take these villages using his own authority, he could do so; it was he who had donated them to the church[25] and he could take them if he wanted, as he had the right to do with them whatever he liked.[26] This case is interesting in many respects. We are at first impressed by the emperor's caution, especially in view of the numerous confiscations we have seen. More than interpreting this as evidence of John V's timidity,[27] I am inclined to consider it proof of the patriarchate's privileged position and a possible indication that up to then the properties of the Great Church had largely escaped confiscation or that they were normally seized after some kind of permission was given by the patriarch. Equally notable is the fact that compensation or restitution is being promised to the patriarch. This act is further interesting because it is one of the rare instances where we get to hear what the owners of properties seized by the state, or that the state wanted to seize, might have to say. The decision of the synod ends with a go-ahead. However, the synod did not just give the villages away. It invoked the legal framework restricting bishops from alienating or renting their church's property. The bishops may indeed have been concerned about acting uncanonically. But there is certainly more to it. The synod would not say no to the emperor, but it could show in this manner its disapproval of the measure. The bishops may have also attempted to suggest to the emperor how far he could go in the future. It is interesting that, although the emperor must have invoked some sort of emergency to justify his plans, nothing of the sort is stated in the synod's decision. Instead the bishops, in order to explain their sanctioning of the seizure, mentioned the fact that the two villages had been donated by the emperor. Of course, many of the Great Church's lands were imperial donations, but many other were not. Did this mean that the emperor should not touch those properties?

From this period also comes one case of proposed confiscation that in fact represents the only general measure of expropriation that is known with certainty.[28] The measure was decided in 1303 in a desperate attempt to repulse the Turkish raids that had almost entirely overrun Byzantine Asia Minor. The lands that constituted the military *pronoiai* in the East had been, to a great extent, lost, causing the soldiers to flee to the West. It was thus decided that peasants attached to the properties of monasteries, churches, and members of the imperial entourage (τοῖς βασιλεῖ παρασπίζουσιν) should be released from their masters and should be turned into soldiers; the latter were expected to stay and protect their possessions against the Turks. This suggests that the state would cede property to the peasants, including probably those lands they already exploited but which belonged until then to their masters. The response of the patriarch to this plan—no doubt given after a request of the emperor—was to send an olive tree branch, without saying a word. This was understood as an acceptance of the measure, which, however, never materialized; the advance of the Turks, in Bithynia in particular, made the plan unfeasible.[29] This case is typical with regard to the justification of the measure: the need to use the land for the military effort. It is noteworthy that Pachymeres dedicates several lines to describe the desperate situation of the emperor, who was left with no other choice but to seize the ecclesiastical properties.[30] It is possible that this passage of Pachymeres reflects the arguments used by the emperor while requesting the patriarch's approval. The extent of the measure, affecting the ecclesiastical lands of an entire province, is explained by the degree of the emergency. In this case too, as in the one dating from 1367, the emperor apparently asked the patriarch before seizing any property. We know that the Great Church had very important possessions in Asia Minor and especially in Bithynia;[31] but no doubt the patriarch was also seen as the representative of the local churches and monasteries. The patriarch's gesture in 1303, to send an olive branch and say nothing, shows that the prelate, although sanctioning the measure, avoided expressing his consent in a more explicit fashion. This attitude bears a certain resemblance to the stance taken by the synod in 1367.

In order to conclude the discussion of this period, we should have a quick look at an imperial act that illustrates the theory put forward concerning the emperor's rights over land. This is the often-cited chrysobull accorded in 1289 to the monastery of Eleousa in Thessaly. In it, Andronikos II declares that he knows "well the right of the emperor and that it is neither possible for an individual, nor for a monastery, to have secure possession of their belongings unless imperial edicts confirm it."[32]

Before we move to the last part of our study, we should make some remarks concerning the period extending from 1259 to 1371. The evidence suggests that important monastic properties were from time to time confiscated. The lands seized were normally ceded as *pronoiai* to servants of the state, most often to soldiers. In many cases, it is possible to relate the expropriations to some military emergency. This is clear in the seizure of Vatopedi's lands done probably before 1259; it may also be assumed concerning the estates confiscated during the civil wars, before the Serbian conquest of 1345, and again in 1350. But there are occasions in which a military crisis seems unlikely, as in the confiscations of properties of Chilandar and Xenophon in the last quarter of the thirteenth century.

Whether done under pressure or not, it is interesting to note that most of the confiscations known were not part of any general measure affecting all owners of an area; rather, they concerned specific estates of some monasteries. I think that this phenomenon is related to the functioning of the *pronoia* system and to the practical needs it entailed. Each time, there must have been only finite lands that could be used to form a *pronoia* since undoubtedly these estates had to satisfy a number of conditions; normally, they had to include productive land and peasants to cultivate it;[33] often, these estates would have to be situated within a specific region of the empire, probably not very far from the base of the *pronoiarios*, if he already had one,[34] or near to where his services would be needed, especially when the *pronoiarios* was going to be settled somewhere by the emperor.[35] Although the state must have always had at its disposal important tracts of land located in different parts of the empire, it may have often been difficult to come by estates fulfilling all the conditions prescribed above—hence the need to expropriate lands.

Our sources suggest that the monasteries affected by the confiscations, although quite wealthy, were not the most influential ones. Especially in the case of the Athonite houses, it may be significant that we hear of no confiscation affecting Lavra, or indeed Chilandar and Vatopedi in the first half of the fourteenth century, by which time these two establishments had become very powerful.

What was the property status of the lands seized? The rights of the monasteries over their lands did not automatically disappear at the moment of confiscation. They seem to have entered a dormant condition ready to be reactivated if the appropriate occasion was offered. The monks complied with the demands of the emperor but did not renounce their rights. Some-times, by invoking these rights, they managed to regain their lands. We saw that in 1355 John V granted a request of Docheiariou, which was based on its ancient rights, and gave some estates back to the monastery.[36] The existence of these dormant rights of the monks, however, does not seem to have limited in any way the full rights the state acquired over the lands confiscated. For example, the same emperor, John V, had issued in 1351 a chrysobull transforming a *pronoia* in Kalamaria, which included lands origi-nally belonging to Docheiariou, into the hereditary possession of the great *adnoumiastes* George Katzaras.[37]

How often were the lands restored or compensation given? In practically all cases dating to this period, the confiscated properties are eventually recuperated or the monasteries receive some other lands instead. However, our evidence is almost certainly misleading in this respect. A confiscation of a land that was never restored to a monastery or for which there was no other reparation would in most cases leave no traces in the monastic ar-chives.[38] This remark has the following logical consequence: The archives, which anyway preserve only a fraction of the total amount of documents they once comprised, most likely limit even further the number of known cases of confiscation, as they only record those for which there was reparation. This means that confiscations probably occurred more frequently than the evidence suggests at first sight. Unattested confiscation could account, per-haps more so than sale, for the not-so-rare disappearance of monastic estates from property lists over time. For the same reason, we may assume that in many cases of seizure no reparation was ever made to the monaster-ies. The examination of the confiscation cases known to us apparently confirms this assumption. Indeed, the Byzantine state does not seem to have been in the habit of restoring the lands seized or offering compensation for them. The restoration of the lands of Docheiariou in 1355 cannot alter this impression. In most of the cases discussed, recuperation is achieved thanks to the intercession of powerful individuals, such as King Milutin of Serbia, or following the donation of the confiscated lands by the *pronoiarioi* who had come to possess them. Of course, these last donations were an alienation of state land, and as such, they had to be approved by the emperor; but they caused no immediate harm to the state treasury, as it is unlikely that the *pronoiarioi* received compensation for the revenues lost. Finally, on three occasions, properties were only restored after Macedonia was conquered by Dušan in 1345. Although only two cases involving the patriarchate survive, we may note here that a considerably better treatment was reserved for the Great Church.

From 1371 to the First Conquest of Thessaloniki by the Ottomans in 1387

We can now turn to the period that begins right after the Battle of Marica in September 1371, at which the ruler of eastern Macedonia, John Uglješa, was defeated and killed by the Ottomans, and after which Byzantium became a tributary state of the Ottomans. Let us briefly recall the main political developments in the region following that event. The outcome of the battle enabled the Byzantines to regain for a short time the control of Macedonia, that is until the 1380s when the Ottomans made their final push taking Serres in 1383, Chalkidiki probably in 1384, and Thessaloniki in 1387. Nevertheless, in 1403, as a consequence of the Battle of Ankara in the previous year, Thessaloniki, along with a part of Macedonia, was recuperated by the Byzantines.[39] With the exception of a two-year-long Turkish occupation of Chalkidiki between 1411 and 1413,[40] the renewed Byzantine rule of the region lasted until the 1420s when the province fell again in the hands of the Ottomans; Thessaloniki, by then under Venetian control, was taken in 1430.[41]

This period is marked by a measure of general confiscation of massive proportions and long-lasting effects. The measure is explained in the *prostagma* that Manuel II issued in favor of the Athonites in 1408. Following is a free translation of the first lines of this act:

> Many years ago, immediately after the death of the despot of Serbia, the late Uglješa, because of the intense and sustained assault made at that time by the Turks, and taking into consideration the common good (σκέψεως γενομένης πρὸς τὸ κοινῇ λυσιτελοῦν), the decision was taken to cede to

pronoiarioi (ἔδοξεν ἵνα προνοιασθῶσι) half the *metochia* of the Athonites, [of the monasteries] of Thessaloniki, and of everybody else, in order to avoid the very real danger of losing everything. It was our intention, and it still is, if by the will of God things get better, to restore the [lands taken] to their [original owners], so that they may possess the entirety of their properties. May God permit this; for it will please us more than it will please those that will receive [the properties]. Since, due to our sins, things did not get any better up to now but on the contrary went worse, these wretched conditions forced us, against our will, to impose further burdens on these [properties]. I am not referring to the period when the Turks completely seized these [lands] and held them, but to the time before and after [that period]. . . . Because [in some estates] the half parts [retained by the monks] have been either partially or entirely confiscated, we decree that [the monks] should possess the halves of these [estates] too, so that things may conform to the initial decision and [the monks] may have the halves of [these estates and no less].[42]

The nature and significance of these confiscations have been the object of discussion. It has been suggested that the measures taken by the Byzantines in 1371 and thereafter did not actually affect the property rights of the monasteries over their lands. According to this theory, only one-half of the revenues of the properties were taken away and assigned to *pronoiarioi*.[43] The study of the already known documents along with a number of unpublished or unexplored ones, most of them from the archives of Vatopedi, may allow us to understand better the nature and extent of these confiscations. Up to now scholars have used testimony coming from the period after 1403, which indirectly informs us about the measures taken after the Battle of Marica. Fortunately, some documents of Vatopedi, dating from the 1370s, contain important data on the question. Two of them, a *paradosis* and a *prostagma* dating most probably from 1377, tell us that some years earlier the land of Vatopedi at Raphalion, in the region of the Lakes Bolbe and Langada, had been given to a company of soldiers under the command of the judge of the army, Sgouros. In 1377, at the orders of John V, the land was restored to the monks.[44] Vatopedi was less fortunate in the case of the estate of Stylarion, north of Kassandra. Apparently half of this vast property acquired in 1369 and measuring 13,000 *modioi* was seized by *protostrator* Chrysos, most likely in 1371 or shortly after. Before 1375, the monks obtained an imperial *prostagma* sanctioning the recuperation of the lands taken.[45] However, it seems that Vatopedi never managed to regain the other half of its estate. Indeed, in 1375, the monastery possessed less than 6,500 *modioi* in Stylarion. At that date, a further confiscation was carried out. A state official, executing imperial orders, rendered to Vatopedi two-thirds of the *paroikoi* and, after carefully drawing the boundaries, two-thirds of the land from Vatopedi's remaining half part, ceding one-third to the state.[46] Thus, as a result of two consecutive confiscations, Vatopedi retained only one-third of the original estate of Stylarion. This situation was no doubt maintained until the arrival of the Ottomans, since it persisted in the fifteenth century.[47]

These are the only confiscations carried out before the first Ottoman conquest of the 1380s that are known thanks to contemporary documents. Evidence from the period after Macedonia's recovery by the Byzantines in 1403 further shows the wide extent of the confiscations in the 1370s and early 1380s. Two more seizures attested in documents from August and September 1404 (that is, from the beginnings of the renewed Byzantine rule) were certainly carried out during the earlier period. The confiscations affected half of Vatopedi's village of Hermeleia and half of Lavra's Drymosyrta, which the state expropriated before Chalkidiki came under the Ottomans.[48] Early fifteenth-century documentation points to several more cases of confiscation likely dating to the 1370s and early 1380s: nine different villages or *metochia* in Chalkidiki belonging to the Athonite monasteries of Docheiariou, Lavra, and Vatopedi.[49] The part of the properties taken by the state ranges from one-half, in most cases, to the entirety of the estate. The fact that our information comes from documents dating to 1409, which do not indicate the time of expropriation, makes it impossible to determine with absolute certainty whether the properties had already been confiscated before 1384—and again in 1403—or whether they were first seized between 1403 and 1409. There are, however, indications that most of these seizures date back to the 1370s or early 1380s.[50] First, the *prostagma* of 1408 states that the confiscation after 1371 was general. Second, another *prostagma* issued after 1403 orders that the Athonites should possess their properties as they did before the Turks took Thessaloniki.[51] Third, in at least one concrete case—the one we just saw concerning Vatopedi's Hermeleia—we know that the Byzantines reinstated in 1404 the measures taken before the Ottoman conquest.[52]

Despite the generality of the measures taken after Marica, there is no doubt that some properties escaped confiscation or were quickly regained by their owners. We already saw that Vatopedi obtained the restoration of Raphalion in 1377. A document of 1404 informs us that the state never took the half part of the *metochion* of Eladiaba, near Hierissos, belonging to the same monastery. The wording of this last document, however, indicates that the fate of Eladiaba was considered exceptional.[53] From the same period we also have some allusions to expropriations of properties belonging to the diocese of Thessaloniki, and maybe also to other churches and monasteries. These were carried out in the autumn of 1383, when Thessaloniki was being threatened by the Ottomans, and were strongly condemned by the metropolitan, Isidore Glabas. The metropolitan protested against the practice of allotting to soldiers what had been dedicated to God. The utility of this economic measure was uncertain, he maintained, while only divine favor could be of help in emergencies. It seems that the diocese managed to secure the favor of the emperor, thus obtaining the restoration of at least one property.[54]

The most eloquent evidence of the debate that developed around the issue of confiscation of ecclesiastical properties in the late fourteenth century is the so-called "anti-Zealot" discourse of Nicholas Kabasilas.[55] The date of original composition of this text has proved impossible to determine. It may have been written any time during the adult lifetime of its author, from the 1340s to the 1390s. Nevertheless, it has been established that Kabasilas revised the text in the last three decades of the fourteenth century, which shows that, even if the discourse was not first written around that time, it was at least considered to be still relevant by its author.[56] The massive confiscation of monastic lands after 1371 would have provided an appropriate historical occasion.[57] The discourse's aim is primarily to condemn the confiscation of monastic properties.[58] In doing so this text reveals both the arguments used to legitimize these actions as well as their refutation by those affected. According to this discourse, the expropriation of revenues, peasants, and villages belonging to monasteries was justified by the use of the following four arguments.

First, those in charge of public affairs, taking into consideration the common good (πρὸς τὸ κοινῇ λυσιτελὲς ὁρῶντας), had both the right and the obligation to administer private properties not according to the wishes of their owners, since the latter often did not know what was best for them, but in the manner that was the most profitable to these owners (§§ 6, 9, 16). Second, the confiscated possessions were not appropriated by some individual but were put to good use; the properties taken from the monasteries were used to feed the poor, to care for priests and churches, and, especially, to arm soldiers and built fortifications. This, in fact, served the objectives of those who had donated these properties; it was better to use these properties in order to equip soldiers rather than let their revenues be wasted by monks and priests (§§ 6, 9, 17–21). Third, the monasteries had vast possessions whose revenues were spent in vain since, unlike soldiers, monks and priests, who stayed at home and faced no danger, had only limited material needs; the properties left to the monks after confiscation would still be enough to cover these needs (§ 6). Fourth, the rights of the monks over their possessions were questionable or limited: contrary to purchase, donation or bequest were not valid ways of ownership acquisition (§ 4; cf. § 11); the monks were not full owners (*despotai*) of their possessions since their alienation right was restricted (§§ 12, 16); the monks were not using the donated properties according to the wishes of the donors (§ 13).

Kabasilas refutes these claims by raising a number of counter-arguments. First, the claims of the state had no legal bearing (§§ 10–20); donation or bequest were as good means of property acquisition as was purchase (§§ 4, 11); the right of the monks to alienate their properties may have been limited but they had full rights over the revenues of these possessions (§ 12). Second, confiscations were against civil law, and the abolishment of laws and the disrespect of private property were tantamount to tyranny; if private property was not protected the economy would collapse (§§ 21, 23–26); those confiscating were not different from thieves (§ 11; cf. §§ 17–20). Third, the efficiency of confiscations was questionable, whereas they certainly brought about spiritual loss; only God could really protect a city from its enemies (§§ 21, 23; cf. § 27). Fourth, confiscations were also against divine law and displeasing to God (§§ 21, 27–32).

Some of the arguments reported or used by Kabasilas are known from other sources. The excessive and badly used wealth of the monks and the idea that what was left to them after confiscation sufficed to cover their needs are old topics of imperial rhetoric.[59] We have already seen the "common good" argument being used before in the Palaiologan period.[60] In fact, what the emperor states in the *prostagma* of 1408 may well reflect what had been said in 1371 to justify the measure: there was a military emergency threatening the common good. It is noteworthy that Kabasilas uses almost the same wording as that of the 1408 *prostagma*.[61] The opponents of these measures questioned their efficiency, emphasizing that only God could really be of help. There is a clear parallel here between Kabasilas and Isidore Glabas.[62] However most of the arguments found in the discourse are encountered nowhere else. One may remark on the insistence of Kabasilas on the strict adherence to the civil laws and to the respect of private property.[63] Even more impressive is the refutation of the confiscations as befitting a tyrannical government. Thanks to the discourse we also see that the state had produced a rather long array of claims in order to justify the measures taken. What is most interesting in this argumentation is that the rights of the monks over their lands are presented as being lesser than the rights of a full owner. This makes monastic possessions less protected than the property of individuals. The fact that such a theory had been produced by imperial propaganda suggests that monastic properties were the main target of confiscation. Is Kabasilas reporting the arguments of his opponents in full? It is doubtful. We are indeed struck by the weakness of what are supposed to be the main arguments of those seeking to legitimize the confiscations. What we see are constructions often based on the blatant misinterpretation of certain laws; they are easily refuted by Kabasilas, who was familiar with both civil and canon law.[64] The argument of the "good use" of the properties seized is equally proven inadequate. This, according to Kabasilas, has no legal relevance; the alienation of ecclesiastical property is illegal irrespective of whether the possessions seized are put to good use. Two important arguments that were being used by the state are conspicuously not mentioned, at least openly. First of all, no explicit reference is made to the pressing needs that obliged the state to have recourse to such measures. Also interesting is the fact that there is no allusion to the rights the emperor claimed to have over his subjects' properties. Nevertheless, although not explicitly listed among the arguments used by the state, they both are refuted. To the indirectly mentioned claim that extraordinary conditions can account for illegal actions,[65] Kabasilas replies that there is no point in time when unlawfulness may be accepted. The right of the emperor to confiscate is also contested. Confiscation of ecclesiastical property for whatever purpose goes against civil and sacred law; whoever orders it is a tyrant.

We can make the following concluding observations with regard to the period extending from 1371 to 1387. All evidence, which, it must be said, is exclusively Athonite, suggests that the measure taken after the Battle of Marica was indeed general, resulting in the confiscation of the half parts of all the *metochia*. The additional confiscations after 1371, mentioned in the *prostagma* of 1408, did take place, as in the case of Stylarion, where a second seizure occurred in 1375.[66] Thanks to the documentation coming from Vatopedi there can be no doubt as to the nature of the confiscation. The state took away lands. This is clear in the case of Raphalion, where only land is mentioned, and even more so in the case of Stylarion, where land is measured and then divided. In some cases, the monasteries may have regained their properties, as in the example of Raphalion. However, the emperor's

statement in the *prostagma* of 1408 that he had been unable to restore the
properties suggests that in most cases the confiscations were upheld. This,
then, was a severe and enduring setback for the monasteries of the Holy
Mountain who in 1371 were probably at their highest point of prosperity,
at least with regard to land acreage.[67]

From 1387 to the End of Byzantine Rule in Macedonia in 1423

The first conquest of Macedonia by the Ottomans was completed in 1387
with the surrender of Thessaloniki. The fate of the ecclesiastical properties
under the new regime is a question that requires further study. It has been
suggested that the Athonites and some other establishments like Prodromos
near Serres obtained early on guaranties from the new rulers and, unlike
other monasteries, managed to preserve their properties.[68] However, the
transition may have not been entirely smooth for the monks of Athos. A
fiscal act dating from 15 September 1404, that is, soon after the Byzantines
took control of Thessaloniki and its region, states that the ancient properties
of the Athonites had been taken from them "by the assault and tyrannical
rule of the impious ones."[69] That this is not rhetoric becomes clear from
the rest of the document by which the assessor surrenders to Vatopedi four
metochia. Concerning one of these *metochia*, Eladiaba near Hierissos, the assessor states that it had been spared by the Ottomans, who decided that the
monastery should keep it, apparently this being an exception. One need
also remember that in his 1408 *prostagma* on behalf of the Athonites Manuel
II describes the immediately preceding period as one "when the Turks
completely seized these [lands] and held them."[70]

    In any event, one of the first actions of the Byzantines after the recovery
of Thessaloniki and its region was to review the property status of the land.
In 1403 the Turks had to abandon many possessions which they had received as timars or in full ownership during the period of Ottoman rule.[71]
One of the most urgent concerns for the Byzantines must have been to mete
out *pronoiai* to soldiers in order to ensure the defense of the country. There
must have also been a lot of requests from individuals and institutions
seeking the confirmation of their possessions or the restoration of their
hereditary lands that had been taken by the Ottomans. Among them were
the monasteries of Mount Athos, which, as a group, were no doubt the greatest landowner of the region after the state. As mentioned above, Emperor
Manuel II issued a *prostagma* addressed to the Athonites, stipulating that the
monks should possess their estates within the region of Thessaloniki in the

same manner as they had done before the capture of the city by the Turks.[72]
This *prostagma* was issued before 29 September 1404, but its exact date is
unknown. In any case, it seems that the decision to reinstate the pre-1387
status only began to be implemented in the summer of 1404: the first preserved official acts concerning monastic properties in the region date from
August and September of that year.[73] The most interesting of these documents is the previously mentioned act of 15 September 1404, concerning
some estates of Vatopedi.[74] This document begins by evoking an imperial
decree ordering the assessor to make a survey of the *metochia* in the theme
of Thessaloniki belonging to the Athonite monasteries and to give to each
one the properties they owned by virtue of chrysobulls, *prostagmata*, and
apokatastaseis. The way this assessor proceeded is probably typical. Relying
no doubt on the documents the monks presented and apparently also using
local witnesses,[75] he established what the situation was before the Ottomans,
surrendering to the monks half or the totality of their estates, depending on
the case.

Let us now review the evidence from the period after 1404 concerning
the confiscated monastic *metochia*. It is best to begin with the already discussed *prostagma* of 1408 that Manuel II issued in favor of the Athonite
monasteries.[76] In it, the emperor remarked that he had not been able to
restore the lands seized, but that on the contrary, additional taxation was
imposed and further confiscations had taken place before and after the
Ottoman rule. By the *prostagma* in question, Manuel II gave some guaran-
tees and conceded some exemptions concerning the taxation of the lands
held by the monks. Moreover, he ordered that the Athonites should possess
no less than half of their estates, as it had been decided originally; what had
been taken in excess of one-half, sometimes resulting in the confiscation of
the entirety of the estates, was to be restored. Apart from the evidence on
the actual extent and duration of the measures, the *prostagma* also contains
interesting information regarding the justification of the confiscations by
the emperor. According to this document, the expropriation was decided
for the common good, that is, in order to hinder the Turks from taking
everything. The emperor stresses the fact that he was forced to take these
measures against his will. We have seen similar arguments used before,
especially in the case of the proposed general confiscation of 1303. What is
original here is that the emperor declares, with great emphasis, that it had
been from the beginning and it still was his intention to restore the properties to their original owners. The implications of such a statement are significant. Occasionally the rights of certain monasteries on their confiscated

properties had been acknowledged in the past by the state, as for example
in the case of Docheiariou in 1355. This is, however, the first attested time
where the property rights of the monasteries were formally recognized by
a general statement. Furthermore, this is also the first known case where the
emperor limits his own rights to seize and hold the properties of his subjects. The measures are only taken because of the emergency; once it is over
the properties have to be restored to their owners.

Considerable information regarding concrete cases of confiscation survives from this period. We have seen that half of Vatopedi's village of
Hermeleia and half of Lavra's Drymosyrta had been expropriated before
1384, the time of the first Ottoman conquest.[77] Irrespective of what its fate
was under the Ottomans, the half part of Hermeleia was again confiscated
in 1404 and was still state property in 1409 and in 1418.[78] The case of
Drymosyrta was different. In 1404, it was ordered that the entire village
should be restored to Lavra. This was apparently not implemented since in
1409 at least part of Drymosyrta belonged to the state. At that point the
village was fully restored, along with some abandoned villages, thanks to
an exchange between Lavra and the state.[79] Most probably also lost before
1384, half of St. Mamas, a village belonging to Vatopedi, was under the
state's control in 1409 and again in 1418.[80] In the same years, in 1409 and
again in 1418, the *paradosis* of one-third of the original estate of Vatopedi's
Stylarion, following the confiscation of the other two-thirds in the early
1370s, was confirmed.[81] The expropriation of eight more villages or *metochia*
belonging to the monasteries of Docheiariou and Lavra is known thanks to
documents dating from 1409. It has been suggested that they had probably
been seized already before 1384. In any case, they were confiscated, for the
second or for the first time, before 1409. An imperial *prostagma* dating from
1409 probably restored the entire village (παροικικὴ κτῆσις) of Mariana,
which had become state property; this *prostagma* was repeated in 1414.[82] A
paradosis of 1409 listing the properties of Docheiariou in Kalamaria gives
further information on the confiscation of this monastery's estates.[83] Half of
Docheiariou's Hermeleia was state property in 1409, a situation apparently
unchanged in 1414.[84] Also, half of Kalokampos remained under the state's
control in 1409. It is noteworthy that in 1409 Docheiariou possessed the
entirety of its estate of Perigardikeia, probably because it had been restored
at some point by the state.[85] The *paradosis* of 1409 does not mention two
estates of the monastery in the area, Atoubla and Longos, something which
may indicate that they had been taken by the state.[86] Information on Lavra's
estates comes from an act of exchange done in 1409 between the monks

and the state and from a fiscal act of 1420 concerning the theme of Thessaloniki.[87] We learn that half of the monastery's village of Gomatou was state property in 1409 and again in 1420. Also originally belonging to Lavra, half of the village of Karbeoi and a part of the village of Siderokausia had been ceded to *pronoiarioi* before 1409; at that date an exchange took place by virtue of which the monastery ceded to the state the possessions it retained in these villages in order to regain possessions elsewhere. Lavra recuperated in particular Drymosyrta, already mentioned above, as well as a part or the entirety of the village of Pinson, and half of the monastery's possessions at Sykai; these properties had also become state property. The exchange in question was initiated by the monks, who preferred to possess entire villages rather than share them with *pronoiarioi*, who caused them great troubles.[88] The 1409 exchange between Lavra and the state was confirmed in 1420.[89] At that date, by virtue of an imperial *horismos*, Lavra recuperated the entirety of its *metochion* of Sykai.[90] A final case concerns Vatopedi. Shortly before 1420 half of that monastery's *metochion* of Sosiana, in Langada, apparently acquired in 1405, was confiscated. It was restored in 1420 following a *horismos* of the despot Andronikos Palaiologos.[91]

In 1404, the Byzantine state decided to return to the situation prevailing immediately before the Ottoman conquest. The measures taken after 1371, which had resulted in the confiscation of one-half or more of monastic *metochia*, were reinstated. Although there is no concrete information, it is possible that further confiscations took place soon after 1404, as it may be understood by the *prostagma* of 1408.[92] It is probable that this act's stipulation that the monks should possess half of their *metochia* and no less was not fully implemented, as the case of Stylarion suggests.[93] Although in most of the surviving cases the estates are divided in two, it is possible that properties were lost to the state altogether, leaving no traces in the archives. There are a few cases of restoration of the totality of the estates to the monasteries. However, these are exceptional. The state clearly maintained the measure until the end and probably carried out some additional confiscations, as in the case of Sosiana, seized shortly before 1420.[94]

Nicolas Oikonomides has remarked that in the acts involving villages half of which had been taken by the state, the assessors recorded almost exclusively peasant taxpayers. His evidence comes from three fiscal documents on behalf of the monasteries of Lavra and Docheiariou.[95] To these documents must now be added three unpublished acts of Vatopedi, where the same phenomenon may be observed.[96] Oikonomides has also observed that when the village of Mariana was restored to Docheiariou in 1409 the emperor explained that what was given to the monastery was the possession of the *paroikoi* (παροικικὴ κτῆσις).[97] The evidence of Lavra and Docheiariou has led Oikonomides to formulate the theory mentioned earlier that the confiscations of 1371 in fact only concerned the revenues of the estates—fiscal revenues and those belonging to the landowner—not the property rights of the monasteries.[98] The logic behind Oikonomides's theory, as I understand it, is the following. The estates were not divided between the state and the monastery, since the acts do not record lands and mention no measuring or setting of boundaries. The only division that took place concerned the *paroikoi*. Half of them were retained by the monastery while the other half would have to pay all their dues to another master, whether the fisc or the *pronoiarios* assigned by the state. It has already been shown that this theory cannot hold for the 1370s: in the case of Vatopedi's Stylarion both lands and *paroikoi* are divided. But could this theory still be valid for the post-1403 period?

A definitive answer to this question cannot be given before the taxation system that prevailed in Macedonia after the first Ottoman conquest has been fully understood. This would allow us to decide whether the method of listing only the *paroikoi* in acts confirming or transferring property is owed to the special status of the estates in question or whether it reflects new taxation practices.[99] At present, I can only point out some evidence that contradicts Oikonomides's theory. In the case of the exchange of villages between Lavra and the state, in 1409, lands are in fact mentioned; several *palaiochoria* (a term normally meaning abandoned villages) water mills, vineyards, a garden, and some arable land change hands or are kept by Lavra. In the case of Sykai, half of this village's *paroikoi*, land and water rights were to be surrendered to the monastery.[100] In the case of the confiscation of Vatopedi's *metochion* of Sosiana, shortly before 1420, land is again mentioned: "half of [Sosiana], with its land, was confiscated according to the customary usage."[101] Finally, it is worth noting again that the *paradosis* of Stylarion, which in fact contains the measuring and division of that estate between the state and Vatopedi, was considered valid in 1409 and 1418.[102]

Conclusion

In the period extending from 1259 to 1371, monastic estates, but maybe also church lands, were occasionally confiscated. It seems that the affected establishments were not the most influential ones. Monastic lands were apparently the ones most often seized. This is indicated by the fact that one of the main arguments in favor of confiscation, as reported by Nicholas Kabasilas, was that the monk's rights over their lands were either invalid or limited. The great wealth that the monasteries controlled explains to some extent why they were the preferred target of expropriation. It is possible that the seizure of estates belonging to monasteries, especially if these had limited influence, was considered the least likely to cause serious reactions. The belief that the monks' wealth was excessive and that they could do with less was probably shared by many in Byzantium. Although we know little about lay properties, it is doubtful that they shared the same fate. The confiscation of an estate belonging to a moderately prosperous layman would represent a very significant reduction of that individual's fortune and would be difficult to legitimize in the eyes of the public. Moreover, a layperson owning wealth comparable to a middle-size monastery would normally be a high-ranking official, a soldier, or a functionary, whose destitution could only follow his removal from service.

The scope of expropriations was normally local and limited and was often carried out to satisfy pressing military needs. Exceptionally, when the situation was more critical, confiscations at a larger scale were decided, as in 1303 and maybe also in 1350. Restoration of the lands expropriated or compensation was apparently the exception rather than the rule. The state did not feel obliged to offer reparation, nor is there evidence of anybody forcing it to do so. No doubt because of its greater influence, the treatment reserved to the Great Church was better than that of the middle-size monasteries of the provinces. The patriarch's permission was asked in advance, and at least in one case restoration was promised.

The period after 1371 began with a massive confiscation measure that affected all the *metochia* of Byzantine Macedonia; these included some of the larger and better-exploited estates of the region. The scale of this measure is unprecedented at least in the Palaiologan period, although other plans or measures—in 1303 and 1350—had anticipated it. From 1371 up to the first conquest of Macedonia by the Ottomans, the measures were maintained overall. With the recovery of Thessaloniki and its region in 1403, the Byzantines reintroduced the measures taken before the Turks came; the confiscations were upheld until the province was definitely lost to Byzantium. The consequences were certainly grave; the monasteries were effectively deprived of one-half of the revenues from what represented the greatest part of their fortune.

Imperial propaganda advocated the emperor's prerogatives over the land of his subjects. He had the right to confiscate it, in particular if no other option was available and if this was done for the common good. He was free to compensate the owners for their losses but was not obliged to, as is shown by the case of Vatopedi in 1265. There was opposition to the confiscations by those affected. The evidence is scarce and problematic, but there are some indications suggesting that contestation became more vocal after the massive expropriations of 1371. In 1367 the synod was still quite diplomatic in showing its discontent with the measure proposed by the emperor. This is in contrast with the attitude adopted by the metropolitan of Thessaloniki, Isidore Glabas, in 1383. The contrast becomes even greater if we assign Kabasilas's discourse to the post-1371 period. This text is indeed radical. The right of the emperor to dispose of the land of his subjects is openly contested. The growing discontent and opposition could account, at least to a certain extent, for the tone and content of the *prostagma* issued by Manuel II in 1408. Emphasizing the difficulties that forced him to take these measures, the emperor recognized the monasteries' property rights, effectively binding himself to restore the confiscated lands as soon as the conditions permitted it.

The case of the expropriations of monastic and church estates is a reflection of the power of central authority and of the extent of the emperor's prerogatives. The evidence examined shows that, in spite of any opposition, the Byzantine state was able to confiscate parts of the monastic wealth whenever necessary and keep it for a long time or permanently. This process counterbalanced to a certain degree the loss of state lands that were acquired, one way or the other, by the monks. Nevertheless, at least until 1371, these confiscations were limited and could not threaten the continuity of monastic prosperity. Even in the last period of its existence, the state was in the position, despite some concessions made in imperial ideology, to seize and hold half of the monastic *metochia* of Macedonia. This evidence then suggests that the Palaiologan state may have been less weak than what is often accepted.[103]

To what extent does the evidence regarding the expropriation of monastic estates in the Palaiologan period support Kazhdan's ideas about the state's "supreme ownership" of land that limited private ownership rights? Does this evidence agree with the arguments of Kyritses concerning the uncertain nature of property in late Byzantium?

There is no doubt that the practice of confiscating estates without any previous court decision and the fact that normally no compensation was given to the dispossessed owners constitute a limitation of the right of property that would be unacceptable in a modern legal system. However, I do not think that this situation warrants Kazhdan's theory. Despite the fact that no court decision was necessary for the expropriations, one can not call these measures arbitrary. Explicitly or not, there is a constant justification of the confiscations: they were done for the common good, normally for the protection of the empire; moreover, the measures are often presented as having been forced upon a state lacking the necessary resources. The very fact that the imperial side felt obliged to justify these actions by using different theoretical constructions or by misinterpreting existing laws shows that these were considered extraordinary measures and that they were never fully accepted as a custom. Indeed, the measures were contested by the parties affected and this no doubt limited to a significant extent the freedom of the emperor in this domain.

The evidence analyzed here cannot support the idea that the notion of property had become obsolete in late Byzantium. What we see in our sources is in fact more in favor of the continued validity of private ownership, even in the case of large estates. The documents abound with mentions of the property rights of the monks, which did not cease to exist at confiscation and sometimes enabled them to recuperate their properties. It should also be stressed here that Kabasilas's opposition to the expropriations largely draws on the legal framework concerning the right to property. With the exception of the period after 1371, the practice of confiscation did not acquire an importance or a regularity that could put the concept of ownership into doubt, just as today the occasional expropriation of lands for projects of public interest does not make people feel insecure about their properties. Even the measures taken after 1371 do not necessarily represent a radical departure from the situation of relative respect of private property that has been suggested for the earlier period. This is so not only because in 1408 the emperor made a statement by which he recognized the property rights of the monasteries, but also because the emergency was such that it fully justified such a measure.

NOTES

I am grateful to Jacques Lefort and Angeliki Laiou for their comments on this article.

1. Georges Ostrogorskij, *Pour l'histoire de la féodalité byzantine* (Brussels: Editions de l'Institut de philologie et d'histoire orientales et slaves, 1954), pp. 92–186.

2. Angeliki Laiou, "Le débat sur les droits du Fisc et les droits régaliens au début du 14e siècle," *REB* 58 (2000): 97–122, esp. pp. 120–21.

3. Demetrios Kyritses, "The 'Common Chrysobulls' of Cities and the Notion of Property in Late Byzantium," *Symmeikta* 13 (1999): 229–43, esp. pp. 241–43.

4. Kazhdan has expressed this view in several books and articles; see most recently Alexander Kazhdan, "State, Feudal, and Private Economy in Byzantium," *DOP* 47 (1993): 83–100; Alexander Kazhdan and Silvia Ronchey, *L'aristocrazia bizantina, dal principio dell'XI alla fine del XII secolo* (Palermo: Sellerio, 1997), pp. 177–85. Essentially in agreement with Kazhdan, Evelyne Patlagean has recently argued that the rights of the state took precedence over those stemming from private law: "Γονικόν. Note sur la propriété allodiale à Byzance," in *Byzantium: State and Society; In Memory of Nikos Oikonomides*, ed. Anna Avramea, Angeliki Laiou, and Evangelos Chrysos (Athens: Institute for Byzantine Research, 2003), pp. 423–34, esp. pp. 433–34, for the late Byzantine period.

5. *Vatopédi* I, no. 16: "ὡς ἐνδεοῦς ὄντος τοῦ δημοσίου τοῦ μέρους ἐξόδων καὶ ἀναλωμάτων χρηματικῶν καὶ ἄλλοι [sic] τῶν ὑπὲρ τοῦ κοινοῦ καταβαλλομένων εἰς τὰς ἐκστρατείας καὶ λοιπὰς δουλείας τὰς Θεοῦ νεύσει πρὸς σύστασιν ἀφορώσας καὶ αὔξησιν καὶ πλατυσμὸν τῶν ρωμαϊκῶν σχοινισμάτων, κατατρόπωσιν δὲ καὶ ἀποδίωξιν παντὸς ἀντικειμένου [sic] μοίρας τῆς πρὸ χρόνων ἤδη πολλῶν τυραννικῶς ἐκ τῆς Ῥωμαίων ἀρχῆς ἐκτεμούσης χώρας ρωμαϊκὰς καὶ καταδουλωσάσης αὐτάς."

6. *Vatopédi* I, p. 164.

7. The kellion of St. Paraskeue in the Skopje region was a donation of King Stefan Uroš I; *Chilandar* I, p. 37.

8. The village of Kastri was an imperial donation made following a request of *župan* Demetrios; *Chilandar* I, pp. 36, 49, and nos. 8 (1271), 10 (1277). On the Serbo-Byzantine relations in this period, see ibid., pp. 39, 44–45.

9. *Xénophon*, no. 5 (1300), lines 7–9; cf. pp. 36–37.

10. In the early 1320s, other parts of the estate of Rosaion or lands that had been restored since 1300–1304 were seized but were given back to Docheiariou soon after: *Docheiariou*, no. 16 (1325–32); cf. p. 140.

11. *Docheiariou*, nos. 18 (1337), 21 (1343). On this affair, see ibid., pp. 140–41.

12. *Docheiariou*, no. 23, lines 29–30. On this expression, cf. *Lavra* I, no. 45 (1084), lines 10–11.

13. *Xénophon*, no. 25 (1338), lines 109–12; cf. no. 30 (1364), lines 9–10, 28–31. On the *prosalentai*, see *Lavra* II, pp. 17–18, and Mark Bartusis, *The Late Byzantine Army: Arms and Society, 1204–1453* (Philadelphia: University of Pennsylvania Press, 1992), pp. 47–48, 158–60.

14. *Esphigménou*, pp. 20, 22–24.

15. Gabriel Millet, "Inscriptions byzantines de Mistra," *Bulletin de correspondance hellénique* 23 (1899): 97–156 (pp. 112–15).

16. Nikos Bees, "Σερβικὰ καὶ βυζαντιακὰ γράμματα Μετεώρου," *Byzantis* 2 (1910–11): 1–100, no. 17 (1348).

17. The Byzantine control of Chalkidiki from 1350 to 1355 has been shown by Nicolas Oikonomides, "Οἱ δύο Σερβικὲς κατακτήσεις τῆς Χαλκιδικῆς τὸν ΙΔ'

αἰῶνα," *Diptycha* 2 (1980–81): 294–99. It seems that, in the western part of the peninsula at least, this rule lasted until 1357/58, as suggested by a recently published document: *Vatopédi* II, no. 111 (1358).

18. *Docheiariou*, no. 29 (1355).

19. *Docheiariou*, no. 33.

20. As suggested by Oikonomides, *Docheiariou*, p. 203.

21. *Lavra* III, no. 129.

22. See Oikonomides, "Οἱ δύο Σερβικὲς κατακτήσεις," pp. 294–95.

23. *Docheiariou*, nos. 29, 33 and notes.

24. On the inalienability of church and monastic property, see Ioannes Koni-dares, *Τὸ δίκαιον τῆς μοναστηριακῆς περιουσίας. Ἀπὸ τοῦ 9ου μέχρι καὶ τοῦ 12ου αἰῶνος* (Athens: A. Sakkoulas, 1979), pp. 254–58; Eleutheria Papagianni, "Legal Institutions and Practice in Matters of Ecclesiastical Property," in *The Economic History of Byzantium: From the Seventh through the Fifteenth Century*, ed. Angeliki Laiou, 3 vols. (Washington, D.C.: Dumbarton Oaks Research Library and Collection, 2002), 3:1061–62. On the prohibition to rent this kind of property to powerful persons, see Koni-dares, *Τὸ δίκαιον*, p. 198.

25. This was indeed the case; they had been donated by Michael VIII in 1272 (JGR, 1:663).

26. Miklosich-Müller, 1:507–8, no. 252. This document is translated and com-mented in Peter Charanis, "Monastic Properties and the State in the Byzantine Em-pire," *DOP* 4 (1948): 51–118 (pp. 115–16). See also Ostrogorskij, *Pour l'histoire de la féodalité byzantine*, pp. 160–61.

27. Charanis, "Monastic Properties," p. 116.

28. Another possible case is the one mentioned above, pp. 61–62, regarding western Chalkidiki in 1350.

29. Pachymérès, *History*, XI.9, in *Georges Pachymérès: Relations historiques*, ed. Al-bert Failler, 5 vols. (Paris: Belles Lettres, 1984–2000), 4:425–27: "ὅσον ἐν προνοίαις ἐτάττετο μοναῖς τε καὶ ἐκκλησίαις." In spite of the term *pronoia* used here, the passage no doubt refers to the estates held in full property by monasteries and churches; cf. the different understanding of Charanis, "Monastic properties," p. 111. For the translation of "τοῖς βασιλεῖ παρασπίζουσιν" as "people of the imperial entourage," see Ihor Ševčenko, "Nicolas Cabasilas' 'Anti-Zealot' Discourse: A Re-interpretation," *DOP* 11 (1957): 79–171 (p. 157 n. 125). On the interpretation of the nature of the measure, concerning peasants and not lands, see Demetrios Kyritses, "Ἀπό χωρικοί, στρατιώτες· ἀλλὸ ἕνα σχόλιο σε γνωστό χωρίο του Παχυμέρη (XI.9)," in *Ψηφίδες. Μελέτες ιστορίας, αρχαιολογίας και τέχνης στη μνήμη της Στέλλας Παπαδάκη-Ökland*, ed. Olga Gratziou and Christos Loukos (Herakleio: Panepistemiakes ekdoseis Kretes, forthcoming.

30. Failler, *Georges Pachymérès*, 4:425.

31. Cf. JGR, 1:661–63.

32. Miklosich-Müller, 5:254.

33. On the composition of *pronoiai* in this period, see most recently Nicolas Oikonomides, "The Role of the Byzantine State," in *The Economic History of Byzantium* (see n. 24, above), 3:1045–46.

34. Cf. Bartusis, *The Late Byzantine Army*, pp. 175–76.

35. Cf. the case of the rowers (*prosalentai* or *proselontes*) who, according both to Pachymeres and to documentary evidence, were assigned lands near the shore: Bartusis, *The Late Byzantine Army*, pp. 47–48.

36. See above, p. 62.

37. *Docheiariou*, no. 27. The land of Docheiariou included in the *pronoia* could be identical to the 900 *modioi* of Rosaion restored to the monastery in 1337 (cf. ibid., pp. 187, 233). This land may have been confiscated again between 1337 and 1345 or in 1350 (cf. ibid., p. 187). Alternatively, Katzaras may have obtained the chrysobull without mentioning that some lands of the *pronoia* had been restored to Docheiariou; this would explain why his son John could not produce any *paradosis* of the estate to his father when his rights on the land were being examined by three imperial officials in 1373 (ibid., no. 41). In any case, what is interesting here is that the main argument of the monks against Katzaras in 1373 is that the land in question had already been restored to them by the emperor in 1337. The reasoning of the officials' decision implies that John could have won the case had he been able to show that the land in question was ceded to his father after 1337, that is, to prove that the land had been confiscated again after 1337.

38. One of the rare cases of apparently uncompensated confiscation known to us from this period, the seizure of some estates of Iviron by the Serbs, is attested only by an act preserved in the archives of another monastery, St. Panteleemon, to which Dušan gave these properties: *Iviron* IV, pp. 13–14.

39. On these dates, see Nicolas Oikonomides, "Le haradj dans l'empire byzantin du XVe siècle," in *Actes du premier Congrès international des études balkaniques et sud-est européennes*, III (Sofia: Editions de l'Académie bulgare des sciences, 1969), pp. 681–88, esp. pp. 681–82 (repr. in Nicolas Oikonomides, *Documents et études sur les institutions de Byzance* [London: Variorum Reprints, 1976]). On Chalkidiki, cf. Nicolas Oikonomides, "The Properties of the Deblitzenoi in the Fourteenth and Fifteenth Centuries," in *Charanis Studies: Essays in Honor of Peter Charanis*, ed. Angeliki Laiou-Thomadakis (New Brunswick, N.J.: Rutgers University Press, 1980), pp. 176–98 (pp. 186–87).

40. See *Docheiariou*, p. 282.

41. For the period 1403–30, see Speros Vryonis, Jr. "The Ottoman Conquest of Thessaloniki in 1430," in *Continuity and Change in Late Byzantine and Early Ottoman Society*, ed. Anthony Bryer and Heath Lowry (Birmingham: Centre for Byzantine, Ottoman and Modern Studies; Washington, D.C.: Dumbarton Oaks, 1986), pp. 281–321 (pp. 282, 304–13; with bibliography).

42. Vladimir Mošin, ed., *Akti iz svetogorskih arhiva* (Belgrade: Srpska Kraljevska Akademija, 1939), pp. 165–67. Cf. the analysis of this document in Ostrogorskij, *Pour l'histoire de la féodalité byzantine*, pp. 161–63.

43. This idea was first launched by Paul Lemerle in *Lavra* IV, pp. 52–53: the state provisionally reclaimed the tax revenues—of the half parts—of the *metochia*, for which the monastery was previously exempted. This theory was developed by Oikonomides in *Docheiariou*, pp. 273–74, where he suggests that the state took away one-half of the fiscal revenues and of the revenues of the landowner. Mark Bartusis (*The Late Byzantine Army*, p. 169) follows the theory as it appears in *Lavra* IV: the state reclaimed the base taxes. Most recently, Oikonomides, apparently abandonning the idea that the landowner's revenues were also withdrawn, has repeated the theory as stated last by Bartusis; Oikonomides, "The Role of the Byzantine State," p. 1048 (referring only to Bartusis and not to *Docheiariou*). On this measure, see also the discussion below, pp. 75–76.

44. See the two unpublished documents preserved in the archives of Vatopedi dating to June 1366 or 1377 and 19 June 1366 or 1377. The first possible date, 1366, is unlikely since the area concerned was probably under Serbian control. The unpublished documents of Vatopedi mentioned here (hereafter *Vatopedi unp.*) will appear in *Actes de Vatopédi III* (forthcoming).

45. *Vatopédi* II, no. 142 (1369–75).

46. *Vatopédi* II, no. 147.

47. See below, p. 74.

48. *Vatopedi unp.*, 15 September 1404, and Franz Dölger, ed., *Facsimiles byzantinischer Kaiserurkunden* (Munich: Mittel- und neugriechisches Seminar der Universität München, 1931), no. 55; *Lavra* III, no. 155.

49. Docheiariou: half of Hermeleia, half of Kalokampos, the entirety of the village of Mariana; Lavra: half of Karbeoi, half of Gomatou, half (?) of Siderokausia, a part or the entirety of Pinson, all the monks' possessions at Sykai; Vatopedi: half of the families of St. Mamas. These cases are discussed in more detail below, pp. 74–75.

50. This view is apparently also accepted in *Docheiariou*, p. 273.

51. See below, pp. 72–73.

52. Cf. also below, p. 74, the case of Vatopedi's estate of Stylarion.

53. *Vatopedi unp.*, 15 September 1404.

54. See George T. Dennis, *The Reign of Manuel II Palaeologus in Thessalonica, 1382–1387* (Rome: Pontificium Institutum Orientalium Studiorum, 1960), pp. 89–91.

55. Ševčenko, "Nicolas Cabasilas' 'Anti-Zealot' Discourse."

56. Ihor Ševčenko, "The Author's Draft of Nicolas Cabasilas' 'Anti-Zealot' Discourse in *Parisinus Graecus 1276*," *DOP* 14 (1960): 187–88; Ihor Ševčenko, "A Postscript on Nicolas Cabasilas' 'Anti-Zealot' Discourse," *DOP* 16 (1962): 407–8. Cf. Peter Charanis, "Observations on the 'Anti-Zealot' Discourse of Cabasilas," *Revue des études sud-est européennes* 9 (1971): 369–76 (p. 375) (repr. in his *Social, Economic and Political Life in the Byzantine Empire* [London: Variorum Reprints, 1973]).

57. Cf. Dennis, *The Reign of Manuel II*, p. 91 n. 30; Ševčenko, "The Author's Draft," p. 188.

58. The other objective of the discourse is to condemn certain practices of the bishops: simony, the appropriation of the possessions of vacant bishoprics and the

imposition of heavy taxes on the faithful and the monasteries (Ševčenko, "Nicolas Cabasilas' 'Anti-Zealot' Discourse," §§ 5, 7, 8, 33–60).

59. See Nikephoros Phokas's novel of 963/64 in *Les novelles des empereurs macédoniens concernant la terre et les stratiotes*, ed. Nikos Svoronos (Athens: Centre de recherches byzantines, 1994), no. 8, and the information regarding the confiscations carried out by Isaac I Komnenos, in *Michaelis Attaliotae Historia*, ed. Immanuel Bekker (Bonn: Weber, 1853), pp. 60–61, and Michel Psellos, *Chronographie ou histoire d'un siècle de Byzance (976–1077)*, ed. Émile Renauld, 2 vols. (Paris: Belles Lettres, 1926–28), 2:120.

60. See above, p. 60.

61. It is indeed likely that Kabasilas's knowledge of the arguments in favor of confiscation came from the preambles of imperial acts or court orations.

62. Cf. Ševčenko, "A Postscript," pp. 405–6.

63. On the defense of private property by Kabasilas, see Angeliki Laiou, "Economic Concerns and Attitudes of the Intellectuals of Thessalonike," *DOP* 57 (2003): 205–23 (pp. 207–8).

64. Cf. Ševčenko, "Nicolas Cabasilas' 'Anti-Zealot' Discourse," p. 87 and n. 27.

65. Ševčenko, "Nicolas Cabasilas' 'Anti-Zealot' Discourse," § 31: "the time of God's law has elapsed . . . ; evil is now dominant."

66. In this context it should be noted that in 1409, some of the monastic *metochia* were in their entirety in the hands of the state, a situation that may reflect pre-1384 conditions: see above, p. 68.

67. The negative effects of the confiscations of 1371 on monastic property have already been emphasized by Ostrogorsky, *Pour l'histoire de la féodalité byzantine*, pp. 161–73. Charanis on the contrary seems to play down their importance: "Monastic properties," pp. 116–17. On the relative prosperity of the Athonites in this period, cf. *Vatopédi* II, pp. 21–24.

68. Nicolas Oikonomides, "Monastères et moines lors de la conquête ottomane," *Südost-Forschungen* 35 (1976): 1–10 (pp. 1–6). The ideas of Oikonomides are generally accepted by scholars. Cf., however, Vassilis Demetriades, "Athonite Documents and the Ottoman Occupation," in *Mount Athos in the 14th–16th centuries*, ed. Kriton Chrysochoides (Athens: Institute for Byzantine Research, 1997), pp. 50–51.

69. *Vatopedi unp*: "ἡ δὲ τῶν ἀσεβῶν ἐπιδρομὴ καὶ περὶ πάντας αὐτῶν δυναστεία καὶ αὐτὰ τὰ αὐτῶν ἀφήρπασε."

70. Mošin, *Akti*, pp. 165–67. On the treatment of monastic properties by the Ottomans during this period, see most recently K. Smyrlis, "The First Ottoman Occupation of Macedonia (c. 1383– c. 1403): Some Remarks on Land Ownership, Property Transactions and Justice," in *Diplomatics in the Eastern Mediterranean, 1000–1500: Aspects of Cross-Cultural Communication*, ed. Alexander Beihammer, Maria Parani, and Christopher Schabel (Leiden: Brill, 2008), pp. 327–48.

71. This was in implementation of the agreements between the Byzantines and Süleyman Çelebi, the eldest son of Bayezid I; see Oikonomides, "Le haradj," p. 682, and Oikonomides, "Ottoman Influence on Late Byzantine Fiscal Practice," *Südost-Forschungen* 45 (1986): 1–24, esp. pp. 2–4. These agreements were included in a

treaty signed in the first months of 1403 by Süleyman, John VII (the nephew of Manuel II), and several other Christian powers of the region. At a later point, in June 1403 or later, Manuel II most probably ratified the terms of this treaty or made a new, similar treaty with Süleyman; see George T. Dennis, "The Byzantine-Turkish Treaty of 1403," *OCP* 33 (1967): 72–88 (pp. 73–77) (repr. in his *Byzantium and the Franks, 1350–1420* [London: Variorum Reprints, 1982]).

72. This *prostagma* is mentioned in a document of 29 September 1404: Arkadios Batopedinos, "Ἁγιορειτικὰ ἀνάλεκτα ἐκ τοῦ ἀρχείου τῆς Μονῆς Βατοπεδίου," *Gregorios ho Palamas* 2 (1918): 449–52, no. 15.

73. *Vatopedi unp.*, August 1404 and 15 September 1404; Dölger, *Facsimiles*, no. 55, 16 September 1404; *Lavra* III, no. 155, August 1404. The delay between the restoration of Thessaloniki to the Byzantines in 1403 and the arrival of the assessors in Chalkidike is probably related to the uncertainty that reigned until the end of 1403 as to who would control the city, Manuel II or John VII; see John W. Barker, *Manuel II Palaeologus (1391–1425): A Study in Late Byzantine Statesmanship* (New Brunswick, N.J.: Rutgers University Press, 1969), pp. 238–45.

74. *Vatopedi unp.*

75. On the use of witnesses, cf. Dölger, *Facsimiles*, no. 55 (1404), line 5.

76. Mošin, *Akti*, pp. 165–67; cf. above, pp. 66–67.

77. See above, p. 68.

78. *Vatopedi unp.*, April 1409 and September 1418.

79. *Lavra* III, nos. 155, 161.

80. *Vatopedi unp.* August 1404 is a *prostagma* confirming to Vatopedi the possession of 28 peasant families in St. Mamas. This number may represent half of the village's population in 1404. By *Vatopedi unp.*, April 1409, the monastery is explicitly given half the families in the village, whose number is 21. In 1418, Vatopedi possessed 20 families in St. Mamas: *Vatopedi unp.*, September 1418. The situation was probably unchanged two years later: *Vatopedi unp.*, August 1420.

81. *Vatopedi unp.*, April 1409 and September 1418.

82. *Docheiariou*, no. 52. On the restoration of Mariana, cf. below, pp. 75–76.

83. *Docheiariou*, no. 53.

84. *Docheiariou*, no. 52.

85. In 1418, the monastery is still in possession of what appears to be the entire village: *Docheiariou*, no. 56.

86. *Docheiariou*, p. 273.

87. *Lavra* III, nos. 161, 165.

88. *Lavra* III, no. 161.

89. *Lavra* III, no. 165.

90. *Lavra* III, no. 165. This document seems to imply that until that day the entirety of Sykai was state property; this is in contradiction with the information coming from the act of exchange of 1409 (no. 161) according to which Lavra is given half of Sykai. If what is said in 1420 reflects the reality, this means that either Sykai was not

restored to Lavra in 1409 or that half of the *metochion* was confiscated again after that date.

91. Arkadios Batopedinos, "Ἁγιορειτικὰ ἀνάλεκτα ἐκ τοῦ ἀρχείου τῆς Μονῆς Βατοπεδίου," *Gregorios ho Palamas* 3 (1919): 209–23, 326–39, 429–41, no. 39 (1420), and *Vatopedi unp.*, August 1420. The *metochion* or *palaiochorion* of Sosiana was most probably created on the lands given in 1405 by Iakobos Tarchaneiotes, that is on half of the *palaiochorion* of Koutales, in Langadas: Batopedinos, "Ἁγιορειτικὰ ἀνάλεκτα," *Gregorios ho Palamas* 3, nos. 37 (1405), 38 (1420).

92. Cf. above, pp. 66–67.

93. In 1409 and 1418, Vatopedi apparently possessed only one-third of the original estate: see above, p. 74. Cf. also the case of the estate of Sykai, n. 90, above.

94. Cf. the remarks of Ostrogorsky in *Pour l'histoire de la féodalité byzantine*, pp. 161–73.

95. *Lavra* III, nos. 161 (1409), 165 (1420); *Docheiariou*, no. 53 (1409).

96. *Vatopedi unp.*, 15 September 1404 (recording the peasants of Hermeleia and mentioning Eladiaba, Prosphorion, and Lantzou); April 1409 (recording the peasants of Lantzou, Eladiaba, Prosphori, Hermeleia, and St. Mamas); September 1418 (recording the peasants of the same villages). Cf. also *Vatopedi unp.*, August 1404: a summary act concerning St. Mamas recording only the number of peasants (*anthropoi*) and widows.

97. *Docheiariou*, no. 52.

98. See above, p. 67.

99. Indeed, Oikonomides argues elsewhere ("Ottoman Influence") that in early fifteenth-century Chalkidiki the Byzantines did not tax, and therefore did not record, land but peasants. Discussing the same acts he used to formulate the theory mentioned above (*Lavra* III, nos. 161, 165; *Docheiariou*, no. 53), the author suggests that the taxation system the Byzantines used in this period was an imitation of the system applied by the Ottomans during their first conquest of the region. According to Oikonomides, one of the main characteristics of the system used after 1403 was that the land itself was no longer a taxable commodity; only the persons who exploited it—the *paroikoi*—had to pay taxes and tithes. This would explain why in the fifteenth-century Byzantine fiscal acts from Chalkidiki there is almost no mention of land (Oikonomides, "Ottoman Influence," esp. pp. 12–13, 22). If we were to accept the Ottoman influence theory, we would also have to accept that the reason why fiscal acts after 1403 mention primarily *paroikoi* in connection to villages, half of which had been taken by the state, may have nothing to do with the villages' property status but rather with the taxation system the Byzantines used at that time in Chalkidiki.

100. *Lavra* III, no. 161, lines 40–50.

101. Batopedinos, "Ἁγιορειτικὰ ἀνάλεκτα," *Gregorios ho Palamas*, no. 39 (1420): "παλαιοχώριον τῆς εἰρημένης θείας μονῆς τὰ Σοσιανὰ εἰς τοῦ Λαγκαδᾶ, οὗ τὰ ἥμισυ μετὰ τῆς γῆς ἐδημοσιεύθη κατὰ τὴν ἄνωθεν συνήθειαν; and a bit

further: εὐεργετοῦμεν αὐτῇ ὃ ᾔτησε, τὸ εἰρημένον ἥμισυ ἡμέτερον τῆς γῆς τοῦ εἰς Λαγκαδᾶ παλαιοχωρίου τῶν Σοσιανῶν, ὥστε ἔχειν ὁμοῦ τὸ ὅλον καὶ τὴν γῆν πᾶσαν αὐτοῦ ἐξ ὁλοκλήρου."

102. *Vatopédi* II, no. 147 (1375), and *Vatopedi unp.*, April 1409 and September 1418.

103. Although Ostrogorsky stresses the severe consequences the measures taken after 1371 had on monastic wealth, he does not consider the implications of this evidence regarding the central authority's power. He sees the whole affair as the last episode of "the long struggle between monasteries and *pronoiarioi*" that ended with the victory of the latter: *Pour l'histoire de la féodalité byzantine*, p. 173.

INTELLECTUAL LIFE AND IDEOLOGY

The Donation of Constantine
and the Church in Late Byzantium

DIMITER G. ANGELOV

It enunciates better than any monument the kind of honors which emperors who do not neglect the pursuit of piety would justly bestow on the church of Christ.

—Matthew Blastares, *Syntagma* (Rhalles-Potles, 6:260)

The Donation of Constantine *(Constitutum Constantini)* is doubtless one of the most famous forgeries of the Middle Ages.[1] The historical genesis of the Donation and the history of its exploitation in the medieval West have been much studied and discussed: the composition during the late fourth or fifth century in Rome of the *Actus Silvestri*, the source of the first part of the Donation (the *confessio*), narrating Emperor Constantine's miraculous recovery from leprosy and subsequent Christian baptism by Pope Sylvester;[2] the forging of the Donation itself (the hagiographical *confessio* and the legally substantive *donatio*), which some scholars have dated to the second half of the eighth century and others have attributed to circles close to the Lateran church in Rome;[3] the textual dissemination of various versions of the document in Latin canon law;[4] the usage of the Donation by the papacy and its ideologues;[5] the commentaries on it by jurists and glosssators;[6] and finally, the definitive exposure of the forgery between 1433 and 1460 by Renaissance humanists and church reformers.[7] The dissemination of the Donation in the Byzantine Empire and the Orthodox East is an intriguing side story in the history of this spurious document. In the East, as in the West, the Donation entered the ideological arsenal of ambitious ecclesiastics. As the words of the fourteenth-century canonist Matthew Blastares suggest, the Donation of Constantine was considered to have established a model for the relationship between emperors and the church. The question naturally arises of how the Donation—a constitutional cornerstone of the papal monarchy after the eleventh century—supported the claims and ambitions of late Byzantine ecclesiastics, whose authority and prestige were steadily rising in the period of the thirteenth, fourteenth, and fifteenth centuries.

The present article tackles this question and in the process raises new ones, some of which will be addressed here, while others go beyond the scope and ambitions of this investigation. Aspects of the reception of the Donation in Byzantium have been treated in seminal studies by George Ostrogorsky,[8] Francis Dvornik,[9] Paul Alexander,[10] Viktor Tiftixoglu,[11] Hans-Georg Krause,[12] and Gilbert Dagron.[13] These studies have been far from exhaustive, however. Scholars have been mostly interested in the circumstances of the initial Byzantine encounter with the Donation in the period before 1204. The role of the Donation after the Latin conquest of Constantinople has received less attention, which is in no way warranted by the wide textual dissemination of the Greek versions of the Donation in the later period. It is to the thirteenth century that the earliest surviving Greek manuscripts of the Donation date. Our study of the late Byzantine responses to the Donation will involve two interrelated investigations. First, we will examine the textual transmission of the Greek versions of the Donation, an examination which sheds illuminating light on contemporary interest in the forgery. Second, we will trace diverse lines of interpretations of the Donation in the domestic context of legal writing, political rhetoric, and court ceremonies, as well as in the broader confessional context of polemic with the Latins. This two-pronged investigation should enable us to draw some general conclusions about the role and place of the Donation in late Byzantium.

Byzantine receptivity to the Donation may appear paradoxical at first sight. The origins of the Donation are traditionally considered to lie in the political climate of eighth-century Rome, a climate close to the Greek East, yet hostile to Byzantine imperial interests in the era of the iconoclast controversy and papal-Frankish rapprochement. As a polemical tool in papal hands from the eleventh century onward, the Donation was a weapon used against the Byzantine church. At the same time, one should not forget that elements of the story of Constantine and Sylvester as reported by the Donation sounded plausible to Byzantine audiences. By the middle Byzantine period, the Sylvester legend had become the dominant version of the baptism of Constantine and had supplanted the historically true, but embarrassing, story of Constantine's baptism on his deathbed by the Arian bishop Eusebius. The Sylvester legend is regularly reported by Byzantine world chronicles composed from the ninth century onward.[14] The story retained vitality in the later Byzantine period, both among historians and hagiographers.[15] The first part of the Donation, the *confessio*, thus presented elements of the Constantine story which were thoroughly familiar to the Byzantines. The second part, the *donatio*, would have sounded more fantastic and certainly less appealing to Byzantine ears. After all, the privileges granted to Pope Sylvester and his successors on the throne of St. Peter meant papal supremacy in Christendom and a quasi-imperial status of the popes. Even so, the *donatio* agreed with the Byzantine ideology of the *translatio imperii* by presenting Constantine as transferring his empire to the East. Furthermore, Byzantine learned audiences and readers of hagiography were aware of a story of how Constantine had acted as a legislator immediately after his miraculous healing and baptism by Sylvester. The source of this story is the Latin *Actus Silvestri*, a hagiographical account translated into Greek probably as early as the sixth century, and continually popular in the middle and late Byzantine periods.[16] The Greek vitae of Sylvester (derived from the translation of the Latin *Actus*) relate how following his baptism Constantine issued a law prescribing partial confiscation of the property of blasphemers and another law entitling poor neophytes to receive from the imperial treasury funds and vestments necessary for their baptism.[17] During the late Byzantine period the story of the baptismal legislative measures enacted by Constantine made its way outside the context of the *Lives of Sylvester*, both in hagiography and historiography.[18] Thus, the *donatio* contained elements of the Constantine story acceptable to the Byzantines. In fact, it was this part of the document rather than the *confessio* that circulated more widely in the Greek East.

Greek Versions of the Donation and Their Circulation in Late Byzantium

Byzantium knew four different versions of the Donation of Constantine: three solely of the *donatio* and one complete with the *confessio*. Three of the versions are translations from Latin, while the fourth version represents an abridged adaptation of what, in all probability, is the oldest surviving Greek translation, the Balsamon version. Several Byzantine scholars and political figures are closely associated, whether through their written works or public careers, with each of the four versions of the Donation. Therefore, for convenience's sake we will refer to these versions as "the Balsamon version," "the Blastares version," "the Kydones version," and "the Chrysoberges version."[19] These handy designations do not imply authorship of the translation or the redaction, an issue which, unfortunately, is not resolvable with certainty for any of the four texts. Hypotheses with varying degrees of plausibility have already been proposed regarding the circumstances of production of each version. It will be our task here to assess these hypotheses and put forward some new ones.

1. THE BALSAMON VERSION (THE *DONATIO* ONLY)

Inc. δέον ἐκρίναμεν μετὰ πάντων τῶν σατραπῶν ἡμῶν καὶ πάσης τῆς συγκλήτου[20]

The earliest Greek translation of the Donation is found in the canonical commentaries of Theodore Balsamon (ca. 1130–40 to after 1195), *nomophylax* and *chartophylax* in the patriarchal bureaucracy of Constantinople during the later years of the reign of Emperor Manuel I Komnenos (1143–80) and subsequently patriarch of Antioch resident in the imperial capital. When commenting on title 8, chapter 1, of the *Nomokanon in Fourteen Titles* (the *Nomokanon* of Pseudo-Photios), which includes the provision that the see of Constantinople ought to enjoy the same prerogatives as those of Rome, Balsamon noted the Donation "presents to us the kind of prerogatives of the see of Rome."[21] Then Balsamon quoted the text of the Donation (the *donatio* only) and followed it up with an interesting commentary regarding the applicability on Byzantine soil of Constantine's concessions to the papacy. The text Balsamon quoted was a translation of the *donatio* as it appears in the famous polemical pamphlet (*libellus*) addressed in 1053 by Pope Leo IX (1049–54) to Patriarch Michael I Keroularios (1043–58) and Archbishop Leo of Ohrid.[22] The authorship of the *libellus* has been attributed to Leo IX's cardinal and envoy to Constantinople, Humbert of Silva Candida.[23] Hans-Georg Krause has shown that the Greek translation was made from a secondary branch of the textual tradition of the *libellus* associated with a group of manuscripts known as "the southern Italian collection."[24]

On the basis of his careful textual study Krause drew far-reaching conclusions. According to him, the translation of the Donation which came to be incorporated into Balsamon's canonical commentaries could not have been produced at the request of Patriarch Michael I Keroularios at the time of the Eastern Schism in 1054, as a traditional theory maintained.[25] Further

Krause argued that Pope Leo's *libellus* never reached Keroularios and that the Donation remained unknown to the Byzantine prelate.[26] The latter argument, in my opinion, overstates Krause's meticulous construction of his case. One needs to distinguish between the time and circumstances surrounding the translation of the Balsamon version, on the one hand, and Byzantine knowledge of the Donation at the time the Eastern Schism, on the other. One ought to agree with Krause that the translation which was incorporated into Balsamon's canonical commentaries should be dated after the confrontation between the papal legates and the Byzantine patriarch in 1054, if we exclude the highly unlikely possibility that the legates brought an already contaminated version of the text. The post-1054 date of the translation of the Balsamon version does not necessarily mean, however, that the legates could not have brought along to Constantinople Pope Leo's *libellus* and that the Donation remained unknown to Keroularios. Circumstantial evidence makes it virtually certain that Keroularios was aware of the Donation. Balsamon explicitly states that Keroularios and "other patriarchs" used the Donation of Constantine to legitimize their political ambitions.[27] Keroularios's political ambitions encroached on imperial prerogative. According to eleventh-century Byzantine historians, Keroularios put on purple imperial buskins, assumed the role of powerful political mediator by arranging for the accession of Isaac I Komnenos (1057–59) on the imperial throne, and asserted the authority of the patriarchal office in managing the wealth of the church.[28] Artistic evidence from the middle of the eleventh century indicates contemporary Byzantine familiarity with the Donation. The illuminations in a Vatican psalter copied in 1058/59 pay unusually high attention to the figure of St. Sylvester and seek to raise the position of priestly authority above secular power, a circumstance which can be explained in the light of current political discussions fueled by the Donation.[29] If Keroularios knew about the Donation, as we are suggesting here, one should assume one of the following two possibilities: either Keroularios became familiar with the Donation through oral communication or the Balsamon version was not the first translation of text into Greek.

There is a wide time span in which the translation of the Balsamon version could have been produced. There is no reason why it could not have come into existence soon after 1054, as the "southern Italian collection" of texts relating to the schism was already put together by about 1070.[30] The translation could also have been made during the twelfth century, when pro-papal circles readily capitalized on the Donation as a proof of the primacy of the see of St. Peter. For example, Pope Paschal II's letter of 1112 to Emperor Alexios I Komnenos (1081–1118) made a reference to the Donation, although without actually citing it.[31] Any of the numerous debates between Byzantine and Western ecclesiastics on healing the schism during the twelfth century could have brought back the *libellus* of Leo IX in its secondary version, which was a basis for the translation. It also cannot be ruled out that the translation could have emerged in the bilingual Greek- and Latin-speaking environment of southern Italy. In any case, familiarity with the Donation increased in Byzantium during the twelfth century. The first allusion to the Donation by a Byzantine historian dates to the twelfth century.[32] To the twelfth century, too, belongs the first use of the Donation in a Byzantine polemical work against the Latins, the *Sacred Arsenal* of Andronikos Kamateros.[33] Whatever the circumstances of production of the Balsamon version, we can securely say that during the lifetime of Balsamon it already circulated independently as a legal document.[34] It is interesting to observe that the Balsamon version does not always adhere closely to the Latin and makes some free interpretations. For example, the translator rendered the Latin expression *corona clericatus* (the clerical crown of Sylvester) rather loosely as "στεφάνη ἤτοι παπαλήθρα" (the latter being a rare word meaning "tonsure"). In approximately the same section of the document the translator did not render literally into Greek the Latin word *phrygium*, which designated the headgear presented by Constantine to Sylvester in lieu of the imperial crown. Instead Constantine placed on the pope's head a *loros*, a mistaken translation of the word *phrygium*, probably induced by the fact that in the Latin original the *phrygium* is said to symbolize the Resurrection, while in Byzantium (according to the tenth-century *Book of Ceremonies* of Constantine Porphyrogennetos) the imperial *loros* was too a symbol of the Resurrection. In reality, the *loros* was not a piece of imperial headgear, but a bejeweled scarf embroidered with gold and worn on ceremonial occasions.[35]

The Balsamon version of the Donation was transmitted after 1204 both in Balsamon's commentaries on the *Nomokanon in Fourteen Titles* and as a self-contained, independently circulating document. Within Balsamon's commentaries on the *Nomokanon*, the special interest which the Donation raised among reading audiences is attested by the occasional appearance of marginalia consisting of the Donation's title[36] or an elaborately drawn index finger meant to attract in an instant the reader's attention to the document.[37] In a thirteenth-century manuscript which is especially important for the history of Balsamon's commentaries (Vaticanus Palatinus 384), the folio containing most of the text of the Donation was torn off and pasted toward the beginning of the manuscript.[38]

A. The Balsamon Version as a Self-Contained Text

The independent circulation of the Balsamon version, which I have been able to trace in more than ten post-1204 manuscripts, highlights in particular a late Byzantine fascination with the Donation. Important patterns in its independent circulation should be mentioned here, while appendix 1 (below) examines the cases in greater detail. The post-1204 copies bear signs of the provenance of the text: a note preceding the Donation and stating that "this [text] has been extracted from the eighth title of [the *Nomokanon* of] the most holy patriarch of Constantinople Photios."[39] The self-contained Balsamon version of the Donation circulated in predominantly legalistic contexts. First, it appears in manuscripts which contain Balsamon's canonical works other than his commentaries on the *Nomokanon in Fourteen Titles*. A representative example is Ambrosianus graecus 682 (Q. 76 sup.) copied in 1287/88.[40] Here the Donation was copied after Balsamon's responses to the inquiries of Patriarch Mark of Alexandria and just before his commentaries on the ecumenical and the local councils; the impression created by this sequence of texts is that the Donation opens Balsamon's commentaries. Second, the Balsamon version was copied in codices transmitting the *Hexabiblos* of Constantine Harmenopoulos and the *Syntagma* of Matthew Blastares, the two most important compendia of secular and religious legislation produced in the late Byzantine period. The Balsamon version was copied in these manuscripts despite the fact that an abridged text of the Donation was an integral part of Blastares' *Syntagma* and that this abridged text was often appended to the *Hexabiblos* of Harmenopoulos, as we will see later on. Third, the Balsamon version made its way into an interpolated late Byzantine redaction of the *Nomokanon in Fifty Titles*, the earliest Byzantine *nomokanon* composed in the late sixth century. Here the Donation was inserted into title 1, which contains legislation of general constitutional nature.[41] Finally, the Balsamon version was copied in miscellaneous manuscripts containing predominantly non-legal texts.

B. Latin Retranslation of the Balsamon Version

A curious aspect of the transmission of the Balsamon version in the late Byzantine world was its copying by Latin prelates resident in the Greek East and the reverse translation of a portion of it into Latin. Soon after 1204 Latin polemicists realized that the Donation, in its Greek version found in Balsamon's canonical commentaries, enjoyed credibility in the eyes of churchmen of the conquered empire. The positive Byzantine attitude to the Donation must have been a welcome discovery. A scribal colophon accompanying the Balsamon version of the Donation in three manuscripts copied in southern Italy provides unique information about the Latin interest. In the years 1205 to 1207 the Roman cardinal Benedict of Sancta Susanna visited Constantinople as a legate of Pope Innocent III and learned of the existence of a Greek text of the Donation. The cardinal commissioned his interpreter, Nicholas of Otranto—a Greek monk from the monastery of St. Nicholas of Casole near Otranto in Apulia—to make a copy of the text. The colophon, of which two slightly different versions survive in the three manuscripts, states that Nicholas of Otranto produced the copy in December 1206 in the Great Palace of Constantinople at the instigation of the Roman cardinal.[42]

The story does not finish here, however. Extracted from its original context, the Balsamon version of the Donation was retranslated into Latin. In 1934 Raymond-Joseph Loenertz showed that the Latin quotation from the Donation in *Tractatus contra Graecos*—a polemical treatise composed by an anonymous Dominican friar resident in Latin-held Constantinople in 1252—does not belong to the Western tradition of the text, but represents a reverse translation into Latin of a part of the Balsamon version.[43] The *Tractatus* of 1252 cites the Balsamon version from its beginning up to the point where Constantine designates the see of Rome as head of the universal church. Then, after a substantial hiatus, the excerpted text jumps to the section where Constantine transfers the capital of his empire to the East, citing henceforward the document until its end.[44] The fate of the retranslation of the Balsamon version was closely related to that of the *Tractatus contra Graecos*. The *Tractatus* was copied in numerous manuscripts and gained immense popularity as a polemical pamphlet against the Greek church, influencing a score of Latin authors of the late Middle Ages.[45] It certainly continued to be read by Dominicans in Constantinople after the re-establishment of a Dominican friary in the imperial capital in 1299, as witnessed by the redaction of the work which Friar Bartholomew prepared there in 1305. The same retranslated segment of the Donation, along with the accompanying commentary in the *Tractatus*, appears in the *Thesaurus veritatis fidei*, a bilingual anti-Orthodox florilegium compiled between 1275 and 1292 on the island of Euboea by the Dominican friar Buonaccorsi (Bonacursius) of Bologna.[46] The Greek text of the Donation in Buonaccorsi's *Thesaurus* follows word-for-word the Balsamon version.[47]

Who was the author of the Latin retranslation? By his own admission, the anonymous Dominican author who composed the *Tractatus* of 1252 combed through Greek manuscripts in libraries in Constantinople and traveled to Nicaea, presumably in order to participate in a religious disputation.[48] These self-referential remarks indicate knowledge of Greek and suggest that the author himself might have translated into Latin some or all of the numerous quotations from Greek patristic authors found in the four books of the *Tractatus*. Was the anonymous author of the *Tractatus* also the translator of the Donation excerpt? Without adducing any evidence, Loenertz considered this a certainty.[49] We would prefer to regard it as a plausible hypothesis rather than an established fact. On the one hand, the Donation excerpt found in the *Tractatus* of 1252 is not related to Nicholas of Otranto's copy of the Balsamon version, because it lacks the salient textual features of the 1206 apograph.[50] Therefore, the translation was clearly not made on this occasion. On the other hand, Latin ecclesiastics in Constantinople are known to have been interested in the Donation soon after 1204 (see below, pp. 114–15, 119), and it is entirely possible that the reverse Latin translation was made by another author well before 1252.

The reverse Latin translation circulated mostly among Dominican friars living in the Greek East rather than audiences in the West. Buonaccorsi's biography exemplifies this readership. Born in Bologna during the first half of the thirteenth century, Buonaccorsi joined the Dominican order in his early youth and spent forty-five years in the Greek-speaking East. In the last years of his life he resided in a Dominican friary on the island of Euboea, where after his death a certain Andreas Doto (a Dominican friar from Crete who visited the place not long before 1323) came across the polemical florilegium and produced an edition of the work, giving it in the process the title *Thesaurus veritatis fidei*, by which it is known today.[51] The anonymous Dominican friar resident in Constantinople who composed in 1305 the polemical treatise *Tractatus contra errores Orientalium et Graecorum* provides another example of the circulation of the retranslation among Dominicans in the East.[52] He cited a brief excerpt from the retranslation of the Balsamon version of the Donation.[53] The author most probably filched the text from the *Tractatus contra Graecos* of 1252, which we know was re-edited in Constantinople in 1305. Indeed, the retranslation had a long history among Latin ecclesiastics settled in the Greek East. In 1442 the Latin archbishop of Crete, Fantinus Vallaresso (ca. 1392–1443), who was trying to enforce the implementation of the Union of Ferrara–Florence on the Venetian-held island, cited parts of the retranslation in his treatise on Christian unity, specifically in the section on Roman primacy.[54]

2. BLASTARES VERSION (ABRIDGEMENT OF THE BALSAMON VERSION) (THE *DONATIO* ONLY)

Inc. θεσπίζομεν σὺν πᾶσι τοῖς σατράπαις καὶ τῇ συγκλήτῳ τῆς ἡμῶν βασιλείας[55]

The late Byzantine period saw the production of a shorter Greek text of the *donatio*. Similar phraseology with the Balsamon version indicates that the briefer text is nothing but an abridged redaction based on the former.[56] The abridged version of the Donation was incorporated into the *Syntagma* of Matthew Blastares completed in 1335, an alphabetically arranged compilation of canons and imperial legislation dealing with matters of predominantly ecclesiastical interest—hence the designation "the Blastares version." The author of this version of the Donation is unknown. Circumstantial evidence seems to point to Blastares and his legal team: the text's succinctness fits with one of the overall objectives of the *Syntagma*, namely, facility of usage; Balsamon's commentaries on the *Nomokanon in Fourteen Titles* are known to have been a source for Blastares' *Syntagma*.[57] Yet internal textual evidence points away from Blastares and should, in my opinion, be given priority over other considerations. The Donation is cited in the *Syntagma* along with a rhetorical preface, which lacks legal substance and begins with the words "having arrived at this point of the oration (*logos*), how could we keep silent about the ordinance of the great Constantine?"[58] The preface continues by praising Constantine for his virtues, mostly piety and respect for the church, but mention is also made of his inner and outer virtues (a component standard for encomia). Only then does the text of the Donation follow. That Blastares calls his work an oration or a speech (*logos*) is worth noticing and suggests that in the preface he is not referring to his legal oeuvre, which he calls elsewhere *syntagma* or more generally *syngramma*.[59] A likely explanation of this inconsistency would be that Blastares extracted the preface and the abbreviated version of the Donation from another work, probably an unknown laudatory oration or saint's life in honor of Constantine the Great, and hence inserted it into the *Syntagma*.[60]

Whoever the author of the Blastares version may have been, the succinct text of the Donation achieved rapid success in legal circles. Soon after its appearance in the *Syntagma*, and without its rhetorical preface, the Blastares version became part of the appendices (the so-called *epimetra*) to Constantine Harmenopoulos's *Hexabiblos*, an important codification of secular law completed in Thessaloniki in 1345.[61] Contemporaries and fellow Thessalonicans, Blastares, and Harmenopoulos must have known about each other's work, and this could explain their shared knowledge of the same succinct version of the Donation. The Donation normally figures as the first appendix to the *Hexabiblos* and is accompanied in some manuscripts by other texts dealing with the relations between secular and ecclesiastical authority: a list of three synodal decrees (*tomoi*) on the excommunication of anti-imperial rebels and the refutation of this practice by Patriarch Philotheos Kokkinos (1353–54, 1364–76). It has been argued that Harmenopoulos himself arranged for the inclusion of the Donation and some of the other appendices during a second publication of the *Hexabiblos* prepared sometime before December 1351.[62] This component of intentionality is important, because it implies that Harmenopoulos and his team wished to disseminate the Donation among contemporary lawyers and considered it an important constitutional document on church-state relations. As an appendix to the *Hexabiblos*, the Blastares version of the Donation circulated widely as a self-contained text and, in rare cases, was also copied in non-legal manuscripts.[63]

The Blastares version of the Donation is more than three times shorter than the Balsamon one, yet it succeeds in giving a summary account of the most important privileges granted by Constantine to the see of Rome. Only a few omissions in content were allowed. The praise of St. Peter, which occupies a large part of the initial section of the *donatio* and adds nothing of legal import, was shortened. Relatively insignificant concessions to the pope were bypassed. For example, no mention is made of the *loros* which (according to the mistranslation in the Balsamon version) Constantine granted to the pope. Nor is there any mention of the military standards—scepters, *signa*, and *banda*—conceded by Constantine to Sylvester. Missing, too, is the entitlement of the clergy of the Roman church to appoint officials of imperial rank, such as *koubikoularioi*, *portarioi*, *exkoubitoi*, even though the permission to use senatorial attire such as white shoes and white caparisons is still there. A slight addition of content was made. According to the Blastares version, Constantine performed groom service to the pope in a specific location, the pope's courtyard, and then led the papal horse by its reins out of the courtyard.

3. KYDONES VERSION[64] (BOTH THE *CONFESSIO* AND THE *DONATIO*)

Inc. (*confessio*): ἐν τῷ ὀνόματι τῆς ἁγίας καὶ ἀδιαιρέτου Τριάδος, τοῦ Πατρὸς δηλαδὴ καὶ τοῦ Υἱοῦ

Inc. (*donatio*): δέον ἐκρίναμεν σὺν πᾶσι τοῖς ἡμετέροις σατράπαις καὶ τῇ συγκλήτῳ

The Kydones version is the only Greek translation of the full text of the Donation. It is found without any accompanying commentary in six Vatican manuscripts.[65] Five of them date to the fourteenth and fifteenth centuries, and the copyist of the text in the fourteenth-century Vaticanus graecus 1102 was none else than the scholar, statesman, and unionist Demetrios Kydones (ca.1324–ca.1398). Since Kydones is not known to have copied works other than his own, Giovanni Mercati has plausibly suggested that Kydones was the author of the translation.[66] Enzo Petrucci has further hypothesized that Kydones prepared the translation during 1369–71, when he was accompanying Emperor John V Palaiologos (1341–91) in the official capacity of his chief minister (*mesazon*) during a visit to Rome.[67] John V traveled to Italy to solicit a crusade against the Turks and converted privately to Catholicism, thus reassuring the pope in the imminent Union of the churches.[68] It is indeed possible that Kydones, who was already a convert to Latin Christianity, became somehow acquainted in Rome with the full text of the Donation and prepared the Greek translation in order to familiarize his Byzantine compatriots with the "original," unbroken version of the document. Kydones (if indeed the translator) succeeded partly in his intention. The full Greek translation was copied in the late fourteenth and the fifteenth century not only by Kydones's Byzantine contemporaries, but it entered the culture of Byzantium's Orthodox neighbors in the Balkans and became the preferred basis for Slavic translations. An old Bulgarian and an old Serbian translation appeared during the later years of the fourteenth century. After the Ottoman conquest of the Balkans, the two translations found their way to Russia, where in the course of time a conflated version appeared; this conflated version was appended in 1653 to the official *nomokanon* of the Russian church.[69] The old Serbian translation of the Kydones version is noteworthy for an interesting change in content unparalleled in any Greek text. Constantine is said to have legislated that all emperors should perform groom service (*officium stratoris*) to the successors of Sylvester rather than that the popes should always wear a *phrygium* (that is, the papal tiara), which is found both in the Latin prototype and in Kydones's translation.[70]

4. CHRYSOBERGES VERSION[71] (THE DONATIO ONLY)

Inc: ὠφέλιμον ἔγνωμεν εἶναι σὺν πᾶσι τοῖς σατράπαις καὶ ἐλλογίμοις ἁπάσης τῆς γερουσίας

The Chrysoberges version circulated least widely from among the four Greek versions of the Donation, yet it is the version which has aroused the most heated discussion. The text is found without any accompanying commentary in three Vatican manuscripts (Vaticani graeci 81, 606, and 1115)

copied in the fourteenth century. As with the Balsamon and the Blastares versions, the Chrysoberges version consists solely of the *donatio* without the *confessio*. Only two incontrovertible facts are certain regarding this text. First, Andreas Chrysoberges, a Greek Dominican and Catholic archbishop of Rhodes, had this version of the Donation at his disposal during the Council of Ferrara-Florence (1438–39)—hence the designation "the Chrysoberges version." The deliberations held in Florence on 20 June 1439 focused on the issue of papal primacy, and on that day the Latins are reported to have raised the subject of the Donation. After the Latin discussants asked the Greeks whether they were familiar with the Donation, Chrysoberges brought forth the Greek text of the document and solemnly read it aloud. Subsequently Chrysoberges made a Latin translation of the text from the Greek codex available to him, Vaticanus graecus 606.[72] The second known circumstance surrounding this mysterious text, definitively established by Krause, is that the Chrysoberges version represents a translation of the *donatio* from the secondary, southern Italian manuscript branch of Leo IX's *libellus* of 1053.[73] In this, the Chrysoberges version is no different from Balsamon's, although the translation is much more precise. For example, the translator rendered correctly the Latin word *phrygium* into Greek, thus avoiding the flight of imagination taken by the translator behind the Balsamon version who called it a *loros*. The Latin expression *corona clericatus* was translated quite literally as "στέμμα ἱερωσύνης," again in contrast to the loose translation in the Balsamon version. Nonetheless, the translator of the Chrysoberges version, too, is responsible for a minor omission and an occasional misunderstanding.[74]

The Chrysoberges version has long been the focal point of controversy, as some scholars considered it closely related to the early medieval origins of the forgery. In 1966 Werner Ohnsorge developed a theory already put forward in a tentative fashion in 1919 by Augusto Gaudenzi. According to Ohnsorge, the Chrysoberges version reflected an eighth-century Greek draft of the *dispositio* of the document. The author of this draft was considered to be none else than Pope Leo III (795–816), who Ohnsorge thought might have been a Greek-speaker.[75] Ohnsorge's interpretation was immediately and justly criticized on philological grounds.[76] Most importantly, as the Chrysoberges version follows a contaminated textual tradition of Pope Leo IX's *libellus*, it is a translation made after 1054 (assuming, again, that in 1054 the papal envoys did not bring a contaminated text).

When and by whom was the Chrysoberges version produced? Unfortunately, we are not, and may never be, in the position to answer this question with certainty, although I would like to offer here some pertinent observations. Petrucci's hypothesis that Cardinal Humbert of Silva Candida arranged for the production of this translation at the time of the onset of the Eastern Schism in 1054 is unsubstantiated.[77] The hypothesis is also highly unlikely. All three manuscripts of the Chrysoberges version date to the fourteenth century, and even though this circumstance alone is not indicative of the period of production of the translation, it increases the probability that this version postdates the widely disseminated Balsamon version. Some of the fourteenth-century audience of this translation is detectable. As Krause has observed, Andreas Chrysoberges, an avid bibliophile, acquired a number of Greek and Latin manuscripts once belonging to his brother Maximos Chrysoberges and to Manuel Kalekas, both students and friends of Demetrios Kydones. Among these manuscripts was Vaticanus graecus 606, the codex which Andreas Chrysoberges used during the Council of Florence for his reverse translation.[78] Thus, the Chrysoberges version circulated during the fourteenth century within the unionist circle of Demetrios Kydones. At that time, the text may have been copied from older manuscripts or may have been produced by members and associates of this intellectual circle. Whatever the case, one can conclude that Byzantine unionists of the late fourteenth century had an agenda similar to that of fourteenth-century lawyers: they wished to popularize and disseminate the Donation among their compatriots.

The examination of the Greek versions of the Donation leads to several conclusions. The Donation circulated widely in the late Byzantine period. Both lawyers and advocates of a union with the Roman church made vigorous efforts to propagate knowledge of the Donation among their contemporaries. Two of the Greek versions, the Balsamon and the Blastares, were the most frequently copied; they circulated mainly in legalistic context. By contrast, the two other versions—the Kydones and the Chrysoberges—belong mostly to the context of unionist activity. This distinction is important, yet it was not absolute when it came to actual usage of the Donation. As we saw, the Balsamon version was known to Dominican polemicists. It was known, too, to Orthodox apologists—in the early fifteenth century, Makarios of Ankara, a Greek polemical author, preferred to quote from the Balsamon version of the Donation rather than from any other version.[79] The wider dissemination of the Balsamon and the Blastares versions hint at the prominent role the Donation played in internal discussions within the Byzantine church, a subject to which we must now turn.

The Donation and the Power Claims of the Church

The domestic use of the Donation, that is, its use in support of the power claims of the church and high churchmen, took three distinct forms in late Byzantium. First, the Donation fostered legal arguments enhancing the standing of the clergy and the church as a corporate body vis-à-vis secular authority. Second, the Donation affected the political rhetoric of ambitious ecclesiastics who saw in it a model of imperial political conduct. Third and finally, it brought symbolic powers to the patriarch of Constantinople through the introduction of the ceremony of groom service (*officium stratoris*) in his honor.

1. LEGALISTIC INTERPRETATIONS

The original forger gave the Donation the outward form of an imperial diploma, calling it an *imperiale constitutum* or *constitutum pragmaticum*.[80] The latter phrase was translated in the Balsamon version as "πραγματικὸν σύστημα," or pragmatic sanction, and imparted legal credibility to the Donation in Byzantine eyes (pragmatic sanctions were a type of imperial legislation commonly enacted in late antiquity).[81] An appropriate starting point for examining the late Byzantine legalistic interpretations of the Donation is the canonical commentaries of Theodore Balsamon. In the twelfth century the Donation evoked different, sometimes contrary, opinions among canonists as to its legal applicability. Within the wide spectrum of views Balsamon appears to have taken the middle ground. He rejected one of the more extreme views immediately after citing the text of the Donation in his commentary on title 8, chapter 1, of the *Nomokanon in Fourteen Titles*. Here Balsamon explained that the Donation entitled the popes to wear every imperial insigne except the imperial crown, and specified that contemporary pontiffs had the habit of riding horses equipped with purple reins and of appointing dignities of exalted imperial rank. Then Balsamon objected to the view (apparently held by some Byzantine churchmen and canonists) that the patriarch of Constantinople, too, held legal title to the same papal privileges on the ground of having been granted "all prerogatives of the pope of Rome" by the Second Ecumenical Council. He pointed to the example of Patriarch Michael I Keroularios and "other patriarchs" who had made an attempt to avail themselves of "all prerogatives" of the papacy, but failed in this effort.[82] The enigmatic reference to "other patriarchs" is not explained; yet, it suggests that the supporters of this extreme view were not solely Keroularios and his associates in the middle of the eleventh century.

While Balsamon did not subscribe to this view, he also did not accept the opposite and equally radical opinion that the Donation lacked any legal validity. In his commentary on canon 28 of the Fourth Ecumenical Council in Chalcedon (which grants the patriarchal see of Constantinople the same primacy of honor as that of Rome), Theodore Balsamon mentioned that some people objected to this canon, because they observed that the patriarch of Constantinople enjoyed none of the privileges conceded by the Donation, and the Donation thus lacked practical implementation in Byzantium. Balsamon rejected this interpretation by saying that as a resident of Constantinople he found such reasoning entirely unacceptable.[83] In his treatise *On the Prerogatives of the Patriarchs* Balsamon again considered this reasoning (based on the lack of practical implementation of the Donation in Byzantium) "useless" when employed as an objection to the view that the pope and the patriarch of Constantinople were equally entitled to the epithet "ecumenical."[84]

Elsewhere Balsamon revealed his own personal opinion on the utility of the Donation, a law which pertained first and foremost to the standing and prerogatives of the patriarchal clergy (the clergy of the Great Church). Only on one occasion did Balsamon use the Donation to defend the status of the patriarch of Constantinople vis-à-vis the emperor: the Donation, according to Balsamon, strengthened the judicial authority of the patriarchal law court, and made its rulings final and not subject to appeal at the imperial tribunal.[85] The main use of the Donation, however, which Balsamon favored, was boosting the authority of the patriarchal clergy, which he considered equal to the college of Roman cardinals. In the section of his commentaries on the *nomokanon* where he cites the text of the Donation, Balsamon notes that "there is nothing to prevent the patriarchal clergy to be honored with [imperial] dignities, although limited ones." Thus, during the feast of the Notary saints Markianos and Martyrios on October 25 the *chartophylax*, a high patriarchal official, was entitled to ride the horse of the patriarch furnished with a white caparison, because the Donation decreed that the clergy of the holy Roman church ought to imitate the senate by riding horses with white caparisons and by wearing white shoes.[86] Balsamon further notes that the *chartophylax*, whose rank was equal to that of "a patriarchal cardinal," had the right to wear a gilded tiara. Balsamon himself served as *chartophylax* for part of his career, and his self-serving agenda is evident. In his treatise *On the Two Offices of Chartophylax and Protekdikos* Balsamon adds that in the recent past the *chartophylax* had used the tiara on many public occasions, for the Donation entitled him to do so, but envious opponents objected to this admirable and legitimate custom. As a consequence, during Balsamon's own day, the gilded tiara was hidden from public view and was kept stored in the chest of the *chartophylax*.[87] Further, Balsamon notes that by virtue of the Donation the status of the *megaloi archontes* of the church (that is, the clergy of the patriarchate) was equal to that of imperial dignitaries, and hence the *megaloi archontes* were freed from the control of the paterfamilias, because imperial dignitaries were also not subject to the power of the paterfamilias according to Byzantine legislation.[88] The logic of this argument is twisted, yet it certainly demonstrates Balsamon's beliefs regarding who should benefit from the privileges of the Donation. Doubtless Balsamon's views of the applicability of the Donation reflect the ideological and political ambitions of the ecclesiastical officials of the Great Church, who in the course of the twelfth century grew to become a highly educated and influential patriarchal bureaucracy.[89]

In comparison with the wide-ranging legalistic discussions of the twelfth century, the reception of the Donation among late Byzantine canonists seems disappointing, even if we take into account the fact that the canonical commentaries produced after 1204 are fewer than the large output of the preceding period. Theodore Balsamon brings up the subject of the Donation nine times in his commentaries, something which no late Byzantine canonist repeated.[90] When between 1356 and 1361 Neilos Kabasilas, the future metropolitan of Thessaloniki, refuted Balsamon's view regarding the supreme status of the patriarchal law court (whose decisions, according to Balsamon, were to be final and irrevocable), he omitted mentioning the Donation.[91] This omission is conspicuous both because his opponent, Balsamon, used the Donation to back up his opinion and since the Donation was widely available to fourteenth-century lawyers.

Still, the Donation continued to attract legal commentary after 1204, with one key difference from the twelfth century. In the late Byzantine period the Donation served predominantly to lend support to the standing of the patriarch of Constantinople and the institution of the patriarchate rather than to enhance the status of the patriarchal clergy. Thus, in his *Syntagma* Matthew Blastares cites the abbreviated version of the Donation in order to support the authority of the patriarch of Constantinople vis-à-vis the autocephalous archbishopric of Ohrid. Special considerations motivated Blastares to invoke the Donation in this context. A legend commonly accepted among the Byzantines since the twelfth century identified the archiepiscopal see of Ohrid with that of Justiniana Prima, a city newly founded by Emperor Justinian I, which in historical reality lay near his village of birth and had ceased to exist during the Slavic invasions of the seventh century.[92] Justinian's novel 131 granted the archbishop of Justiniana Prima the right to ordain bishops of dioceses lying in the western Balkans (the prefecture of Illyricum) and mentioned, rather vaguely, that the see of Justiniana Prima had the rights of the pope in this area. In the early thirteenth century, during the meteoric rise of the state of Epiros, the archbishop of Ohrid and Justiniana Prima Demetrios Chomatenos availed himself of what he considered to be "papal rights" granted by Justinian's novel 131 and went so far as to claim the prerogative of crowning and anointing emperors.[93] Blastares dismissed any high ambitions of the see of Ohrid. After citing the provisions of novel 131 regarding the see of Justiniana Prima he noted that judicial disputes in Illyricum were "under the jurisdiction of the patriarch of Constantinople and his synod which enjoy the prerogatives of the ancient Rome" (a statement based on *Codex Iustinianus*, 1.2.6). It is in order to support this opinion that Blastares cited the text of the Donation along with its rhetorical preface.[94] The context in which Blastares invoked the Donation is partly traditional and partly new. One can find the same provision of *Codex Iustinianus*, 1.2.6, stating that "arising judicial disputes in Illyricum ought not to be settled against the will of the archbishop of Constantinople and its synod which enjoys the prerogatives of the ancient Rome," in title 1, chapter 8, of the *Nomokanon in Fourteen Titles* (this is the very same chapter and title where, in his commentaries, Balsamon cited the text of the Donation).[95] Yet Blastares invoked the Donation for a different reason than what had been Balsamon's agenda. Blastares wished to restrict the judicial autonomy of the see of Ohrid and strove to strengthen the power of the patriarch over the episcopal hierarchy rather than support the standing of the patriarchal officials.

The same view of the patriarch of Constantinople as beneficiary of the Donation is implicit in an anonymous commentary transmitted in a fifteenth-century Harmenopoulos manuscript (BnF, Cod. gr. 1388).[96] The Balsamon version of the Donation was copied at the very beginning of the codex as a self-contained text preceding Harmenopoulos's *Hexabiblos*. Thus, the Donation created the impression of special constitutional significance, an impression reinforced by the fact that one of the other excerpted legal texts preceding the *Hexabiblos* is the famous preamble of Justinian's novel 6 on the twin powers of kingship (*basileia*) and priesthood (*hierosyne*).[97] Immediately after the text of the Donation one finds the gloss "read the

twenty-eighth canon of the six hundred and thirty holy fathers of the Fourth
Ecumenical Council." Then follows the whole of the mentioned canon
of Chalcedon, which legislates that the see of Constantinople, New Rome,
ought to have the same primacy of honor as the papacy being second in
rank after it.[98] This gloss on the Donation does not specify any precise
application, yet the implication is clear: the privileges granted to the see of
Rome by Constantine should pertain to the see of Constantinople by virtue
of being the New Rome.

Another late Byzantine law collection, the interpolated redaction of
the *Nomokanon in Fifty Titles,* also implies that the Donation of Constantine
pertains to the authority of the patriarch, although, again, further details
as to more precise applicability are missing. The *Nomokanon in Fifty Titles* is
the earliest Byzantine *nomokanon* produced in the late sixth century.[99] In
the fourteenth century a new redaction of the *Nomokanon* appeared, which
features additional legal texts, mostly pieces of imperial legislation.[100] The
Balsamon version of the Donation was inserted into title 1, which carries
provisions on general issues about the relations between imperial and ecclesiastical authority, between laws and canons.[101] Thus, title 1 opens with the
mentioned preamble of novel 6 of Justinian and features the ruling of
Justinian's novel 131 that the canons of the first four ecumenical councils
ought to have the force of law. The fourteenth-century interpolator inserted
the Donation and a few other laws dealing with aspects of church-state relations, including excerpts from the ninth-century legal collection *Eisagoge*
of Patriarch Photios, specifically from title 1 ("On Laws and Justice"), title 2
("On the Emperor"), and title 3 ("On the Patriarch"). Indeed, one of the two
extant manuscripts of the interpolated redaction of the *nomokanon* features
the Donation and the provisions of the *Eisagoge* copied next to each other.[102]
The implied relationship between the two legal texts is significant. Photios's
Eisagoge grants the ecumenical patriarch of Constantinople ideological attributes and legislative rights traditionally reserved for imperial authority,
something which is unparalleled in the entire Byzantine legal literature.[103]
Therefore, the joint inclusion of the chapters from the *Eisagoge* and the Donation in the *Nomokanon in Fifty Titles* suggests that the goal of the compiler
was to bolster up the authority of the patriarch of Constantinople vis-à-vis
the imperial office.

The use of the Donation as a source of empowerment of the patriarchal
clergy was more limited in late Byzantium than it had been in the twelfth
century. No surviving canonical text of the period advocates this line of
interpretation. To find fading echoes of this approach, one needs to look

beyond legal literature. An imperial ordinance (*prostagma*) issued in 1270 by Emperor Michael VIII Palaiologos and addressed to Patriarch Joseph I Galesiotes (1266–75, 1282–83) ruled that the judicial post of *dikaiophylax*, which Michael VIII had revived after 1261 and assigned initially to the imperial clergy, should rank among the leading officials of the patriarchal administration (the so-called *exokatakoiloi*). According to the justification used in the ordinance, the Donation of Constantine decreed "not unclearly, but in the best fashion" that the ecclesiastical hierarchy of officials should mirror the imperial one.[104] One should not seek here any general legal implications. The imperial charter pertains solely to the specific case of the appointee, Theodore Skoutariotes, and paradoxically presents the emperor as acting contrary to the hierocratic spirit of the Donation. Michael VIII's decision to reform the hierarchy of officials in the Great Church is justified through his priestly epithet of *epistemonarches*, which refers to the emperor's powers over ecclesiastical administration.[105]

The textual history of the Balsamon version of the Donation also hints at a lingering view in late Byzantium that the Donation could pertain to the clergy of the Great Church. Several late Byzantine apographs of the Balsamon version feature an interesting variant reading in a section of the text which refers to the ceremonial privilege of the clerics of the Roman church to ride horses outfitted with a white caparison. Instead of the original text (a literal translation from Latin) "θεσπίζομεν καὶ τοῦτο, ἵνα οἱ κληρικοὶ τῆς ἁγίας ῾Ρωμαίων ἐκκλησίας καβαλικεύωσιν ἄλογα κεκοσμημένα διὰ ὀθονίων λευκῶν," four manuscripts of the Balsamon version transmit the phrase differently, as "θεσπίζομεν καὶ τοῦτο, ἵνα οἱ κληρικοὶ τῆς μεγάλης ἐκκλησίας καβαλικεύωσιν ἄλογα κεκοσμημένα διὰ ὀθονίων λευκῶν."[106] In other words, "the clerics of the holy church of the Romans" have become "the clerics of the Great Church." This variation, in my view, is not an innocent slip committed by a scribe. The clerics of the Great Church are synonymous with the patriarchal clergy and officialdom, and the substitution highlights the role of the patriarchal clergy as a beneficiary from the Donation. We may be reminded here of Balsamon's view that the Donation entitled the *chartophylax* to ride the patriarchal horse with a white caparison and to wear a gilded tiara. Only the eventual critical edition of Balsamon's commentaries may provide an answer as to the likely time of introduction of this textual variation. It is to be emphasized for the time being that all four manuscripts containing this reading date to the period between the thirteenth and the fifteenth century, and in all cases they transmit the Donation as a self-contained text outside the *Nomokanon in Fourteen Titles*.

It is perhaps noteworthy that the same variant reading, although in another part of the text, appeared in a manuscript of Balsamon's commentaries on the *Nomokanon in Fourteen Titles* copied in 1311 in Trebizond.[107]

2. POLITICAL RHETORIC OF CHURCHMEN

The second kind of domestic use of the Donation was at the level of what can be called political rhetoric. Late Byzantine churchmen were willing and eager to tout the Donation as a historical example of how emperors should respect, endow, and submit to the church. No political rhetoric fueled by the Donation is attested before 1204, even though this silence of the sources does not necessarily indicate a change of approach to the Donation in the later period, if we trust Balsamon's words that Michael I Keroularios and "other patriarchs" wished to obtain all the prerogatives which could be derived from the Donation. The political rhetoric which we can assume only hypothetically to have existed during the eleventh century found its fulfillment in late Byzantium. The saintly patriarch Athanasios I (1289–93, 1303–9) is a case in point. Athanasios is well-known for his far-reaching plans for social and monastic reform during his second patriarchate as well as for his hierocratic thinking.[108] At a time when the Turks were overrunning Byzantine Asia Minor and refugees swamped the imperial capital, Athanasios organized social support networks, presided over a law court judging cases of social oppression, and drafted an imperial novel dealing with secular issues.[109] The patriarch eventually had to resign from his office after facing opposition from the imperial authorities and his own administration. In his letter of resignation (1309) Athanasios claimed that the emperor had given him honors comparable only to the privileges which Constantine had granted to Pope Sylvester.[110] Athanasios thus looked up to the relations between Pope Sylvester and Constantine as a model for his powerful position.

The preface to the Donation in Matthew Blastares' *Syntagma* also portrays Constantine and Pope Sylvester as having established a model relationship between emperors and the church. The preface extols lavishly the Donation. It is said that no contemporary could know "a more divine ordinance" and "a worthier thing to be announced in public." The Donation is further said to "enunciate better than any monument the kind of honors which emperors who do not neglect the pursuit of piety would justly bestow on the church of Christ." Having issued the Donation, Constantine "set himself in public as a good example of piety to everyone."[111] The preface thus puts forward the view that contemporary rulers should follow up in the footsteps

of Constantine and the church should benefit from the support, both symbolic and financial, from secular authority.

The Donation is also presented as an example worth emulating by Archbishop Symeon of Thessaloniki (d. 1429). Born and raised in Constantinople, Symeon spent most of his life in the imperial capital having taken the
habit of a Hesychast monk, most probably in the monastery of the Xanthopouloi.[112] In 1416 or 1417 Symeon was ordained archbishop of Thessaloniki
and led the church of the second city of the empire shortly before its second
and final fall to the Turks in 1430. In his large epitome of Orthodox faith
and liturgical practice entitled *Dialogue in Christ* Symeon assumes a hostile
perspective to imperial involvement in church matters.[113] Symeon refers
twice to the Donation of Constantine. He mentions, as we will shortly see,
the ceremony of groom service to the patriarch of Constantinople and also
invokes the Donation to criticize the conduct of those Byzantine emperors
whom he considered disrespectful toward the church. He makes this critical
comment in his treatise *On the Sacred Ordinations* (a part of the *Dialogue
in Christ*) while giving an account of the custom by which newly ordained
bishops traveled to Constantinople from the provinces to present themselves
to the emperor and deliver a prayer. Symeon describes both the current
ritual, of which he disapproved, and "the God-pleasing and appropriate
way" in which the ritual had been conducted in the past.[114] According to
Symeon, in the past a reception took place in the palace, where the newly
ordained bishop delivered the prayer and censed the emperor. Then the
emperor bowed his head and the bishop blessed him. After exchanging a
kiss, the bishop in turn bowed his head out of respect for the emperor's
secular authority and departed from Constantinople, oftentimes loaded
with lavish gifts. Symeon points to ancient models for such pious imperial
conduct. He refers his readers to the Greek lives of St. Ambrose for an
example of how emperors bowed their heads to ecclesiastics.[115] Then he
points to the Donation of Constantine which, according to him, established
a paragon for imperial generosity toward the church. According to Symeon,
Constantine granted generous gifts not only to Sylvester, but to almost every
bishop in the synod, presumably the patriarchal synod of Constantinople.[116]
This was in contrast to the emperors of Symeon's day, who did not carry out
the ceremony in the proper way and fell short of the ancient models of
imperial piety. In a manner which Symeon found scandalous, they made
bishops bow without themselves bowing and had bishops kiss their callous
and unholy hands.[117] Symeon thus used the Donation to teach his readers
a lesson of how emperors should conduct themselves in the company of high
ecclesiastics.

3. RITUAL GROOM SERVICE IN BYZANTIUM

A usage of the Donation in late Byzantium, which contrasts most prominently with the period before 1204, is the adoption of the Western ceremony of ritual groom service (*officium stratoris*). The Donation describes how Constantine displayed his respect for Pope Sylvester by attending him as his groom (*stratoris officium illi exhibuimus*). This account in the Donation inspired a special ritual, which appears in the coronation ceremony of the Western emperor during the ninth century, and which was regularly performed from the twelfth century onward in ceremonial encounters between popes and emperors as well as between popes and other secular rulers.[118] Twelfth-century Byzantine attitudes to *officium stratoris* seem to have been mostly dismissive and derisory. In his *History* John Kinnamos ridiculed the way the Western emperor acted as the pope's squire "in a fashion unworthy of himself." According to Kinnamos, this ritual served to demonstrate that the pope and the Western emperor were decorated with false titles.[119] By the middle of the thirteenth century, however, Byzantine views of the ritual had changed, and there was willingness to adopt the ceremony as a way of rendering honor to the patriarch of Constantinople. The earlier doubts regarding the legitimacy of this ritual did not disappear fully, however. Rather, one can distinguish over the course of the fourteenth and the fifteenth century the emergence of a clerical perspective favoring the ritual and an imperial one which opposed it.

The historian George Pachymeres describes an episode of ritual squire service on behalf of the patriarch of Constantinople in Nicaean exile, which was performed in the city of Magnesia in Asia Minor during the early autumn of 1258.[120] When Patriarch Arsenios Autoreianos (1254–60, 1261–64) came from Nicaea to meet for the first time Michael Palaiologos, the newly elected regent of the underage Nicaean emperor John IV Laskaris, Palaiologos honored the arriving leader of the church by holding the reins of his mule and led him in a solemn procession to the palace in the city, where Patriarch Arsenios took residence in a sumptuous "imperial tent" (βασιλικὴ σκηνή). Pachymeres does not provide any explanation as to when and by whom this ceremony was adopted in the empire of Nicaea, nor does he mention how contemporaries viewed it. Writing much later, Pachymeres reports the episode matter-of-factly, almost in passing, in the context of his disapproving description of how Palaiologos curried Arsenios's favor in preparation of his usurpation of the throne. The ceremony is doubtless a re-enactment of the *officium stratoris* as practiced in the medieval West, with the difference that Arsenios was riding a mule, not a horse—and with the

further distinction that Palaiologos was not yet a supreme ruler, but still a
regent.

The reason for the thirteenth-century change in attitude toward *officium
stratoris* lies, in my opinion, in the continual popularization of the Donation
among ecclesiastics and especially in the closer contacts between Latins and
Greeks after 1204. The Latin origin of *officium stratoris* was never forgotten.
After the conclusion of the Union of Lyons in 1274 Michael Palaiologos,
now emperor, became target of criticism for his Latin-mindedness. An anti-
Latin pamphlet attributed to a certain Panagiotes describes the ritual squire
service as a foreign, Latin rite. It ridicules the unionist Byzantine emperor,
who is said to have held the reins of a mule carrying an image of Pope
Gregory X (1271–76).[121] Interestingly, the Byzantine polemicist dates this
episode to the patriarchate of Arsenios, something which could never have
occurred in reality—Arsenios was deposed in 1264, seven years before
Gregory X was elected pope in 1271.

Latin customs were well known to the two main participants in the ritual
in Magnesia in 1258, Michael Palaiologos and Patriarch Arsenios. Palaiologos had made his career in the Nicaean army as *megas konostaulos*, a military office whose main function was command over the Latin mercenaries
in imperial service. Patriarch Arsenios had participated in a Nicaean embassy to Rome in the early 1250s, which discussed the possibility of a union
with Pope Innocent IV (1243–54).[122] At that time the Nicaean delegation
was ready to restore the unity of the church by recognizing papal primacy
in exchange for the return of Constantinople.[123] Arsenios's visit to Rome
coincided with dramatic events in the struggle between the papacy and
the Hohenstaufen over political hegemony in Italy. At the first Union of
Lyons in 1245, Innocent IV had taken the extreme measure of deposing
Frederick II Hohenstaufen from the imperial office. Innocent IV, who received Arsenios and fellow Nicaean diplomats, was a systematic proponent
of the hierocratic papal doctrine and made use of the Donation in the
ideological struggle with the Western emperor.[124] During his pontificate, for
instance, scenes from the Donation of Constantine, including that of *officium
stratoris*, were depicted in the church of SS. Quattro Coronati in Rome,
which was dedicated in 1246 as a visual statement of papal propaganda.[125]

In the same decade of the 1250s Latin ecclesiastics in the Empire of
Constantinople propagated legends about the acceptability of *officium stratoris* in Byzantium in the distant past. The *Tractatus contra Graecos*, composed
in 1252, mentions a curious story of how before the schism Byzantine emperors regularly rendered honor to papal legates in Constantinople, whom

they served ceremonially as squires and whose horses they led on foot to a palace called "the Cardinals' Palace." Thus, Byzantine emperors are said to have imitated Constantine's act described in the Donation.[126] The *Tractatus* dates the beginning of the schism to about AD 872 (that is, in the era of Patriarch Photios), and thus imparts longevity and historical credibility to the ceremony of *officium stratoris*.[127] The story, of course, is invented, yet it makes sense when set in the context of the Latin Empire of Constantinople. Roman cardinals serving as papal legates to the Latin Empire held higher authority than the Latin patriarchs of Constantinople. For example, in contrast to the patriarchs, papal legates held the exclusive right to excommunicate the Latin emperor.[128] The legates wore sumptuous red garments and shoes, an entitlement which they explained by referring to the Donation.[129] It is in my view not an accident that the earliest case of *officium stratoris* rendered to the Byzantine patriarch dates to 1258, shortly after the composition of the *Tractatus contra Graecos*. Confronted with stories of the historicity of *officium stratoris* and contemporary Western examples, the Byzantines became amenable to adopting the foreign ritual.

The encounter between Palaiologos and Arsenios in Magnesia in 1258 did not lead to the permanent introduction of Donation-based ceremonial into the Palaiologan court. The mid-fourteenth-century ceremonial handbook of Pseudo-Kodinos is silent about the ritual. At about the same time, Emperor John VI Kantakouzenos distanced himself from the performance of ritual groom service when visiting Serbia. The episode occurred during the famous encounter between Kantakouzenos and the Serbian king Stephan IV Dušan at Tao near Pristina in 1342. At that time, the king met on foot the arriving archbishop of Serbia, Ioannikios, held the reigns of his horse, and led him to the house where Kantakouzenos was waiting. In the meantime, Kantakouzenos insisted on waiting inside the house and thus, as he himself explains, followed "the custom of the Byzantine emperors." It appears that the *officium stratoris* had made its way to Serbia, and Kantakouzenos considered it a foreign custom which he did not recognize, or at least did not wish to witness.[130]

Yet, Kantakouzenos's flat refusal to witness the performance of ritual groom service seems to reflect only the imperial perspective on the matter. In the early fifteenth century Byzantine ecclesiastics continued to regard the emperor's groom service to the patriarch of Constantinople as legitimate and acceptable. Symeon of Thessaloniki refers to *officium stratoris* in his work *On the Holy Ordinations*, specifically in a section describing the ceremony of election and investiture of the ecumenical patriarch of Constantinople. The reported electoral procedure differs in nothing from the traditional: the emperor nominates the patriarch from among three candidates proposed by the synod and invests him with the bishop's staff and pallium.[131] After the election a festive procession follows—a procession which Symeon describes somewhat differently from the version found in the ceremonial book of Pseudo-Kodinos. According to Pseudo-Kodinos, the patriarch mounts his horse outside the imperial palace and leads imperial officials and dignitaries in a procession to the church of Saint Sophia. In Symeon of Thessaloniki's version, after his investiture the patriarch mounts his horse inside the imperial courtyard, and then a special groom leads on foot the patriarch's horse out of the imperial courtyard and proceeds in this fashion publicly to the patriarchate (near the church of Saint Sophia). In addition to imperial officials, the emperor's son is said to take part in the procession. Symeon explains that the groom represented the emperor and rendered the patriarch the same homage which Constantine once had rendered to Sylvester.[132] Thus, Symeon added new elements to a well-known ceremony and interpreted them through the Donation of Constantine.

The question arises of whether Symeon described a real ceremonial procession with the staging of *officium stratoris* or made up an attractive story. After all, it was Symeon's agenda throughout his commentaries to attack and humble imperial authority. There is no reason, in my view, to cast doubt on Symeon's testimony. In the first place, as monk resident in Constantinople before he was ordained archbishop of Thessaloniki in 1416 or 1417, Symeon should be considered a credible eyewitness to events in the imperial capital and especially to church rituals. The ordination of at least five ecumenical patriarchs must have been in Symeon's living memory: Patriarch Anthony IV in 1391; Kallistos II Xanthopoulos in 1397; Matthew I in 1397; Euthymios II in 1410; and Joseph II in 1416. Two of these patriarchs are particularly worthy of note. Patriarch Kallistos II was one of two Xanthopouloi brothers (Ignatios and Kallistos), influential Hesychast monks, in whose monastery in Constantinople Symeon is likely to have resided. Therefore, Symeon would have been close to this patriarch.[133] Patriarch Joseph II is known to have been ordained on the feast day of Saints Constantine and Helena, that is, 21 May 1416.[134] The celebration of the memory of Constantine would fit perfectly well with the staging of Donation-based ritual during the ordination. Therefore, it is plausible to suggest that Symeon saw the ceremony he described at least once, shortly before his departure for Thessaloniki. In the second place, Symeon's description is not the only piece of evidence that the ceremony of *officium stratoris* was acceptable for late

Byzantine ecclesiastics. We are reminded here of the episode of 1258, and therefore we should not hasten to belittle Symeon's testimony as suspect. In fact, when comparing Symeon's and Pachymeres' descriptions, we may observe a compromise on how to apply the Donation to Byzantine court ceremonial. Unlike the case of Michael Palaiologos and Arsenios, the secular dignitary no longer attended to the patriarch as his squire. Instead, a special agent performed the groom service in lieu of the emperor—a substitution which seems to have had the purpose of ensuring that the emperor avoided a public humiliation. In the third place and most importantly perhaps, Symeon's account displays curious closeness with the abridged Blastares version of the Donation. This version introduces the unique detail of how Constantine, serving Sylvester as his squire, led the papal horse out of the imperial courtyard. The detail corresponds to the patriarch being led out of the imperial palace in Symeon's account and is likely to reflect a conscious effort to fashion *officium stratoris* in a way fitting its original model, the Donation of Constantine.

The Donation in Anti-Latin Polemics: From Lukewarm Adoption to Outright Rejection

Confronted with the Donation in their polemics with the Latins, Byzantine ecclesiastics devised an ingenious way of challenging its pro-papal spirit. The Donation naturally lent support to the thesis that the Roman primacy was of human, not divine origin. For according to the Donation, the papacy received its exalted status from the Byzantine emperor Constantine by means of imperial legislation.[135] This anti-Latin interpretation of the Donation is first seen during the second half of the twelfth century. In his *History* John Kinnamos, the official chronicler of Emperor Manuel I, used the Donation to argue that Constantine the Great had created the dignity of the pope. In addition, as Paul Alexander suggests, Kinnamos might have alluded to the Donation in two other instances in his *History*: in his contention that the true imperial office was Constantinople's and in his claim that the pope lacked the right to appoint emperors, having once accepted the move of the seat of the empire to the East.[136] Kinnamos's central argument is found also in Andronikos Kamateros's *Sacred Arsenal*—a polemical collection supporting the emperor's debates with representatives of the Roman and the Armenian church conducted during the 1170s.[137] The *Sacred Arsenal* presents Manuel I as explaining to the Roman cardinals that the primacy of Rome derived from its associations with the imperial office rather than from St. Peter and that the Donation pointed to the great privileges the papacy gained from imperial authority.[138]

The twelfth-century Byzantine argument persisted after 1204, as is clearly seen in Nicholas Mesarites' account of the disputations between Greeks and Latins in 1214. Holding the twin title of metropolitan of Ephesos and exarch of Asia, Mesarites represented the interests of the persecuted Orthodox clergy during negotiations he conducted in Constantinople in 1214 with the Roman cardinal Pelagius of Albano. After the end of the negotiations Mesarites set off for the city of Herakleia Pontike in Paphlagonia in the company of a two-man delegation consisting of a learned Spanish lawyer and his interpreter, Nicholas of Otranto. In a new disputation that took place in Herakleia Pontike Mesarites made a frontal attack on the doctrine of papal primacy. He denied the validity of the Petrine claim by arguing that St. Peter was not the only apostle and Rome was not the only city he honored with his presence. He argued that the popes could claim supremacy over the universal church only through their associations with Rome and the Roman imperial office, as the Donation of Constantine clearly demonstrated. Mesarites evidently adopted his arguments from Kamateros's *Spiritual Arsenal,* which he seems to have read in preparation for the disputation.[139]

After 1214 we have to wait for one hundred years to encounter another case of Byzantine polemical usage of the Donation. In the 1330s Barlaam of Calabria referred to the Donation (the "chrysobull of Constantine," as he called it) in one of the anti-Latin treatises on papal primacy that he composed while serving as Emperor Andronikos III's envoy and negotiator, and before his eventual conversion to Catholicism.[140] Barlaam argued that Constantine could have bestowed on the pope only something that the latter lacked. Therefore, the grant of primacy through the Donation meant that previous popes had not enjoyed supreme status in Christendom and that they had been equal to all other bishops of the early church. Just as Andronikos Kamateros and Nicholas Mesarites had, Barlaam used the Donation to diminish the importance of the Petrine claim and the divine origin of papal power.[141]

The rarity of late Byzantine polemical use of the Donation contrasts starkly with the situation on the Latin side. Latin polemical authors made exceedingly frequent references to the Donation and formulated various arguments on its basis. In the following pages I will discuss the most prominent cases and identify distinct lines of Latin polemical interpretation and commentary in the period 1204–1453.

The earliest attested Latin use of the Donation after the conquest of Constantinople dates to 1206 when the Roman cardinal Benedict of Sancta Susanna ordered Nicholas of Otranto to make a copy of the document from Balsamon's commentaries. That this copy was produced with polemical purposes in mind is suggested by its preface found in Vaticanus gr. 1416, according to which the Donation shows that "every church is administered by the pope of Rome."[142] In the Latin Empire of Constantinople, the Donation played the double role of lending support to the doctrine of papal primacy in the eyes of the subject population and of backing the authority of Roman legates and cardinals sent to the Latin Empire. We already saw the emergence of the legend of a "traditional" groom service rendered to Roman cardinals visiting Constantinople. Nicholas Mesarites' report of the negotiations in 1214 illustrates how the Donation served the purposes of the Roman legates. As metropolitan of Ephesos and exarch of Asia, Mesarites voiced his annoyance at the poor reception for a man of his rank that he received from Cardinal Pelagius during an official audience at the Great Palace: the cardinal and papal legate did not stand up to meet the Nicaean bishop, but remained sitting on a sumptuous throne. Furthermore, Pelagius was wearing red shoes and a red robe, and explained to Mesarites that the cardinal bishops of Rome were entitled to use the imperial red color on account of the privileges the Donation granted to the popes and the papal clergy. Mesarites' response is most interesting. The Nicaean prelate reports that once he heard the words of the cardinal, he turned inside out the upper part of his simple-looking shoes and pointed to the red-colored leather stitched to the inside. In this way, Mesarites showed that Byzantine high ecclesiastics enjoyed, too, some of the insignia of imperial power, yet they behaved more humbly than their Roman counterparts. (Earlier in his report, Mesarites mentions how on arriving in Constantinople he demonstratively declined to mount a horse equipped with red saddle and red reins.) Mesarites wished thus to embarrass the cardinal and to show that the privileges granted by the Donation to the Roman church devolved also on the Byzantine one, although they did so much less conspicuously.[143]

The fall of the Latin Empire of Constantinople in 1261 put an end to the usage of the Donation for the benefit of visiting Roman cardinals. Instead, the Donation continued to play a role as a key document supporting papal primacy during disputes between Latins and Greeks. Latin polemical treatises that mention the Donation do so always in the context of a discussion of papal primacy. It should come no surprise that the two unions between the churches—the Union of Lyons (1274) and the Union of Ferrara-Florence (1438–39)—witnessed pro-Latin use of the Donation. We have already seen how in 1439, during the sessions of the Council of Florence, the Latin party brought up the subject of the Donation, and the Chryso-berges version was read and retranslated.[144] As for the Council of Lyons, we need to turn to the activities of Humbert de Romans (ca. 1200–77), who was one of the chief ideologues of the union and a fervent crusade propagandist. Commissioned by Pope Gregory X to articulate the objectives of the union, Humbert de Romans composed between 1272 and 1274 his *Opus tripartitum,* where he mused upon the future of the crusading movement, the attainment of the union, and the reform of the church. Humbert believed that the success of the union passed through Byzantine recognition of papal primacy and referred to the Donation as evidence that the Byzantines had, in fact, accepted papal primacy in the past.[145]

The Latins approached imaginatively the polemical potential of the Donation. The four treatises that cite the retranslation of the Balsamon version, starting with *Tractatus contra Graecos* of 1252, state that Constantine had promulgated the Donation in Latin as well as in Greek.[146] This statement reflects the bilingual circulation of the Donation and advertises its relevance with regard to the Eastern churches. All four treatises add that after the promulgation of the Donation, the First Ecumenical Council followed in its footsteps and decreed that Rome ought to be the head of all churches. The *Tractatus* of 1305 goes as far as claiming that "the universal councils" confirmed the validity of the Donation itself.[147] The legend of the role of the First Ecumenical Council in sanctioning papal primacy appears in a polemical context already in Pope Leo IX's *libellus* of 1053, and therefore it is not surprising that Latin polemicists of the late Middle Ages continued to link the two important "historical" events of the reign of Constantine.[148]

Latin authors flaunted fondly the Donation as evidence in support of the Petrine theory, in complete contrast to the Greek claim that the Donation served to show the exact opposite, namely, the human origin of papal primacy. For the Donation indeed describes Constantine's veneration for the apostles Peter and Paul and refers to Pope Sylvester as St. Peter's successor. The pro-Petrine interpretation emerges clearly in the thirteenth-century anonymous polemic *De erroribus graecorum,* a practical guide on conducting disputations with the Greeks, which Dondaine attributes to Buonaccorsi of Bologna and dates to the year 1292.[149] In the section on papal primacy, it is said that the Greeks could argue on the basis of the Second and the Fourth Ecumenical Councils as well as the Quinisext Council (not recognized in the West) that the see of Constantinople ought to have the same rights as Rome. Buonaccorsi advises the Latin disputants to counter-argue that the primacy of Rome was not derived from the imperial dignity, but stemmed from the Petrine doctrine, as "the privilege of Constantine manifestly testifies."[150] In this way, a response emerged to the Byzantine interpretation of the Donation.

The polemical treatise of Manuel Kalekas (d. 1410) commonly known as *Contra Graecos* also invokes the Donation in support of the Petrine theory. A Byzantine teacher and theologian whose adamant anti-Palamism and close association with his teacher, Demetrios Kydones, led to his conversion to Catholicism, Manuel Kalekas composed the treatise in Greek, completing it in the period 1403–10 when he resided at a Dominican friary on Genoese Lesbos.[151] This treatise in four books deals mostly with the issue of the procession of the Holy Spirit and addresses briefly other points of disagreement, including papal primacy, where Kalekas refers to the Donation.[152] He states that by issuing the Donation at the time of his conversion, Constantine acknowledged a prior "custom" of the Christians, namely, that the pope headed the universal church by virtue of being the successor of St. Peter. In order to illustrate how the Donation supported the Petrine theory, Kalekas refers to relevant passages, which, surprisingly, do not correspond to any known Greek text. While this may suggest the existence of yet another Byzantine version of the Donation, the question should be left open for the time being, for there are indications that Kalekas might have simply para-phrased very loosely the Kydones version.[153]

The massive Latin usage of the Donation provides the background for understanding the remarkable refutation of its genuineness by a Byzantine polemical author, the metropolitan of Ankara Makarios, in the early fif-teenth century. Makarios was not the first person in the Middle Ages to put into doubt the authenticity of the Donation. In the West such doubts were voiced as early as 1001 in a charter issued by Emperor Otto III (996–1002). A few additional attacks on the Donation followed in the twelfth century, although none was carefully argued and could establish effectively the fact that the Donation was a forgery unworthy of credence.[154] In Byzantium itself, the twelfth century also witnessed such questioning. In his treatise *On the Prerogatives of the Patriarchs* Theodore Balsamon cites the opinion of unnamed adversaries who diminished the rank of the patriarch of Constan-tinople vis-à-vis the pope; they are said to have used the "alleged" Donation ("τὸ νομιζόμενον θέσπισμα"), deemed by them inapplicable on Byzantine soil and relevant only to the Roman see, to argue for the inferior status of the patriarch of Constantinople.[155] Balsamon's language implies doubts as to the authenticity of the Donation. It must be stressed, however, that elsewhere Balsamon regarded the Donation as a valid imperial law. One may plausibly suppose that in his treatise *On the Prerogatives of the Patriarchs* Balsamon was reporting views current among fellow canonists (whose identity, unfortunately, we do not know) rather than his own conviction. And it is noteworthy that neither Balsamon nor any of his contemporaries is known to have picked up on the spirit of questioning the authenticity of the Donation.[156]

By contrast, during the early fifteenth century Makarios of Ankara embarked on a decisive and well-argued refutation of the Donation's authenticity in his work *Against the Latins*. His exposure of the forgery has been noticed by scholars, although so far there has been no analysis of the argumentation.[157] Precious little is known of the biography of Makarios (fl. ca. 1400), including his mysterious family background and life span.[158] He originated from Thessaly and came to Constantinople sometime during the second half of the fourteenth century, taking the monastic habit and joining the official Palamite faction of the church. In inner church politics Makarios displayed extraordinary zeal and contentiousness, which appear to have been prominent traits of his character. In 1397, having already been placed once under ecclesiastical interdict, Makarios became metropolitan of Ankara resident in Constantinople. He was close enough to Emperor Manuel II Palaiologos (1391–1425) to join his entourage during his long sojourn in the West in 1400–1403. On his return to Constantinople, Makarios had the misfortune of re-involving himself in the controversy over the legitimacy of Patriarch Matthew I (1397–1410), whose ordination was seen as uncanonical, because this was the third episcopal see he had occupied. Makarios opposed vigorously the patriarch by producing lengthy canonical writings, and his opposition led ultimately to his own undoing. In 1405 Makarios was deposed from the metropolitan bishopric of Ankara and in 1409 was excommunicated. His traces in the documentary record disappear after this year.

Makarios completed his polemical treatise *Against the Latins* during the years 1403–4, shortly after his return from the West.[159] There are solid reasons for dating the work to this period. His treatise makes it seem apparent that he has traveled to the West.[160] At the same time, the specific views Makarios embraced bespeak a date prior to his close entanglement in the church controversy over the legitimacy of Patriarch Matthew. In *Against the Latins* Makarios defended the administrative powers of the Byzantine emperors over the church and the quasi-priestly character of imperial authority, whereas during the controversy over the legitimacy of Patriarch Matthew, Makarios criticized the emperor's support of his opponent and composed a treatise seeking to limit the emperor's ecclesiastical rights.[161] It is probable that Makarios began composing *Against the Latins* while journeying in the West with the emperor. During his stay in Italy, France, and England Manuel II fostered the spirit of Christian unity in the hope of motivating western monarchs to rally to Constantinople's defense, yet he did not favor any doctrinal concessions by the Byzantine church. Manuel II's writings composed at the time include a treatise explaining the Orthodox position on the procession of the Holy Spirit and papal primacy.[162] A member of the emperor's traveling suite, Makarios adopted a similar intransigent attitude toward the union.

Makarios opens *Against the Latins* by attacking the doctrine of papal primacy and soon comes to tackle the subject of the Donation. In chapter 3 he remarks that the fathers of the Council of Nicaea did not ever mention the "so-called Donation" either because they considered it invalid or because the document was forged subsequently when it was deceitfully attributed to Constantine.[163] The latter comment anticipates the full-scale exposure of the forgery in chapter 6, which is entitled "On the So-Called Ordinance of the Holy and Great Emperor Constantine." Makarios starts by adducing historical arguments discrediting the authenticity of the Donation and continues with canonical ones aimed at showing its legal invalidity. Constantine, Makarios notes, issued the Donation before founding Constantinople, and therefore could not have legislated on the order of precedence of the five patriarchates, including the patriarchate of Constantinople.[164] Nor could Emperor Constantine have granted the papacy judicial primacy in Christendom, for this judicial primacy was not honored by the First Ecumenical Council, nor was it by any other ecumenical council.[165] Further, Makarios notes, Constantine did not leave Rome and the West to be ruled by popes, as the Donation claims, but appointed his third son, Constans, as an emperor over Rome, Italy, and southern Gaul, and entrusted his first son, Constantine, with the governance of northern Gaul. When the latter died, Constans took over the rule of the entire Western empire. Additionally, Makarios notes, the successors of Constantine and Constans continued to reside inside the city of Rome, a circumstance contradicting the provisions of the Donation.[166]

The legalistic discussion which follows seems to address a segment of Makarios's readership still left unconvinced by the historical attack on the forgery. Citing the designation of the Donation in the Balsamon version as "a pragmatic sanction" (πρακτικὸν σύστημα), Makarios notes that it was never confirmed by subsequent canons and therefore lacked legal force. In support of this interpretation he refers to the eighth canon of the Third Ecumenical Council in Ephesos, which states that "if someone shall bring forward a rule contrary to what is here determined, the synod decrees it shall be to no effect."[167] He notes that a similar provision was found in the acts of the Fourth Ecumenical Council and cites specifically "an ordinance of Justinian," stating that "the privileges of the churches ought to be maintained, but the pragmatic sanctions that are contrary to the canons ought to be rejected" (*Codex Iustinianus* 1.2.12).[168]

Makarios of Ankara is among the first authors of the waning Middle Ages to subject the Donation to systematic historical criticism. It is remarkable that Makarios composed his work more than twenty years before the series of attacks on the Donation undertaken in the Renaissance West, which began with Nicholas of Cusa's *Concordantia catholica* presented at the Council of Basel in 1433.[169] Seven years later, in 1440, the Italian humanist Lorenzo Valla composed his famous treatise which exposed, in greater detail and in a more vitriolic fashion, the Donation as a forgery.[170] In the 1450s Aeneas Sylvius Piccolomini, the future Pope Pius II (1458–64), and Reginald Pecock followed in the footsteps of Valla, in Italy and England, respectively.[171] Did Makarios's work influence these Latin humanists of the later fifteenth century? No trace is found of Makarios's arguments against the Donation during the deliberations of the Council of Ferrara-Florence, neither among the Latins nor among the Greeks. We hear of no protest of the Byzantine delegation against the use of the Donation. While it is unlikely, in my view, that Makarios influenced his quattrocento contemporaries, it is interesting to note that the latter debunked the forgery by using a similar historical approach and historical arguments. Nicholas of Cusa, for example, argued that the Donation could not be genuine, because the jurisdiction of the Roman emperors prevailed in Italy long after the grant to the pope was supposed to have been made.[172] Makarios of Ankara had stated just the same. In a manner similar to Makarios of Ankara, Lorenzo Valla wondered how the Donation could speak of Constantinople as one of the patriarchal sees, when it was not yet a patriarchate, nor a Christian city, nor named Constantinople, nor founded and planned.[173] These objections against the authenticity of the Donation are rational and rest on an acute historical and chronological consciousness. Makarios of Ankara shared with his renowned Renaissance contemporaries a common historical approach to textual critique, a central feature of the new age of humanism.[174]

Conclusion

The Donation of Constantine reached the peak of its popularity in Byzantium during the period after 1204, when it became well known to a wide array of churchmen ranging from canonists and compilers of legal manuscripts to bishops and patriarchs of Constantinople. The Donation circulated among late Byzantine audiences in the form of four Greek versions, versions copied in numerous manuscripts and in various contexts well beyond the legalistic. Two or possibly three of these versions were produced during the late Byzantine period. The textual history of the Greek versions demonstrates by itself a contemporary fascination with this "document," which was thought to have been issued by the eponymous and saintly founder of Constantinople.

The Donation mattered for the late Byzantine church from both a constitutional and an ideological point of view. The range of its discussion and application broadened in this period. The Donation fueled the rhetoric of politically assertive high ecclesiastics, something which we can only suppose for earlier times, and inspired churchmen to adopt from the West the ceremony of groom service, which in Byzantium was to render honor to the ecumenical patriarch of Constantinople. The general tendency of the legal and ceremonial uses of the Donation in the period was toward enhancing the powers of the patriarch of Constantinople vis-à-vis imperial authority and the episcopal hierarchy. Thus, the predominant domestic application of the Donation corresponded to the centralization of the Byzantine church under the patriarchate of Constantinople in the course of the fourteenth century.[175] The use of the Donation was one of the ideological expressions and underpinnings of this historical process.

Still, in spite of its rising popularity, late Byzantine attitudes toward the Donation were marked by ambivalence. For one, use of the Donation was far more common in a domestic context than it ever became on the pages of confessional polemic with the Latins. The reason for this tendency appears to have been the natural realization, one never explicitly expressed, that the Donation served more effectively the polemical goals of the Latin opponents. Indeed, the Donation assisted numerous Latin authors of the late Middle Ages in advocating the subject status of the Byzantine church. It is, therefore, not surprising that the twelfth-century line of Orthodox polemical interpretation petered out in the course of time, and eventually in the early fifteenth century a Byzantine author sought to disprove the authenticity of the Donation. One may even wonder whether the pro-papal spirit of the

Donation did not impede it from attaining a more critical internal importance in Byzantium. In any case, the ambivalent attitude toward the Donation is also evident from the fact that the legal commentaries on it never matched the promise of the twelfth century, despite the massive copying of the legalistically oriented Balsamon and Blastares versions. Finally, the ambivalence of late Byzantine attitudes is seen in the hesitant adoption of the ceremony of groom service to the patriarch of Constantinople, a ceremony that faced opposition from imperial circles and was unable to establish itself as a regularly staged court ritual, apart from what appears to have been a brief moment in the late fourteenth and the early fifteenth centuries.

Even so, for an anti-Byzantine forgery imported fairly recently into the Greek-speaking East, the Donation left an extraordinarily deep imprint on late Byzantine law, ceremonial, and political imagination. The Donation buttressed the ideological status of the patriarch of Constantinople at a time when, outside the empire, it actively served to undermine Orthodox doctrine. The Donation worked its way into Byzantium largely against the current, and in this its success is doubly remarkable.

Appendix 1

The Balsamon Version of the Donation: Codicological and Textual Observations

The observations here do not rest on a complete study of all manuscripts of the Balsamon version of the Donation, but aim to provide a basis for future work and critical edition. The following eighteen manuscripts of the Balsamon version of the Donation have been consulted:

MSS of the *Nomokanon in Fourteen Titles* (*Nomokanon* of Pseudo-Photios):

Basel, Universitätsbibliothek, A III 6 (13th c.)
British Library, Arundel 533 (14th c.)
Barocci gr. 205 (14th c.)
Esphigmenou, 4 (13th c.)
Vaticanus Palatinus gr. 384 (13th c.)
Vaticanus gr. 844 (13th–14th c.)
Vaticanus Reginensis gr. 51 (16th c.)

MSS of the Balsamon version of the Donation as a self-contained text:

Ambrosianus gr. 682 (Q. 97 sup.) (copied in 1287/88)
BnF, Codex gr. 1263 (14th or 15th c.)
BnF, Codex gr. 1388 (15th c.)
Laurentianus gr. 8, 17 (15th or 16th c.)
Laurentianus lat. 16, 40 (16th c.)
Vaticanus gr. 1416 (16th c.)
Vaticanus gr. 1276 (13th c.)
Vaticanus gr. 640 (14th c.)
Vaticanus Reginensis gr. 57 (copied in 1358/59)
Vindobonensis juridicus gr. 6 (15th c.)
Vindobonensis historicus gr. 34 (copied in 1430)

1. THE GENESIS OF BALSAMON'S COMMENTS ON THE DONATION IN THE *NOMOKANON IN FOURTEEN TITLES*

There still is no critical edition of Theodore Balsamon's commentaries on the *Nomokanon in Fourteen Titles*. The best edition so far is the one by Rhalles and Potles published in Athens in 1852 in the first volume of their

Σύνταγμα τῶν ἱερῶν καὶ θείων κανόνων. The two editors compared earlier editions of the *nomokanon* and Balsamon's running commentaries on it (editions by Christophore Justel in 1610, Gentian Hervet in 1650, and Henri Justel and Gulielmus Voellius in 1661) with the version of the text found in what today is Cod. 1379 of the National Library of Greece in Athens, itself a copy of a manuscript produced in Trebizond in 1311. Rhalles and Potles's edition does not make use of some of the earliest textual witnesses. An early redaction of Balsamon's commentaries datable to ca. 1179 is found in a thirteenth-century manuscript, to which Viktor Tiftixoglu first drew our attention: Vaticanus Palatinus gr. 384. This early redaction features marginal glosses by Balsamon, some of which entered the subsequent final redaction, while others did not. It is the second redaction which has become widely known through the printed editions.[176] The text of the Donation in Vaticanus Palatinus gr. 384 begins on folio 21r–v. and continues on folio 37v. The reason for this sequence is that the current folio 21 has been torn off and pasted toward the front of the manuscript before the beginning of the *nomokanon*. Folio 37 has also been torn off and has been rebound vice versa, that is, the recto has become verso, and the verso recto. My examination of the text of the Donation in Vaticanus Palatinus gr. 384 has not revealed any significant variations from the printed text by Rhalles and Potles. What is different is that the entire known text of Balsamon's commentary on the Donation is absent. In other words, we do not find Balsamon's statements that Michael I Keroularios and other patriarchs attempted to use the Donation for their own benefit, that the Donation should pertain to the rights of the patriarchal *chartophylax*, etc. Instead Vaticanus Palatinus gr. 384 features marginal glosses on the upper and right-hand margins of folio 37v. Unfortunately, most of the marginalia are not legible in the current state of binding of the manuscript, because the folio has been reversed and the glosses of the right-hand margin make space for the stub and thus lie hidden from sight. In addition, the three lines of glosses on the upper margin have largely faded and the uppermost line has been partially destroyed on account of clipping. I was able to make out only a few words: "ἐνομοθετήθη . . . οὔτε γὰρ οἱ ἀρχιερεῖς διὰ τούτων πατριαρχικοὺς εἰς τὴν βασιλεῦσαν ἐνδημοῦσαν . . . οὕτω τῆς μεγαλοπόλεως . . . ἀπὸ πολὺν δὲ χρόνον ἐν αὐτῇ διατρίβοντι οὐδεμίαν κάκωσιν ὑπομένουσι. . . ." Fragmentary as it is, this legible text in the upper margin clearly does not correspond to the known commentary of Balsamon. Furthermore, it is notable that four of the six examined manuscripts of Balsamon's commentaries on the *Nomokanon in Fourteen Titles* omit the commentary on the Donation and do not feature any marginalia. The codices in question are Basel, Universitätsbibliothek, Cod. A III 6; British Library, Cod. Arundel 533; Cod. Barocci gr. 205; Esphigmenou, Cod. 4. Only two of the examined MSS—Vat. gr. 844 and Vat. Regin. gr. 51—transmit Balsamon's commentaries of the Donation known to us from the printed editions.

The following conclusions naturally arise. Balsamon quoted the text of the Donation in both redactions of his commentaries on the *Nomokanon in Fourteen Titles* at title 8, chapter 1. He made different comments in each edition. The comments in the first edition are still to be identified fully, which is to be achieved through the disassembling of the quire and examination of the marginal glosses trapped in the stub. Dependent on the first edition are a number of early manuscripts of the *nomokanon*, which do not copy the marginal glosses and omit entirely Balsamon's early comments on the Donation. In his subsequent, final redaction of his commentaries Balsamon voiced his well-known opinion, from which another group of manuscripts is derived.

An important note needs to be made regarding the intentionality of Balsamon when he cited the Donation in the *Nomokanon in Fourteen Titles*. The anonymous Byzantine canonist of Sinaiticus gr. 1112, who was Balsamon's rival and contemporary during the 1180s and commented on the *nomokanon*, followed Balsamon in mentioning that the Donation demonstrated the privileges enjoyed by the church of old Rome.[177] However, he omitted to quote the text of the Donation and instead referred his readers elsewhere to "Title 557" of an unknown legal collection: "οἷα δέ εἰσι τὰ προνόμια τῆς ἐν τῇ παλαιᾷ Ῥώμῃ ἁγίας ἐκκλησίας παρίστησιν ἡμῖν τὸ παρὰ τοῦ ἰσαποστόλου ἁγίου μεγάλου Κωνσταντίνου γεγονὸς ἔγγραφον θέσπισμα πρὸς τὸν ἁγιώτατον Σίλβεστρον τὸν τότε πάπαν τῆς Ῥώμης, ὅπερ ζήτει ἐν τίτλῳ φνζ΄."[178] The anonymous canonist of Sinaiticus gr. 1112 seems to have envisaged a mysterious collection of imperial laws and patriarchal decisions with uniquely high title numbers.[179] The reference to this collection indicates that the Balsamon version of the Donation circulated as an independent, self-contained legal document already before or at least during the time of Balsamon.

2. TEXTUAL VARIATIONS

The examination of the late Byzantine manuscripts of the Balsamon version of the Donation has not uncovered any large-scale contamination of the text. Two curious cases of variation are worthy of note here, as they are suggestive of contemporary interpretations. The first is the substitution of the phrase "οἱ κληρικοὶ τῆς μεγάλης ἐκκλησίας" for the correct expression "οἱ κληρικοὶ τῆς Ῥωμαίων ἐκκλησίας" in a section of the Donation referring to the ceremonial privileges of the clerics of the Roman church. This variation crops up in four codices transmitting the Balsamon version as a self-contained text: Ambros. gr. 682 (Q. 76 sup.), fol. 19r; BnF, Cod. gr. 1388, fol. 3v; Laur. gr. 8, 17, fol. 456r; and Vindob. hist. gr. 34, fol. 373r–v. Another interesting variation appears in two late Byzantine manuscripts of the *Nomokanon in Fourteen Titles*. In most codices, as well as in the Rhalles and Potles edition (1:147, lines 6–7), the successors of Sylvester on the papal throne are referred to as "πᾶσι τοῖς διαδόχοις αὐτοῦ μακαρίοις ἐπισκόποις." However, Esphigmenou, Cod. 4, and Vatic. gr. 844 feature an interpolation: "πᾶσι τοῖς διαδόχοις αὐτοῦ *ὀρθοδόξοις* μακαρίοις ἐπισκόποις." We can plausibly hypothesize that this modification, too, was likely to have been provoked (whether consciously or not) by confessional considerations rather than being an innocent copying slip. The specific reference to Sylvester's successors as "orthodox" excluded the popes from being worthy recipients of privileges of the Donation.[180]

In addition to textual variants informed by contemporary realities, there are variations that are less significant from a purely historical point of view; nonetheless they contribute to the establishment of distinct textual families and thus help the eventual establishment of a *stemma* of the Balsamon version. I note below some unique textual features in manuscripts of the late Byzantine interpolated redaction of the *Nomokanon in Fifty Titles* (see below, appendix 1, part 3C) and in the Nicholas of Otranto group of manuscripts (see below appendix 2, part 2).

3. THE SELF-CONTAINED BALSAMON VERSION: CONTEXTS OF CIRCULATION

A. Balsamon Codices without the *Nomokanon in Fourteen Titles*

Ambrosianus gr. 682 (Q. 97 sup.). The codex has been described in Martini and Bassi, *Catalogus*, 2:780–88. See also Turyn, *Dated Greek Manuscripts of the Thirteenth and Fourteenth Centuries in the Libraries of Italy*, 1:57–58. Copied in 1287/88, probably in Cyprus, this codex contains various canonical writings of Balsamon without his commentaries on the *Nomokanon in Fourteen Titles*. The Donation was copied on folios 18v–19v after Balsamon's canonical responses to Patriarch Mark of Alexandria and immediately before the beginning of his commentaries on the canons of the councils. The Donation thus gives the impression of opening Balsamon's commentaries.

Vaticanus Reginensis gr. 57. The fourteenth-century codex has been described in Henry Stevenson, *Codices manuscripti Graeci reginae Svecorum et Pii PP. II* (Rome: Ex Typographeo Vaticano, 1888), pp. 48–51. See also Alexander Turyn, *Codices Graeci Vaticani saeculis XIII e XIV scripti annorumque notis instructi* (Vatican City: Biblioteca Apostolica Vaticana, 1964), pp. 154– 56. The great bulk of the codex (fols. 47–489) was executed in 1358/59. This was the time when the Donation was copied near the end of the codex on folios 454v –55v together with various other legal texts. The codex contains various canonical writings, such as the *Nomocanon in Fourteen Titles*, although without Balsamon's commentaries, as well as the canons of the councils and the apostles, with the commentaries of Zonaras.

B. Harmenopoulos and Blastares Codices

Moscow, State Historical Museum (formerly Sinodal'naya biblioteka), no. 327. This codex containing Blastares' *Syntagma* has been described by Arkhimandrit Vladimir, *Sistematicheskoe opisanie rukopisei Moskovskoi sinodal'noi biblioteki* (Moscow: Sinodal'naia tipografia, 1894), pp. 476–77. I have not been able to examine a reproduction of this manuscript. See also Pavlov, "Podlozhnaia darstvennaia gramota," pp. 22–23, who refers to the codex as no. 149. The codex has been dated to 1342 on the basis of the copyist's note, that is, still during the lifetime of Blastares and soon after the completion of the *Syntagma* in 1335. The Donation is found on folio 1 and is followed immediately by the text of Blastares' *Syntagma*, thus serving as a prolegomenon to the *Syntagma*. It is certain that this version is the Balsamon one, because the accompanying note published by both Arkhimandrit Vladimir and Pavlov states that the text has been excerpted from the *Nomokanon of Photios* (that is, the *Nomokanon in Fourteen Titles*).

Vindobonensis hist. gr. 34. This codex, a legal miscellany copied in 1430, has been described in Herbert Hunger, *Katalog der griechischen Handschriften der Österreichischen Nationalbibliothek*, Teil 1, *Codices historici, codices philosophici et philologici* (Vienna: Prachner, 1961), pp. 35–38. Hunger mistakenly identified this version of the Donation with the one edited by Augusto Gaudenzi, *Bullettino dell'Istituto Storico Italiano* 39 (1919): 108–112, which in fact is the *donatio* of the Kydones version, not the Balsamon version. The opening work in the codex is Blastares' *Syntagma* (fols. 1r–164r), which is followed shortly by Harmenopoulos's *Hexabiblos* (fols. 177r–310r). The latter work does not feature the abbreviated Blasteres version of the Donation in its appendices. The Donation (fols. 372v–74r) was copied at a great distance from the *Hexabiblos*. One wonders whether the compiler of the manuscript included the Balsamon version as an afterthought, having had no access to the abbreviated one.

Vindobonensis jur. gr. 6. The miscellaneous codex, copied in the fifteenth century and featuring the legal works of Harmenopoulos, has been described by Herbert Hunger, *Katalog der griechischen Handschriften der Öster-reichischen Nationalbibliothek*, Teil 2, *Codices juridici, codices medici* (Vienna: Prachner, 1969), pp. 11–13. The Balsamon version of the Donation is copied on folios 194v–95v at a certain distance after Harmenopoulos's *Hexabiblos* (fols. 2v–136v) and his epitome of the canons (fols. 141r–182r). As in the above case, Harmenopoulos's *Hexabiblos* does not feature the abbreviated version of the Donation in its appendices.

BnF, Cod. gr. 1388. This fifteenth-century codex containing Harmeno-poulos's *Hexabiblos* and other legal works has been described in Omont, *Inventaire*, 2:34–35. The *Hexabiblos* of Harmenopoulos does not feature the abbreviated Blastares version of the Donation in its appendices. The Balsamon version of the Donation (fols. 2v–4v) is the opening work copied in the codex.

C. Interpolated Redaction of the *Nomokanon in Fifty Titles*

Vaticanus gr. 640. This codex, a judicial miscellany dating to the four-teenth century, has been described by Robert Devreesse, *Codices Vaticani Graeci*, vol. 3, *Codices 604–833* (Vatican City: Biblioteca Apostolica Vaticana, 1950), pp. 60–63. See also Beneševič, *Sinagogá v 50 titulov*, p. 187 and n. 1. The Donation is found on folios 43v–45r and forms part of several legal documents interpolated into title 1 of the *nomokanon*. The Donation is pre-ceded, although not immediately, by excerpts from the first three titles of Photios's *Eisagoge* (fols. 39v–40r).

BnF, Cod. gr. 1263. This codex, a judicial miscellany dating to the four-teenth or the fifteenth century, has been described by Omont, *Inventaire*, 1:281. See also Beneševič, *Sinagogá v 50 titulov*, p. 187 and n. 1. Unlike the Vatican manuscript, the interpolations are not incorporated into the text, but are written in the margins of the manuscript. The Donation is found on folios 25r–27r. Again unlike the Vatican manuscript, the Donation is preceded immediately by the excerpts from Photios's *Eisagoge* on folios 23r–24v.

The apographs of the Donation in the two manuscripts of the *Nomokanon in Fifty Titles* belong to the same textual family. Both contain the variant reading "διὰ ταύτην τὴν θείαν κέλευσιν καὶ πραγματικὸν θέσπισμα ἐψηφίσαμεν" instead of the correct "διὰ ταύτην τὴν θείαν κέλευσιν καὶ πραγματικὸν σύστημα ἐθεσπίσαμεν" (Rhalles-Potles, 1:148, lines 4–5). This variation is found also in the fifteenth-century Vindob. jur. gr. 6, fol. 195v. (See above, appendix 1, section 3B)

D. Miscellany

Laurentianus gr. 8, 17. The codex has been dated to the fourteenth century and described by Angelo Maria Bandini, *Catalogus codicum manuscriptorum Bibliothecae Mediceae Laurentianae varia continens opera Graecorum patrum*, 3 vols. (Florence, 1764; repr. Leipzig: Zentralantiquariat der Deutschen Demokratischen Republik, 1961), 1:358–62. Contrary to Bandini, Jean Verpeaux, *Pseudo-Kodinos: Traité des offices* (Paris: CNRS, 1966), p. 351 n. 1, dated the manuscript to the fifteenth or the sixteenth century. Marco Petta, "Codici greci della Puglia transferiti in biblioteche italiane ed estere," *Bollettino della Badia Graeca di Grottaferrata*, n.s., 26 (1972): 83–129 (p. 118), assigned the production of this manuscript to the scriptorium of the abbey of St. Nicholas of Casole near Otranto in Apulia, although this attribution is doubtful, as it is based on the hypothesis, no longer sustainable (see below, appendix 2), that the text of the Donation here belongs to the Nicholas of Otranto group. The manuscript contains mostly works of John Chrysostom along with other theological and miscellaneous works, including the account of the coronation of Manuel II Palaiologos in 1392 on folios 421r–23r. The Donation of Contantine was copied at the very end of the codex on folios 454r–57v and does not seem to bear any relation with other works copied.

E. The Copy by Nicholas of Otranto (1206) and the Southern Italian Tradition

(see appendix 2)

Appendix 2

Nicholas of Otranto's Group of the
Balsamon Version of the Donation

Nicholas of Otranto copied the Balsamon version of the Donation when serving as an interpreter to the Roman cardinal and papal legate Benedict of Sancta Susanna during his official embassy to Constantinople in the years 1205–7. This apograph was subsequently brought to Apulia, where Nicholas was a monk in the monastery of St. Nicholas of Casole near Otranto, and was further reproduced together with two slightly different notes, stating that Nicholas copied the Balsamon version in December 1206 at the Great Palace of Constantinople after being commissioned to do so by the papal cardinal and legate. Johannes Hoeck and Raymond-Joseph Loenertz, *Nikolaos-Nektarios von Otranto, Abt von Casole: Beiträge zur Geschichte der ost-westlichen Beziehungen unter Innozenz III. und Friedrich II.* (Ettal: Buch-Kunstverlag, 1965), p. 53 n. 11, thought that the copy made by Nicholas of Otranto survived in four manuscripts: Vaticanus gr. 1416, Vaticanus gr. 1276, Laurentianus gr. 8, 17, and Laurentianus lat. 16, 40. In fact, the Nicholas of Otranto family should be restricted to three manuscripts. Laurentianus gr. 8, 17 clearly does not belong to this group. Not only does this codex lack the note on the circumstances of production of Nicholas of Otranto's copy, but it does not present the salient textual features which all three remaining manuscripts share (see below, appendix 2, part 2).

1. THE CODICES OF THE NICHOLAS OF OTRANTO GROUP

A. Vaticanus gr. 1276

The codex dates to the thirteenth century and was copied in the abbey of St. Nicholas of Casole near Otranto. Although this manuscript has not yet been described in the series *Codices Vaticani Graeci*, relevant information as to its features can be found in Robert Devreesse, *Les manuscrits grecs de l'Italie méridionale* (Vatican City: Biblioteca Apostolica Vaticana, 1955), pp. 19, 45; Petta, "Codici greci della Puglia," pp. 88, 91, 115, 124–25; Hoeck-Loenertz, *Nikolaos-Nektarios von Otranto*, pp. 22–23, 113–16. A large fragment of the Balsamon version of the Donation is found on folios 96r–97v, with the beginning missing, doubtless because of the loss of a folio. The colophon on the date and circumstances of execution of Nicholas of Otranto's copy found on folios 97v–98r. has been published by Petrucci, "I rapporti," p. 59 n. 2.

B. Vaticanus gr. 1416

This codex has been dated to the late sixteenth century by Petrucci, "I rapporti," p. 57. The relevant volume from *Codices Vaticani Graeci* is still outstanding. The Balsamon version of the Donation on folios 121r–24r features a preface (see below, part 3) and is followed by a note on the date and circumstances of execution of Nicholas of Otranto's copy published by Petrucci, "I rapporti," p. 59 n. 2. The *confessio* from the Kydones version was copied on folios 127–32.

C. Laurentianus lat. 16, 40

This little codex (partly Latin, partly Greek) dates to the sixteenth century and has been described by Antionio Maria Bandini, *Catalogus codicum latinorum Bibliothecae Mediceae Laurentianae*, 5 vols. (Florence: n. pub., 1774–78), vol. 1, cols. 295–96. The Donation is found on folios 5r–12r. It is followed (fols. 12r–v) by the same note as the one in Vat. gr. 1416.

2. COMMON CHARACTERISTICS OF THE GROUP

The three manuscripts of the group refer to the Lateran palace in Rome as "τὸ ἡμέτερον βασιλικὸν παλάτιον τὸ Λατερανένσιον" (Vat. gr. 1276, fol. 96r, Vat. gr. 1416, fol. 122r, Laur. lat. 16, 40, fol. 7v). By contrast, the form "τὸ Λατερανέσιον" (Rhalles-Potles, 1:146, line 12) appears in all other examined manuscripts of the Balsamon version. The word Λατερανένσιον is a Latinism formed by analogy with the adjective *lateranensis* and evokes the bilingual environment of southern Italy. In addition, this group of manuscripts features two cases of *lectio simplicior* that are unique to it: a scribal error known as *saut du même au même* or omission due to *homoteleuton*, that is, the omission of text framed between identical words or endings.[181]

The boldface text below framed by the word τὴν γῆν indicates the words that dropped out in the copying process due to this scribal error. (Note that the entire section quoted below is missing from the fragment of the Donation preserved in Vat. gr. 1276.)

Rhalles-Potles, 1:145, lines 3–10: "[Δέον ἐκρίναμεν . . .] ἵνα ὡς ὁ ἅγιος Πέτρος ἐκ προσώπου τοῦ υἱοῦ τοῦ Θεοῦ ἐστιν εἰς τὴν γῆν, **οὕτω καὶ οἱ ἐπίσκοποι, οἱ διάδοχοι τοῦ κορυφαίου τῶν Ἀποστόλων ἀρχικὴν**

ἐξουσίαν εἰς τὴν γῆν ἔχωσι, πλέον παρ᾽ ὃ ἔχει ἡ βασιλεία τῆς δόξης ἡμῶν, καὶ τοῦτο παρεχωρήθη ἀφ᾽ ἡμῶν καὶ ἀπὸ τῆς βασιλείας ἡμῶν. Καὶ θέλομεν. . . ."

Vat. gr. 1416, fol. 121r, and Laur. lat. 16,40, fol. 5r: "[Δέον ἐκρίναμεν . . .] ἵνα ὡς ὁ ἅγιος Πέτρος ἐκ προσώπου τοῦ υἱοῦ τοῦ Θεοῦ ἐστιν εἰς τὴν γῆν, ἔχων πλέον παρ᾽ ὃ ἔχει ἡ βασιλεία τῆς δόξης ἡμῶν καὶ τὸ παρεχωρηθὲν ἀφ᾽ ἡμῶν καὶ ἀπὸ τῆς βασιλείας ἡμῶν. Καὶ θέλομεν. . . ."

In another case cited below, the phrase in boldface text, "διὰ τοῦτο δὲ χρήσιμον ἐννοήσαμεν," has been omitted on account of the similar ending –σαμεν in the verbs παρεχωρήσαμεν and ἐννοήσαμεν. It is interesting that the omission of the phrase through a scribal error (hardly intentional) modifies the text in such as way as to create the impression that the pope was given the imperial office itself! The Donation never makes such a radical statement. The syntax of the sentence has become garbled as result of the omission, yet an attempt was made to fix this in the version of the text in Vat. gr. 1276. Here the infinitive μεταφέρειν dependent on χρήσιμον ἐννοήσαμεν has been modified into an indicative, and the verb ἐσπουδεύσαμεν has been inserted to smooth the flow of the text.

Rhalles-Potles, 1:148, lines 4–11: "διὰ ταύτην τὴν θείαν κέλευσιν καὶ πραγματικὸν σύστημα ἐθεσπίσαμεν διαμένειν, καὶ τοῖς ἀνδράσι τῆς ἁγίας τῶν Ῥωμαίων ἐκκλησίας εἰς τὸν αἰῶνα παρεχωρήσαμεν. **Διὰ τοῦτο δὲ χρήσιμον ἐννοήσαμεν** τὴν βασιλείαν ἡμῶν καὶ τὸ κράτος τῆς βασιλείας εἰς τὰς ἀνατολικὰς χώρας μεταφέρειν, καὶ ἐν τῇ Βυζαντίῳ χώρᾳ, τόπῳ χρησίμῳ, τὴν πόλιν ἐπὶ τῷ ὀνόματι ἡμῶν ἱδρυθῆναι καὶ τὴν ἡμῶν βασιλείαν ἐκεῖ συστῆναι."

Vat. gr. 1416, fol. 123v, and Laur. lat. 16,40, fol. 11r–v: "διὰ ταύτην τὴν θείαν κέλευσιν καὶ πραγματικὸν σύστημα ἐθεσπίσαμεν διαμένειν, καὶ τοῖς ἀνδράσι τῆς ἁγίας τῶν Ῥωμαίων ἐκκλησίας εἰς τὸν αἰῶνα παρεχωρίσαμεν [sic] τὴν βασιλείαν ἡμῶν καὶ τὸ κράτος τῆς βασιλείας, εἰς τὰς ἀνατολικὰς χώρας μεταφέρειν καὶ ἐν τῇ Βυζαντίᾳ χώρᾳ, τόπῳ χρησίμῳ, τὴν πόλιν ἐπὶ τῷ ὀνόματι ἡμῶν ἱδρυνθῆναι καὶ τὴν ἡμῶν βασιλείαν ἐκεῖ συστῆναι."

Vat. gr. 1276, fol. 97v: "διὰ ταύτην τὴν θείαν κέλευσιν καὶ πραγματικὸν σύστημα ἐθεσπίσαμεν διαμένειν, καὶ τοῖς ἀνδράσι τῆς ἁγίας τῶν Ῥωμαίων ἐκκλησίας εἰς τὸν αἰῶνα παρεχωρήσαμεν τὴν βασιλείαν ἡμῶν καὶ τὸ κράτος τῆς βασιλείας εἰς τὰς ἀνατολὰς μεταφέρομεν καὶ ἐν τῇ Βυζαντίῳ χώρᾳ, τόπῳ χρησίμῳ, τὴν πόλιν ἐπὶ τῷ ὀνόματι ἡμῶν ἱδρυνθῆναι ἐσπουδεύσαμεν καὶ τὴν ἡμῶν βασιλείαν ἐκεῖ συστῆναι."

3. THE PREFACE TO THE DONATION IN VAT. GR. 1416

The copy of the Balsamon version of the Donation in the sixteenth-century Vat. gr. 1416 contains a unique preface, according to which the Donation demonstrates that the universal church should be subject to the see of Rome. Most of the preface, in fact, is an excerpt from title 8, chapter 1, of the *Nomokanon in Fourteen Titles* and the attendant commentaries of Theodore Balsamon. It is probable, therefore, that the original apograph of Nicholas of Otranto in 1206 consisted of the Donation along with the attendant text in the work from which it was excerpted. It is important again to note that the entire opening part of the Donation is missing in the thirteenth-century Vat. gr. 1276, the earliest of the three manuscripts of the group.

A. Vaticanus gr. 1416, fol. 120r–121r:

Διαθήκη τοῦ μεγάλου Κωνσταντίνου

Ἐκ τοῦ νομοκανόνος τῆς βίβλου τῆς συνοψισθείσης[182] ἐκ προτροπῆς τοῦ μακαριωτάτου πατριάρχου Κωνσταντινουπόλεως κυροῦ Μιχαὴλ καὶ θεοσεβοῦς βασιλέως κυροῦ Μανουὴλ παρὰ
5 Θεοδώρου τοῦ Βαλσαμὼν τοῦ πρώτου διακόνου τῆς μεγάλης ἐκ-κλησίας καὶ χαρτοφύλακος χρηματίσαντος, ὅτε καὶ τὴν βίβλον ταύτην συνέθετο, ὕστερον δὲ γεγονότος πατριάρχου μεγάλης Ἀν-τιοχείας, ἀποδεικνύοντος, ὅτι πᾶσα ἐκκλησία ὑπὸ <τοῦ> πάπα Ῥώμης δικαιοῦται, ὡς ἐκ τοῦ μεγάλου Κωνσταντίνου διατάξεως
10 ἔξεστιν εἰδεῖν· τῆς δὲ βίβλου ἡ ἀρχὴ "πείθεσθε τοῖς ἡγουμένοις" ἐστίν, ἥτις διαιρεῖται εἰς ιδ' τίτλους. ἐν δὲ τῷ ὀγδόῳ δηλοῦται ταῦτα, ἅτινα βασανίζων οὕτω φησίν.

Ἡ στ' διάταξις τοῦ β' τίτλου τοῦ α' βιβλίου τοῦ κώδικός φησιν, ὅτι τὰς ἀναφυομένας κανονικὰς ἀμφισβητήσεις ἐν ὅλῳ τῷ Ἰλλυρικῷ[183]
15 οὐ δεῖ τέμνεσθαι παρὰ γνώμην τοῦ ἀρχιεπισκόπου Κωνσταντινου-πόλεως καὶ τῆς αὐτοῦ συνόδου, ἥτις ἔχει τὰ προνόμια τῆς ἀρχαίας Ῥώμης . . .[184] οἷα δέ εἰσι τὰ προνόμια τῆς ἐν παλαιᾷ Ῥώμῃ ἁγίας ἐκκλησίας, παρίστησιν ἡμῖν τὸ ἰσαπόστολον ἁγίου μεγάλου Κων-σταντίνου γεγονὸς ἔγγραφον θέσπισμα πρὸς τὸν ἅγιον Σίλβεστρον
20 τὸν τότε πάπαν τῆς Ῥώμης, ὃ καὶ ἔχει οὕτως. Δέον ἐκρίναμεν μετὰ πάντων τῶν σατραπῶν ἡμῶν καὶ πάσης τῆς συγκλήτου καὶ τῶν ἀρχόντων [the text of the Donation follows].

138   DIMITER G. ANGELOV

NOTES

1. Horst Fuhrmann, ed., *Das Constitutum Constantini, Konstantinische Schenkung*, MGH: Fontes iuris Germanici antiqui in usum scholarium 19 (Hannover: Hahn, 1968). An English translation can be found in Mark Edwards, trans., *Constantine and Christendom* (Liverpool: Liverpool University Press, 2003), pp. 92–115. See also Johannes Fried, *Donation of Constantine and Constitutum Constantini: The Misinterpretation of a Fiction and Its Original Meaning*, with a contribution by Wolfram Brandes (Berlin: de Gruyter, 2007), pp. 129–37 (Latin text); 138–45 (English translation).

2. Wilhelm Levison, "Konstantinische Schenkung und Silvester-Legende," *Aus rheinischer und fränkischer Frühzeit* (Düsseldorf: Schwann, 1948), pp. 390–473, esp. pp. 409–10; Wilhelm Pohlkamp, "*Privilegium ecclesiae Romanae pontifici contulit*: Zur Vorgeschichte der Konstantinischen Schenkung," in *Fälschungen im Mittelalter: Internationaler Kongress der Monumenta Germaniae Historica, München 16.–19. September 1986*, vol. 2, *Gefälschte Rechtstexte—Der bestrafte Fälscher* (Hannover: Hahn, 1988), pp. 413–90, esp. pp. 482–86; Wilhelm Pohlkamp, "Textfassungen, literarische Formen und geschichtliche Funktionen der römischen Silvester-Akten," *Francia* 19, no. 1 (1992): 115–96, esp. p. 149 n. 160.

3. For a discussion of some of the extensive historiography on the date of the Donation, see Horst Fuhrmann, "Das frühmittelalterliche Papsttum und die Konstantinische Schenkung," in *I problemi dell'Occidente nel secolo VIII*, 2 vols., Settimane di studio del Centro italiano di studi sull'alto medioevo 20 (Spoleto: Presso la sede del Centro, 1973), 1:257–92. On its association with the Lateran church, see Nicolas Huyghebaert, "La Donation de Constantin ramenée à ses véritables dimensions: À propos de deux publications récentes," *Revue d'histoire ecclésiastique* 71 (1976): 45–69; Nicolas Huyghebaert, "Une légende de fondation: Le *Constitutum Constantini*," *Le Moyen Âge* 85 (1979): 177–209; Raymond-Joseph Loenertz, "Le *Constitutum Constantini* et la basilique du Latran," *BZ* 69 (1976): 406–10. Fried, *Donation of Constantine and Constitutum Constantini*, pp. 53–72, has recently argued, however, for a Frankish origin of the forgery. The Donation was originally forged in Latin, not Greek, as an earlier theory held. See here p. 103.

4. Johanna Petersmann, "Die kanonistische Überlieferung des *Constitutum Constantini* bis zum Dekret Gratians: Untersuchung und Edition," *Deutsches Archiv* 30 (1974): 356–449.

5. Frank Zinkeisen, "The Donation of Constantine as Applied by the Roman Church," *English Historical Review* 9 (1894): 625–63; Walter Ullmann, *The Growth of Papal Government in the Middle Ages* (London: Methuen, 1955), pp. 74–86, 144–48, 160, 326, 416–18; Michael Wilks, *The Problem of Sovereignty in the Late Middle Ages* (Cambridge: Cambridge University Press, 1963), pp. 543–47; Fried, *Donation of Constantine and Constitutum Constantini*, pp. 11–33.

6. Domenico Maffei, *La Donazione di Costantino nei giuristi medievali da Graziano a Bartolo* (Milan: Giuffrè, 1958); Cecil Woolf, *Bartolus of Sassoferrato: His Position in

the History of Medieval Political Thought (Cambridge: Cambridge University Press, 1913), pp. 94–100, 315–23, 343–50.

7. See here p. 124.

8. George Ostrogorsky, "Zum Stratordienst des Herrschers in der byzantinisch-slavischen Welt," *Seminarium Kondakovianum* 7 (1935): 187–204, drew attention to the importation of the papal ceremony of groom service *(officium stratoris)* and traced the continual application of this ritual under different circumstances in seventeenth-century Russia.

9. Francis Dvornik, *The Idea of Apostolicity in Byzantium and the Legend of the Apostle Andrew* (Cambridge, Mass.: Harvard University Press, 1958), pp. 252, 288–99, pointed to cases of usage of the Donation in polemical exchanges between Latins and Greeks.

10. Paul Alexander, "The Donation of Constantine at Byzantium and Its Earliest Use against the Western Empire," *ZRVI* 8 (1963): 11–26, demonstrated that the first mention of the Donation by a Byzantine historian dates to the twelfth century and not earlier as had traditionally been assumed.

11. Viktor Tiftixoglu, "Gruppenbildungen innerhalb des konstantinopolitanischen Klerus während der Komnenenzeit," *BZ* 62 (1969): 25–72, esp. pp. 60–72, examined the twelfth-century canonical debate on the implications of the Donation.

12. Hans-Georg Krause, "Das Constitutum Constantini im Schisma von 1054," in *Aus Kirche und Reich: Festschrift für Friedrich Kempf*, ed. Hubert Mordek (Sigmaringen: Thorbecke, 1983), pp. 131–58, studied meticulously the circumstances of the earliest Byzantine translation of the Donation.

13. Gilbert Dagron, *Empereur et prêtre: Études sur le "césaropapisme" byzantin* (Paris: Gallimard, 1995), pp. 248–55 (Gilbert Dagron, *Emperor and Priest: The Imperial Office in Byzantium*, trans. Jean Birrell [Cambridge: Cambridge University Press, 2003], pp. 240–47) argued that the Donation inspired the ambitious Patriarch Michael I Keroularios and discussed aspects of the domestic Byzantine usage of the Donation in the eleventh and the twelfth century.

14. John Malalas (sixth century), *Ioannis Malalae chronographia*, ed. Ioannes Thurn (Berlin: de Gruyter, 2000), p. 243; George the Monk (ninth century), *Georgii monachi chronicon*, ed. Carolus de Boor, 2 vols. (Leipzig: Teubner, 1904), 2:485–87; Theophanes (ninth century), *Theophanis chronographia*, ed. Carolus de Boor, 2 vols. (Leipzig: Teubner, 1883–85), 1:17–18, who says that he finds the version of Constantine's baptism by Sylvester more believable than the version of his baptism by Eusebius; John Zonaras (twelfth century), *Ioannis Zonarae epitomae historiarum libri XIII–XVIII*, ed. Theodor Büttner-Wobst (Bonn: Weber, 1897), pp. 7–12 (a particularly lengthy report).

15. Ephraim of Ainos (fourteenth century), *Ephraem Aenii historia chronica*, ed. Odysseus Lampsides (Athens: Academy of Athens, 1990), pp. 17–18; John Kantakouzenos (fourteenth century), *Ioannis Cantacuzeni eximperatoris historiarum libri IV*,

ed. Ludwig Schopen, 3 vols. (Bonn: Weber, 1828–32), 3:18, lines 5–9. The earliest extant Greek vitae of Constantine featuring the Sylvester legend date to the ninth century. See Alexander Kazhdan, "'Constantin Imaginaire': Byzantine Legends of the Ninth Century about Constantine the Great," *Byzantion* 57 (1987): 196–250, esp. pp. 200–202, 239–40. In late Byzantium, the Sylvester legend is reported in the vitae of Constantine by Constantine Akropolites (see Constantine Simonides, *The Panegyric of That Holy, Apostolic, and Heaven-Crowned King Constantine the Great, Composed by His Head Logothetes Constantine Acropoliti* [London: Longman, Brown, Green, and Longmans, 1853], pp. 15–17), and John Chortasmenos (see below, n. 18). Constantine Acropolites also mentions Constantine's baptism by Sylvester in his life of St. Zotikos. See Timothy Miller, "The Legend of Saint Zotikos According to Constantine Akropolites," *Analecta Bollandiana* 112 (1994): 352–53.

16. Levison, "Konstantinische Schenkung," pp. 445–54, pointed to Latinisms in the Greek text of the vita. Cf. also Louis Duchesne, *Liber pontificalis*, 2 vols. (Paris, 1886–92; repr. Paris: Boccard, 1955), 1:cix–cx, cxv. Garth Fowden, "Constantine, Silvester and the Church of S. Polyeuctus in Constantinople," *Journal of Roman Archaeology* 7 (1994): 274–84 (p. 279), has argued that the *Actus Silvestri* was known in Constantinople already in the early sixth century. In any case, the earliest Greek manuscripts are tenth-century, and the Greek vita survives in over ninety manuscripts. For a brief overview of the Greek and Syriac translations, see Levison, "Konstantinische Schenkung," p. 396; Pohlkamp "Textfassungen," pp. 136–37.

17. The various Greek vitae of Sylvester have been surveyed by François Halkin, *Bibliotheca hagiographica graeca*, 3rd ed. (Brussels: Société des Bollandistes, 1957), nos. 1628–34; François Halkin, *Auctarium* (Brussels: Société des Bollandistes, 1969), nos. 1629–34. For the legislation of Constantine as repored in the middle Byzantine vitae, see *Illustrium Christi martyrum lecti triumphi*, ed. François Combefis (Paris: A. Bertier, 1660), pp. 282–83 (based on a tenth-century manuscript); *Le ménologe impérial de Baltimore*, ed. François Halkin (Brussels: Société des Bollandistes, 1985), pp. 26–27 (eleventh-century imperial *menologion*); John Zonaras's twelfth-century vita in *Roma e l'Oriente* 6 (1913): 346–47. A difference between the Byzantine East and the Latin West is worthy of note. In its original Latin redaction (A1), the *Actus Silvestri* reports an eight-day period of legislation after Constantine's baptism; on the fourth day Constantine is said to have instituted the pope as the head of all priesthood. This part of the *Actus Silvestri* stirred the imagination of papal ideologues, including the forger of the Donation, yet it is missing from the Greek vitae of Sylvester, because the Greek translation rests on the abridged Latin redaction (B1), which in fact never circulated widely in the West. See Levison, "Konstantinische Schenkung," pp. 446–49. Pohlkamp, "*Privilegium ecclesiae Romanae*," p. 420 n. 1, notes that the original A1 redaction probably remained unknown in Byzantium and supplies (pp. 445 n. 120 and p. 467) the much briefer Latin text of redaction B1, corresponding to the eight-day period of legislation found in redaction A1. A study of the textual history the Greek vitae and their relations to the *Actus Silvestri*

is a desideratum following the critical edition of the Latin versions announced by Wilhelm Pohlkamp.

18. We find this story in the ecclesiastical history of Nikephoros Kallistos Xanthopoulos (d. ca. 1335), PG, vol. 145, cols. 1284C–85B, and in the vita of Constantine by John Chortasmenos (ca. 1370–before 1439), in Theophilos Ioannou, ed., *Mnemeia Hagiologica* (Venice, 1884; repr. Leipzig: Zentralantiquariat der Deutschen Demokratischen Republik, 1973), pp. 185–86. For the attribution of the authorship of this vita to Chortasmenos, see Herbert Hunger, *Johannes Chortasmenos (ca. 1370– ca. 1436/37): Briefe, Gedichte und kleine Schriften* (Vienna: Österreichische Akademie der Wissenschaften, 1969), p. 8.

19. Most of these designations have been introduced by Krause, "Das Constitutum Constantini," pp. 147–48.

20. Published in Rhalles-Potles, 1:145–48 (reprinted in Werner Ohnsorge, "Das Constitutum Constantini und seine Entstehung," *Konstantinopel und der Okzident* [Darmstadt: Wissenschaftliche Buchgesellschaft, 1966], pp. 108–22); PG, vol. 104, cols. 1077B–81D, which purports to be a reprint from Gulielmus Voellius and Henri Justel, *Bibliotheca iuris canonici veteris*, 2 vols. (Paris: L. Billaine, 1661), 2:929–33.

21. Rhalles-Potles, 1:148. On the *Nomokanon in Fourteen Titles*, see Hans-Georg Beck, *Kirche und theologische Literatur im byzantinischen Reich* (Munich: Beck, 1959), pp. 146, 423, with further bibliography.

22. Already in 1896 Aleksei Pavlov, "Podlozhnaia darstvennaia gramota Konstantina Velikago pape Silvestru v polnom grecheskom i slavianskom perevode," *VV* 3 (1896): 24–29, showed that Balsamon's text is a translation from the *libellus*. For the Latin text of the Donation in the *libellus*, see *Acta et scripta quae de controversiis ecclesiae Graecae et Latinae saeculo undecimo composita extant*, ed. Cornelius Will (Leipzig, 1861; repr. Frankfurt am Main: Minerva, 1963), pp. 72–74 (= PL, vol. 143, cols. 753B–55D).

23. Anton Michel, *Humbert und Kerullarios*, 2 vols. (Paderborn: Schöningh, 1924–30), 1:44–53, 66–76, attributed authorship of the *libellus* to Humbert.

24. Krause, "Das Constitutum Constantini," pp. 143–47, 152–53. For the designation "southern Italian collection," see Anton Michel, "Lateinische Aktenstücke und -sammlungen zum griechischen Schisma (1053/54)," *Historisches Jahrbuch* 60 (1940): 46–64, esp. pp. 62–64. A critical edition of Leo IX's *libellus* still remains a *desideratum*. Cf. Krause's observations on the manuscript tradition (differing from Michel's) in *Historische Zeitschrift* 217 (1974): 671–77.

25. For this traditional theory, see Augusto Gaudenzi, "Il Costituto di Costantino," *Bullettino dell'Istituto Storico Italiano per il medio evo e Archivio Muratoriano* 39 (1919): 9–112 (p. 70); Enzo Petrucci, "I rapporti tra le redazioni latine e greche del Costituto di Costantino," *Bullettino dell'Istituto Storico Italiano per il medio evo e Archivio Muratoriano* 74 (1962): 45–160 (p. 58).

26. Krause, "Das Constitutum Constantini," pp. 153–56.

27. Rhalles-Potles, 1:148–49. Tiftixoglu, "Gruppenbildungen," p. 62 n. 37, considers that Balsamon's testimony means that Keroularios was acquainted with the Donation. *Contra*, see Alexander, "The Donation of Constantine at Byzantium," pp. 25–26. Franz Tinnefeld, "Michael I. Kerullarios, Patriarch von Konstantinopel (1043–1058): Kritische Überlegungen zu einer Biographie," *JÖB* 39 (1989): 95–127, esp. pp. 105–7, considers the possibility that the written text of the *libellus* never reached Keroularios, who knew about the Donation by word of mouth.

28. Michael Attaleiates, *Historia*, ed. Wladimir Brunet de Presle and Immanuel Bekker (Bonn: Weber, 1853), p. 60; Scylitzes Continuatus, in Eudoxos Tsolakes, ed., Ἡ συνέχεια τῆς χρονογραφίας τοῦ Ἰωάννου Σκυλίτση (Thessaloniki: Hetaireia Makedonikon Spoudon, 1968), p. 105.

29. Ioli Kalavrezou, Nicolette Trahoulia and Shalom Sabar, "Critique of the Emperor in the Vatican Psalter gr. 752," *DOP* 47 (1993): 195–219, esp. pp. 212–15. Cf. Dagron, *Emperor and Priest*, pp. 240–41.

30. Michel, "Lateinische Aktenstücke," p. 63.

31. *Acta Romanorum Pontificum*, vol. 1, *A S. Clemente I, an. c.90, ad Celestinum III*, ed. Aloysius Tăutu, Pontifica commissio ad redigendum codicem iuris canonici orinetalis, ser. 3 (Vatican City: Typis Polyglottis Vaticanis, 1943), p. 797. On the date of the letter, see Jean Darrouzès, "Les documents byzantins du XIIe siècle sur la primauté romaine," *REB* 23 (1965): 42–88 (p. 52). For other twelfth-century Latin polemicists who referred to the Donation when urging the subordination of the Eastern churches to Rome, see Jannis Spiteris, *La critica bizantina del primato romano nel secolo XII* (Rome: Pontificium Institutum Orientalium Studiorum, 1979), pp. 119–20, 125, 191–93.

32. See here p. 117 and n. 136.

33. See here p.117 and nn. 137–38.

34. See the testimony of the anonymous commentator of Sinaiticus gr. 1117 in appendix 1, part 1, p. 129.

35. The differences are most clearly seen in Ohnsorge's facing edition of various versions of the Donation: the Balsamon, the Chrysoberges, the text of the Donation in Leo IX's *libellus* of 1053 (based on Cornelius Will's edition) and the text of the *donatio* from the full text of the Donation (based on Karl Zeumer's 1888 edition). See Ohnsorge, "Das Constitutum Constantini und seine Entstehung," pp. 114–15 (§ 14), 118–19 (§ 16). Cf. ibid., pp. 157–60, for Ohnsorge's good observations on the translation and the identification of other misunderstandings. On the *loros* and its symbolism, see Maria Parani, *Reconstructing the Reality of Images: Byzantine Material Culture and Religious Iconography (11th–15th Centuries)* (Leiden: Brill, 2003), pp. 18–27.

36. In Cod. A. III. 6 of the Universitätsbibliothek, Basel (thirteenth century), fol. 18v, one reads in the margins "τὸ πρὸς τὸν ἅγιον Σίλβεστρον πάπαν Ῥώμης

θέσπισμα τοῦ μεγάλου καὶ ἰσαποστόλου βασιλέως τοῦ ἁγίου Κωνσταντίνου." In another manuscript of Balsamon's commentaries of the *Nomokanon in Fourteen Titles*, Vat. gr. 844 (thirteenth–fourteenth century), fol. 30r, Balsamon's words "τοῦ μεγάλου Κωνσταντίνου γεγονὸς ἔγγραφον θέσπισμα" are underlined for the sake of drawing attention.

37. Cod. Barocci 205 (fourteenth century), fol. 44r.

38. See appendix 1, part 1, pp. 128–29. On the special importance of this codex, see Viktor Tiftixoglu, "Zur Genese der Kommentare des Theodoros Balsamon mit einem Exkurs über die unbekannten Kommentare des Sinaiticus gr. 1117," in *Byzantium in the 12th Century: Canon Law, State and Society*, ed. Nicolas Oikonomides (Athens: Society of Byzantine and Post-Byzantine Studies, 1991), pp. 483– 532, esp. p. 484 n. 5, and pp. 489–90.

39. Ambros. gr. 682 (Q. 76 sup.), fol. 18v: παρεξεβλήθη ἀπὸ τοῦ η′ τίτλου τοῦ παναγιωτάτου πατριάρχου Κωνσταντινουπόλεως κῦρ Φωτίου ταῦτα. The same note precedes the self-contained text of the Donation in the Balsamon version in Laur. gr. 8, 17, fol. 454r (fifteenth–sixteenth century) and in Moscow, State Historical Museum (formerly Sinodal'naya biblioteka), Cod. gr. 327, fol. 1r (fourteenth century). See appendix 1, part 3, pp. 131, 133.

40. Alexander Turyn, *Dated Greek Manuscripts of the Thirteenth and Fourteenth Centuries in the Libraries of Italy*, 2 vols. (Urbana: University of Illinois Press, 1972), 1:57–58, mentions that the handwriting has Cypriot appearance, and it is probable that the manuscript originates from Cyprus. Cf. Emidio Martini and Domenico Bassi, *Catalogus codicum graecorum Bibliothecae Ambrosianae*, 2 vols. (Milan: Hoepli, 1906), 2:780–88.

41. See Vladimir N. Beneševič, *Sinagogá v 50 titulov i drugie juridičeskie sborniki Joanna Scholastika* (St. Petersburg, 1914; repr. Leipzig: Zentralantiquariat der Deutschen Demokratischen Republik, 1972), p. 187 n. 1. Cf. appendix 1, part 3, pp. 132–33. On the date of production of the interpolated redaction of the *Nomokanon in Fifty Titles*, see below, n. 100.

42. The two versions have been published by Petrucci, "I rapporti," p. 59 n. 2. For a further discussion of the copy made by Nicholas of Otranto, see appendix 2, pp. 134–37.

43. PG, vol. 140, cols. 536B–37A. See Raymond-Joseph Loenertz, "Autour de traité de fr. Barthélémy de Constantinople contre les Grecs," *Archivum Fratrum Praedicatorum* 6 (1939): 361–71, esp. pp. 366–68. Dvornik, *The Idea of Apostolicity*, p. 293, wrongly calls the excerpt found in the *Tractatus contra Graecos* of 1252 "the full text of the *Donatio Constantini*."

44. The excerpted text corresponds to Rhalles-Potles, 1:145, line 3; 1:146, line 2; 1:148, lines 7–14.

45. The fundamental study on the *Tractatus* remains Antoine Dondaine, "'Contra Graecos', premiers écrits polémiques des Dominicains d'Orient," *Archivum Fratrum*

Praedicatorum 21 (1951): 320–446. Dondaine disproved Loenertz's attribution of authorship (see above, n. 43), listed twenty known manuscripts, and traced the impact of the work on Latin polemical literature. Friedrich Stegmüller, "Bonacursius Contra Graecos: Ein Beitrag zur Kontroverstheologie des XIII. Jahrhunderts," in *Vitae et Vertitati: Festgabe für Karl Adam* (Düsseldorf: Patmos-Verlag, 1956), p. 58 n. 1, signaled yet another manuscript.

46. This section of the *Thesaurus* (yet unpublished in its entirely) was edited by Franz Reusch, *Die Fälschungen in dem Traktat des Thomas von Aquin gegen die Griechen* (Munich: Königliche Akademie der Wissenschaften, 1889), pp. 702–4. On the date of composition of the *Thesaurus*, see Dondaine, "Contra Graecos," pp. 409–18. Buonaccorsi cites Theoktistos, unionist metropolitan of Adrianople active at the time of the Union of Lyons, which provides an idea of the date of the *Thesaurus*. See the considerations of Vitalien Laurent, "Un théologien unioniste de la fin de XIIIe siècle: Le métropolite d'Adrinople Théoctiste," *REB* 11 (1953): 187–204 (pp. 192–96).

47. The original redaction of the *Tractatus contra Graecos* of 1252 appears, too, to have been bilingual, although bilingual manuscripts have not survived. See Dondaine, "Contra Graecos," p. 328.

48. PG, vol. 140, cols. 528A and 566C.

49. See Loenertz, "Autour de traité," p. 368.

50. On these features, see appendix 2, part 2, pp. 135–36.

51. Information about Buonaccorsi's life comes from Andreas Doto's preface to the *Thesaurus veritatis fidei*. See Jacques Quétif and Jacques Echard, *Scriptores Ordinis Praedicatorum*, 2 vols. (Paris, 1719; repr. New York: Franklin, 1961), 1:158. Andreas Doto's redaction is found in BnF, Cod. gr. 1251, a codex which he presented with special dedication to Pope John XXII in Avignon in 1326 while serving as an envoy of Andronikos II in the course of unionist negotiations (1324–27). See Philippe Hoffmann, "Contribution à l'étude des manuscrits du 'Thesaurus veritatis fidei' de Buonaccorsi de Bologne, O.P.: description et histoire des *Parisini graeci* 1251 et 1252," *Bollettino della Badia Greca di Grottaferrata*, n.s., 46 (1992): 65–99; Angeliki E. Laiou, *Constantinople and the Latins: The Foreign Policy of Andronicus II, 1282–1328* (Cambridge, Mass.: Harvard University Press, 1972), pp. 315–29.

52. On the date of composition, see Dondain, "Contra Graecos," pp. 418–22. The text has been published by Friedrich Stegmüller, "Ein lateinischer Kontroverstraktat gegen die Griechen aus der Universitätsbibliothek Uppsala," *Kyrkohistorisk Årsskrift* 1 (1954): 123–50. The author was most probably Guilelmus Bernardi de Gaillac, who founded in 1299 Dominican houses in Constantinople and Pera. See Marie-Hélène Congourdeau, "Note sur les dominicains de Constantinople au début du 14e siècle," *REB* 45 (1987): 175–81 (pp. 176–78).

53. Stegmüller, "Ein lateinischer Kontroverstraktat," p. 145, lines 4–7. Stegmüller did not notice that the Donation-excerpt came from the Latin retranslation of the Balsamon version. One may observe minor variant readings between the *Trac-*

tatus contra errores Orientalium et Graecorum of 1305 and the *Tractatus contra Graecos* of 1252 (readings from the latter are given in brackets): "Terrenam [*aeternam:* PG, vol. 140, col. 536B] sedem sanctam cathedram beati Petri volumus exaltari et glorificari. Et decernentes [*discernentes:* PG, vol. 140, col. 536C] sancimus, ut habeat potestatem principalem, et sit ipsa caput quattuor sedium, scilicet [*sedis: add.* PG, vol. 140. col. 536C] Alexandriae, Antiochiae, Hierosolymorum et Constantinopolis."

54. Fantinus Vallaresso, *Libellus de ordine Generalium Conciliorum et Unione Florentina,* Concilium Florentinum: documenta et scriptores, ser. B, 2, fasc. 2, ed. Bernard Schultze (Rome: Pontificium Institutum Orientalium Studiorum, 1944), chap. 68, p. 91, line 23–p. 92, line 4. Bernard Schultze noticed that the Latin text is a translation of the Balsamon version. Cf. p. liii.

55. Published in Matthew Blastares, *Syntagma,* in Rhalles-Potles, 6:261–62, and in *Const. Harmenopuli Manuale legum, sive, Hexabiblos,* ed. Gustav Ernst Heimbach (Leipzig: Weigel, 1851), pp. 820–22.

56. Compare, for example, the expression "ὠμοφόριον ὅπερ περικυκλοῖ τὸν βασιλικὸν τράχηλον" in the Balsamon version (Rhalles-Potles, 1:146, lines 14–15) to "τὸ κυκλοῦν τὸν τράχηλον ὠμοφόριον" in the Blastares version (Rhalles-Potles, 6:261, lines 10–11).

57. Spiros Troianos, "Περὶ τὰς νομικὰς πηγὰς τοῦ Ματθαίου Βλάσταρη," *EEBS* 44 (1979–80): 305–29.

58. Rhalles-Potles, 6:260: "ἀλλ' ὧδε τοῦ λόγου γενόμενος, τὸ τοῦ μεγάλου θέσπισμα σιωπήσωμεν Κωνσταντίνου"; the fourteenth-century Serbian translation of the *Syntagma* renders *logos* quite literally as *slovo.* See Stojan Novaković, *Matije Vlastara Sintagmat* (Belgrade: Srpska Akademija Nauka i Umetnosti, 1907), p. 273.

59. See Blastares' preface to the *Syntagma* in Rhalles-Potles, 6:27.

60. Such saints' lives are known to have been produced during the period. See above, nn. 15 and 18.

61. The text in Blastares' *Syntagma* and the appendix to Harmenopoulos are nearly fully identical. Only the sworn promise of Constantine to observe the provisions of the Donation found in Blastares' *Syntagma* (Rhalles-Potles, 6:262, lines 1–2: "πίστεις ἐνόρκους ποιούμεθα, ἢ μὴν ὅλως πάντα ταῦτα μὴ παραβῆναι") is missing from the appendix to the *Hexabiblos* as published by Heimbach. On the date of publication of the *Hexabiblos,* see Marie Theres Fögen, "Die Scholien zur Hexabiblos im Codex vetustissimus Vaticanus Ottobonianus gr. 440," *Fontes Minores* 4 (1981): 256–345.

62. On the basis of BnF, Cod. gr. 1361 copied in the year 1351, Konstantinos Pitsakes, *Κωνσταντίνου Ἀρμενοπούλου Πρόχειρον νόμων ἢ Ἑξάβιβλος* (Athens: Dodone, 1971), pp. 48–50 (Greek pagination of the preface), has argued that Harmenopoulos himself arranged for some of the appendices, including the Donation and the Farmer's law, which appear in this manuscript. See Henri Omont, *Inventaire*

sommaire des manuscrits grecs de la Bibliothèque nationale, 4 vols. (Paris: Picard, 1886–98), 2:24.

63. See, for example, BnF, Cod. gr. 1310 (XV c.), fols. 407v–8r and Ambros. 598 (O 123 sup.) (XVI c.) fol. 58r–v. Cf. Henri Omont, *Inventaire*, 1:295–97; Martini and Bassi, *Catalogus,* 2:689–94.

64. Published on the basis of Vat. Ottob. gr. 309 (sixteenth century) by Pavlov, "Podlozhnaia darstvennaia gramota," pp. 59–80, and on the basis of Vat. gr. 789 and Vat. gr. 614 (both fourteenth century) by Gaudenzi, "Il Costituto di Costantino," pp. 87–97, line 28, and pp. 108–12.

65. Vat. gr. 614, 778, 789, 973, 1102, and Vat. Ottob. gr. 309. See Petrucci, "I rapporti," pp. 56–57.

66. Giovanni Mercati, *Notizie di Procoro e Demetrio Cidone, Manuele Caleca e Teodoro Meliteniota ed altri appunti per la storia della teologia e della letteratura bizantina del secolo XIV* (Vatican City: Biblioteca Apostolica Vaticana, 1931), pp. 162–65. Cf. Erich Gamillscheg, *Repertorium der griechischen Kopisten 800–1600*, vol. 3, *Handschriften aus Bibliotheken Roms mit dem Vatikan*, Teil A, *Verzeichnis der Kopisten* (Vienna: Verlag der Österreichischen Akademie der Wissenschaften, 1997), p. 74; Franz Tinnefeld, *Demetrios Kydones: Briefe*, 4 vols. (Stuttgart: Hiersemann, 1981–2003), 1:69–70.

67. Petrucci, "I rapporti," pp. 151–60.

68. Frances Kianka, "Byzantine-Papal Diplomacy: The Role of Demetrius Cydones," *International History Review* 7 (1985): 175–213, esp. pp. 194–200. See also John W. Barker's article in the present volume, pp. 159–64.

69. Francis Thomson, "The Intellectual Difference Between Muscovy and Ruthenia in the Seventeenth Century: The Case of the Slavonic Translations and the Reception of the Pseudo-Constantinian *Constitutum (Donatio Constantini),*" *Slavica Gandensia* 22 (1995): 63–107, esp. pp. 67–70.

70. Ostrogorsky, "Zum Stratordienst des Herrschers," p. 201 n. 43; Thomson, "The Intellectual Difference," p. 68. In Serbia the Donation was known already through the translation of Blastares' *Syntagma* produced during the reign of Stephan IV Dušan.

71. Published by Gaudenzi, "Il Costituto di Costantino," p. 97, line 29, and p. 107, hence reprinted in Ohnsorge, "Das Constitutum Constantini," pp. 108–23, and Helmut Boese, "Die Konstantinische Schenkung in den Verhandlungen des Florentiner Konzils," *Deutsches Archiv* 21 (1965): 586–92. Krause, "Das Constitutum Constantini," pp. 149–50 n. 93, has corrected Gaudenzi's critical apparatus.

72. See the Latin account of the acts of the council by Andreas de Santacroce, *Acta Latina Concilii Florentini*, ed. Georg Hofmann, Concilium Florentinum: documenta et scriptores, ser. B, 6 (Rome: Pontificium Institutum Orientalium Studiorum, 1955), p. 247, lines 34–39. Helmut Boese, "Die Konstantinische Schenkung," pp. 576–92,

edited the Latin retranslation along with the Greek prototype and commented on the circumstances of its production. Krause, "Das Constitutum Constantini," p. 151 n. 91, has shown that the Latin retranslation was based on the version in Vat. gr. 606. On Andreas Chrysoberges, see Raymond-Joseph Loenertz, "Les dominicains byzantins Théodore et André Chrysobergès et les négociations pour l'union des églises grecque et latine de 1415 à 1430," *Archivum Fratrum Praedicatorum* 9 (1939): 5–61. Joseph Gill, *The Council of Florence* (Cambridge: Cambridge University Press, 1959), did not mention the use of the Donation. Deno Geanakoplos errs when saying that during the Council of Ferrara-Florence "papal champions made no use of the famous Donation of Constantine to support papal claims of supremacy." See Deno John Geanakoplos, "The Council of Florence (1438–39)," *Church History* 24 (1955): 324–46 (p. 331) (reprinted with revisions in Deno John Geanakoplos, *Constantinople and the West* [Madison: University of Wisconsin Press, 1989], pp. 224–54 [pp. 238–40]).

73. Krause, "Das Constitutum Constantini," pp. 152–53.

74. The phrase *pro reverentia beati Petri* found in the Latin text at the point where Constantine renders groom service to Pope Sylvester was omitted in the Chrysoberges version. See the facing reprint of the Greek and Latin texts in Ohnsorge, "Das Constitutum Constantini und seine Entstehung," p. 118 (§ 16). For a minor misunderstanding in the translation, see Krause, "Das Constitutum Constantini," pp. 155–56 n. 133.

75. Ohnsorge, "Das Constitutum Constantini und seine Entstehung," pp. 93–162. On the ethnic origins of Pope Leo III see Hans-Georg Beck, "Die Herkunft des Papstes Leo III.," *Frühmittelalterliche Studien* 3 (1969): 131–37.

76. Horst Fuhrmann, "Konstantinische Schenkung und abendländisches Kaisertum," *Deutsches Archiv* 22 (1966): 63–178, esp. pp. 103–9. Cf. the response by Werner Ohnsorge, "Zur Dispositio des Constitutum Constantini in den Codd. Vat. Graec. 81 und 1115," *BZ* 61 (1968): 277–84.

77. Petrucci, "I rapporti," pp. 145–51.

78. Krause, "Das Constitutum Constantini," p. 151; Mercati, *Notizie*, pp. 159–60. Cf. Mercati, *Notizie*, pp. 165–66, regarding Vat. gr. 1115, a codex which contains the Chrysoberges version and also belonged to Kydones.

79. Makarios of Ankara, *Against the Latins*, chap. 5, in Patriarch Dositheos, *Tomos katallages* (Iasi, 1692), p. 9, lines 7–12. On this work, see pp. 121–24.

80. Fuhrmann, *Das Constitutum Constantinum*, p. 57, line 11; p. 94, line 268.

81. Franz Dölger and Ioannes Karayannopulos, *Byzantinische Urkundenlehre* (Munich: Beck, 1968), pp. 78–79, note that the term first appears at the beginning of the sixth century. See also Adolf Berger, *Encyclopedic Dictionary of Roman Law* (Philadelphia: American Philosophical Society, 1953), p. 648.

82. Rhalles-Potles, 1:148. An English translation of Balsamon's interesting comments can be found in Dagron, *Emperor and Priest*, pp. 244–45.

83. Rhalles-Potles, 2:285–86.

84. Rhalles-Potles, 4:553.

85. Rhalles-Potles, 3:149–50 (on the patriarchal court of justice; commentary on canon 12 of Antioch).

86. Rhalles-Potles, 2:149. On the feast day of Saints Markianos and Martyrios called "the Notary saints," see *Synaxarium Ecclesiae Constantinopolitanae*, in *Propylaeum ad AASS Novembris*, ed. Hippolyte Delehaye (Brussels: Société des Bollandistes, 1902), cols. 161–62.

87. Rhalles-Potles, 4:540.

88. Rhalles-Potles, 1:79–80. See also Balsamon's opinion based on the Donation that the ecclesiastical officials of the Great Church should belong to the same rank as bishops and imperial dignitaries in Rhalles-Potles, 2:323–24.

89. See Tiftixoglu, "Gruppenbildungen," pp. 53–60.

90. Rhalles-Potles, 1:79, 80, 148–49; 2:175, 285, 324; 3:149; 4:539, 553.

91. Albert Failler, "Une réfutation de Balsamon par Nil Kabasilas," *REB* 32 (1974): 211–23 (p. 221). After invoking the acts of the Fourth Ecumenical Council and the Apostolic Canons, Kabasilas argued that the decisions of the patriarchal tribunal ought to be subject to appeal before the emperor, who should refer the matter for adjudication to a supreme court consisting of bishops and high dignitaries. It is likely that this supreme court consisting of laymen and ecclesiastics was the General Judges of the Romans, although Kabasilas did not mention them by name.

92. Günter Prinzing, "Entstehung und Rezeption der Justiniana-Prima-Theorie im Mittelalter," *Byzantinobulgarica* 5 (1978): 269–87.

93. *Demetrii Chomateni Ponemata diaphora*, ed. Günter Prinzing, Corpus Fontium Historiae Byzantinae 38 (Berlin: de Gruyter, 2002), pp. 376–77, no. 114. See Günter Prinzing, "A Quasi Patriarch in the State of Epiros: The Autocephalous Archbishop of 'Boulgaria' (Ohrid) Demetrios Chomatenos," *ZRVI* 41 (2004): 165–82; Ruth Macrides, "Bad Historian or Good Lawyer? Demetrios Chomatenos and Novel 131," *DOP* 46 (1992): 187–96.

94. Rhalles-Potles, 6:260, lines 3–6: "Τὰς ἀναφυομένας κανονικὰς ἀμφισβητήσεις ἐν ὅλῳ τῷ Ἰλλυρικῷ οὐ δεῖ τέμνεσθαι παρὰ γνώμην τοῦ ἀρχιεπισκόπου Κωνσταντινουπόλεως, καὶ τῆς αὐτοῦ Συνόδου, ἥτις ἔχει τὰ προνόμια τῆς ἀρχαίας Ῥώμης."

95. Rhalles-Potles, 1:143.

96. See appendix 1, part 3, p. 132.

97. Cf. Francis Dvornik, *Early Christian and Byzantine Political Philosophy: Origins and Background*, 2 vols. (Washington, D. C.: Dumbarton Oaks, 1966), 2:815–18; John Meyendorff, "Justinian, the Empire and the Church," *DOP* 22 (1968): 43–60.

98. Paris, BnF, Cod. gr. 1388, fols. 4v–5r. See Rhalles-Potles, 2:280–81.

99. Beck, *Kirche und theologische Literatur*, pp. 145–46, 423; Ruth Macrides, "*Nomos* and *Canon* on Paper and in Court," in *Church and People in Byzantium*, ed. Rosemary Morris (Birmingham: Centre for Byzantine, Ottoman and Modern Greek Studies, 1990), pp. 62–85 (p. 67).

100. The production of this interpolated edition of the *Nomokanon in Fifty Titles* should be dated to the fourteenth century for the following reasons. The interpolated legal texts (see Beneševič, *Sinagogá v 50 titulov*, pp. 185–89) contain several late Byzantine documents: a synodal *tomos* of 1229, a *prostagma* of Andronikos II of 1312 and the treatise of John Pediasimos *On Marriage*. The *prostagma* of Andronikos II of 1312 on the inviolability of church properties provides a *terminus ante quem non*. On this *prostagma*, see Franz Dölger, *Regesten der Kaiserurkunden des oströmischen Reiches von 565–1453*, vol. 4, *Regesten von 1282–1341* (Munich: Beck, 1960), no. 2336. The earliest manuscript of the interpolated edition (Vat. gr. 640) dates to the fourteenth century (see appendix 1, part 3, p. 132), which is, therefore, the century of production of the interpolated redaction.

101. Gulielmus Voellius and Henri Justel, *Bibliotheca iuris canonici veteris*, 2 vols. (Paris: L. Billaine, 1661), 2:604–7. See the synopsis in Beneševič, *Sinagogá v 50 titulov*, p. 293.

102. *Eisagoge*, 1.1–6; 2.1–12; 3.1–11, in JGR, 2:240–43. On BnF, Cod. gr. 1263, see appendix 1, part 3, p. 132.

103. See *Eisagoge*, 3.1–3, in Zepos, JGR, 2:242. Andreas Schminck, *Studien zu mittelbyzantinischen Rechtsbüchern* (Frankfurt am Main: Löwenklau, 1986), pp. 12–14, has shown that the original title of the legal collection was *Eisagoge*, not *Epanagoge* as previously thought. On the connection between Photios and the *Eisagoge*, see J. Scharf, "Photios und die Epanagoge," *BZ* 49 (1956): 385–400. On the ideological attributes and constitutional rights with which the *Eisagoge* vests the patriarch of Constantinople, see Dagron, *Emperor and Priest*, pp. 229–35; Spyros Troianos, "Nomos und Kanon in Byzanz," in *Kirche und Staat im christlichen Osten*, Kanon 10 (Vienna: Verband der wissenschaftlichen Gesellschaften Österreichs, 1991), pp. 39–42.

104. Miklosich-Müller, 5:247–48. On the office of *dikaiophylax*, see Ruth Macrides, "Dikaiophylax," in *The Oxford Dictionary of Byzantium*, ed. Alexander Kazhdan, 3 vols. (New York: Oxford University Press, 1991), 1:634.

105. On the title of *epistemonarches*, see Dagron, *Emperor and Priest*, pp. 252–53, with further bibliography.

106. See Ambros. gr. 682 (Q. 76 sup.) (dated to 1287/88), fol. 19r; BnF, Cod. gr. 1388 (fifteenth century), fol. 3v; Laur. gr. 8, 17 (fourteenth century), fol. 456r; Vindob. hist. gr. 34 (dated to 1430), fol. 373r–v. For the standard text, see Rhalles-Potles, 1:146, line 32.

107. See Rhalles-Potles, 1:146 n. 3. Rhalles and Potles used an apograph of the manuscript copied in 1311 in Trebizond, which is now lost.

108. Alice-Mary Talbot, "The Patriarch Athanasius (1289–1293; 1303–1309) and the Church," *DOP* 27 (1973): 11–28; John Boojamra, *Church Reform in the Late Byzantine Empire: A Study in the Patriarchate of Athanasios of Constantinople* (Thessaloniki: Patriarchal Institute of Patristic Studies, 1982). On the political ideas of Athanasios, see Dimiter Angelov, *Imperial Ideology and Political Thought in Byzantium, 1204–1330* (Cambridge: Cambridge University Press, 2007), pp. 393–409.

109. George Pachymeres, *History*, XI.1, in *Georges Pachymérès: Relations historiques*, ed. Albert Failler, 5 vols. (Paris: Belles Lettres, 1984–2000), 3:405, lines 1–32, speaks of Athanasios both transmitting appeals to the emperor as well as adjudicating cases of social oppression. The novel of Athanasios has survived in a long version (Zepos, JGR, 1:533–36) and a short one (Heimbach, *Manuale Legum sive Hexabiblos*, pp. xxii–xxviii). The form of the novel is that of petition presented by the synod to the emperor with a list of legislative measures.

110. Alice-Mary Talbot, ed. and trans., *The Correspondence of Athanasius I, Patriarch of Constantinople* (Washington, D.C.: Dumbarton Oaks, 1975), p. 286, no. 112. Patriarch Athanasios may be referring here to the emperor's formal promise to follow the reform program, a promise made at the beginning of Athanasios's second patriarchate. See Vitalien Laurent, "Le serment de l'empereur Andronic II Paléologue au patriarche Athanase Ier, lors de sa seconde accession au trône oecuménique (Sept. 1303)," *REB* 23 (1965): 124–39.

111. Rhalles-Potles, 6:260.

112. David Balfour, "Saint Symeon of Thessalonike as a Historical Personality," *Greek Orthodox Theological Review* 28 (1983): 55–72.

113. On Symeon of Thessaloniki as a hierocrat, see Angelov, *Imperial Ideology and Political Thought*, pp. 392, 415–16.

114. Symeon of Thessaloniki, *De Sacris Ordinationibus*, PG, vol. 155, cols. 429D–33A.

115. Halkin, *Bibliotheca hagiographica graeca*, nos. 67–70.

116. Symeon of Thessaloniki, PG, vol. 155, col. 432B: "Κωνσταντῖνος ὁ Μέγας οὐ τὸν θεῖον Σίλβεστρον μόνον, ἀλλὰ καὶ τοὺς ἐν τῇ συνόδῳ πάντας σχεδὸν προπέμπων αὐτοὺς καὶ τιμῶν καὶ δωρούμενος καθεωρᾶτο."

117. In the middle of the fourteenth century Pseudo-Kodinos mentions bishops kissing the emperors cheek and hand during the Holy Friday, while only the patriarch exchanged a kiss with the emperor on the mouth. See Jean Verpeaux, ed. and trans., *Pseudo-Kodinos: Traité des offices* (Paris: Editions du Centre national de la recherche scientifique, 1966), p. 238, line 20, and p. 239, line 2.

118. Ullmann, *Growth of Papal Government*, p. 160. The earliest case of *officium stratoris* on behalf of the pope is said to have occurred in 754 at Ponthion before the

Pippin the Short's coronation as king of the Franks. See ibid, pp. 56, 59. The classical study on this ritual is by Robert Holtzmann, *Der Kaiser als Marschall des Papstes* (Berlin: de Gruyter, 1928).

119. John Kinnamos, *Ioannis Cinnami epitome rerum ab Ioanne et Alexio Comnenis gestarum*, ed. Augustus Meineke (Bonn: Weber, 1836), p. 219.

120. George Pachymeres, *History*, 1.26, in *Georges Pachymérès*, 1:103. Cf. Ostrogorsky, "Stratordienst," pp. 191–92.

121. See *Anecdota Graeco-Byzantina, pars prima*, ed. Afanasii Vasil'ev (Moscow: Universitas Caesarea, 1893), p. 179. Cf. Deno John Geanakoplos, "A Greek *Libellus* against Religious Union with Rome after the Council of Lyons (1274)," *Interaction of the "Sibling" Byzantine and Western Cultures in the Middle Ages and Italian Renaissance (330–1600)* (New Haven: Yale University Press, 1976), pp. 156–70.

122. Antonio Franchi, *La svolta politico-ecclesiastica tra Roma e Bisanzio (1249–1254). La legazione di Giovanni da Parma. Il ruolo di Federico II* (Rome: Pontificium Athenaeum Antonianum, 1981), pp. 138–39, 232, with further sources on the participants in the Byzantine embassies.

123. The proposals of the Greek delegation have been discussed by Joseph Gill, *Byzantium and the Papacy, 1198–1400* (New Brunswick: Rutgers University Press, 1979), pp. 92–96.

124. See Innocent IV's encyclical letter *Eger Cui Lenia*, in Peter Herde, ed., "Ein Pamphlet der päpstlichen Kurie gegen Kaiser Friedrich II. von 1245/46 ('Eger cui lenia')," *Deutsches Archiv* 23 (1967): 468–538 (pp. 521–22), published earlier by Eduard Winkelmann, ed., *Acta imperii inedita saeculi XIII et XIV*, 2 vols. (Innsbruck, 1880–85; repr. Aalen: Scientia, 1964), 2:696–98, translated in part in Brian Tierney, *The Crisis of Church and State 1050–1300* (Englewood Cliffs, 1964; repr. Toronto: University of Toronto Press, 1988), pp. 147–49. Cf. Maffei, *La Donazione di Costantino*, pp. 46–49, 76–81.

125. John Mitchell, "St. Silvester and Constantine at the Ss. Quattro Coronati," in *Federico II e l'arte del Duecento italiano*, ed. Angiola Romanini, 2 vols. (Galatina: Congedo, 1981), 2:15–32.

126. *Tractatus contra Graecos*, PG 140, cols. 537D–38A. The text printed in PG refers to Emperor Constantius I, although one should read Constantine. The Latin retranslation of the Balsamon version is cited immediately afterward.

127. *Tractatus contra Graecos*, PG 140, col. 539A–B, makes mention of "three hundred and eighty years or more" having elapsed since the beginning of the schism. The expression "or more" brings us to the time of the Photian Schism (863–69). The dating of the beginning of the schism to the era of Photius is not surprising. See Tia Kolbaba, "The Legacy of Humbert and Cerularius: The Tradition of the 'Schism of 1054' in Byzantine Texts and Manuscripts of the Twelfth and Thirteenth Centuries," in *Porphyrogenita: Essays on the History and Literature of Byzantium and the Latin East in Honour of Julian Chrysostomides*, ed. Charalambos Dendrinos,

Jonathan Harris, Eirene Harvalia-Crook, and Judith Herrin (Aldershot: Ashgate, 2003), pp. 47–61.

128. See Leon Santifaller, *Beiträge zur Geschichte des lateinischen Patriarchats von Konstantinopel (1204–1261) und der venezianischen Urkunde* (Weimar: Böhlaus Nachfolger, 1938), p. 196 (letter of Pope Honorius III to King Robert of Courtenay dated 27 September 1222)

129. See here p. 119 and n. 143.

130. John Kantakouzenos, *Ioannis Cantacuzeni*, 2:274: "κατὰ τὸ Ῥωμαίων βασιλέων ἔθος ὑπήντα τε ἔνδον τοῦ οἰκήματος." According to Ostrogorsky, "Zum Stratordienst des Herrschers," pp. 203–4, the introduction of this ceremony into the Serbian court was related to the appearance of a Serbian translation of the *Syntagma* of Matthew Blastares.

131. Symeon of Thessaloniki, *De Sacris Ordinationibus*, PG, vol. 155, cols. 437C–44B.

132. PG, vol. 155, col. 441D: "Καὶ ὑπὸ πεζοῦ τοῦ κόμητος τὸν χαλινὸν τοῦ ἵππου κατέχοντος ἄντι τοῦ βασιλέως αὐτοῦ, ὡς ὁ μέγας ἐν βασιλεῦσι Κωνσταντῖνος τῷ ἱερῷ πεποίηκε Σιλβέστρῳ." Cf. Verpeaux, *Pseudo-Kodinos*, pp. 281–82.

133. Balfour, "Saint Symeon of Thessalonike," p. 59. See Raymond Janin, *La géographie ecclésiastique de l'Empire byzantin*, vol. 3, *Les églises et les monastères*, pt. 1, *Le siège de Constantinople et le patriarcat oecuménique*, 2nd ed. (Paris: Institut français d'études byzantines, 1969), pp. 378–79; Venance Grumel, "Notes sur Calliste II Xanthopoulos," *REB* 18 (1960): 199–204.

134. Vitalien Laurent, *Les "Mémoires" du grand ecclésiarque de l'Eglise de Constantinople Sylvestre Syropoulos sur le Concile de Florence (1438–1439)* (Paris: Editions du Centre national de la recherche scientifique, 1971), p. 104, lines 17–20. See Jean Darrouzès, *Les regestes des actes du patriarcat de Constantinople*, vol. 1, *Les actes des patriarches*, fasc. 7, *Les regestes de 1410 à 1453* (Paris: Institut français d'études byzantines, 1991), no. 3300. The election and ordination of Patriarch Joseph II in 1416 was preceded by discussions and ratification of the traditional privileges of the emperor in ecclesiastical administration. See Laurent, *Les "Mémoires,"* pp. 102–4; Darrouzès, *Les regestes*, no. 3299.

135. A point rightly emphasized by Dvornik, *The Idea of Apostolicity*, p. 288.

136. See John Kinnamos, *Ioannis Cinnami epitome*, pp. 219–20; Alexander, "The Donation of Constantine at Byzantium," pp. 19–22. Cf. Ostrogorsky, "Zum Stratordienst," p. 190.

137. On the *Sacred Arsenal* of Andronikos Kamateros, see Paul Magdalino, *The Empire of Manuel I Komnenos, 1143–1180* (Cambridge: Cambridge University Press, 1993), pp. 290–91; Darrouzès, "Les documents byzantins du XIIe siècle," pp. 72–78.

138. Andronikos Kamateros, *Sacred Arsenal*, in Monacensis gr. 229, fol. 11r.: "μετὰ γὰρ τὸ κήρυγμα πάντως ἀκόλουθον ἂν ἦν ἑπομένως τῇ βασιλείᾳ καὶ τὴν

ταύτης ἱερωσύνην, τήν τε τιμὴν καὶ τὴν τῶν ἄλλων ἁπασῶν ἐκκλησιῶν προκαθεδρίαν κληρώσασθαι · μὲν οὖν γε καὶ μείζονα προσεπιφιλοτιμηθῆναι ταύτην αὐτῇ παρὰ τοῦ μεγάλου Κωνσταντίνου γνωρίζομεν ἐκ τῆς αὐτοῦ διατάξεως ἐκτεθείσης ὅτ᾽ ἐξ ἐκείνης πρὸς ταύτην τὴν μεγαλόπολιν τὰ τῆς βασιλείας πάντα παράσημα μετεβίβασε, τῷ οἰκείῳ τιμίσας ταύτην ὀνόματι καὶ βασιλίδα καταξιώσας καλεῖσθαι τῶν πόλεων." I am grateful to Dr. Alessandra Bucossi for enabling me to consult the text of Kamateros's work, part of which she has edited in her "Prolegomena to the Critical Edition of Hiera Hoplotheke—Sacred Arsenal by Andronikos Kamateros" (PhD dissertation, Oxford University, 2006).

139. August Heisenberg, *Neue Quellen zur Geschichte des lateinischen Kaisertums und der Kirchenunion*, vol. 3, *Der Bericht des Nikolaos Mesarites über die politischen und kirchlichen Ereignisse des Jahres 1214* (Munich: Bayerische Akademie der Wissenschaften, 1923), pp. 34–35. For a probable reference to the Sylvester legend, see ibid., p. 9, lines 20–23 (fragmentary text). Yannis Spiteris, "I dialoghi di Nicolas Mesarites coi Latini: opera storica o finzione letteraria," *Orientalia Christiana Analecta* 204 (1977): 181–86, considered Mesarites' report fictional rather than real on account of the similarities of the arguments with those reported by Kamateros, although a simpler explanation would be that the disputation in Herakleia Pontike was carried along familiar lines.

140. Tia Kolbaba, "Barlaam the Calabrian: Three Treatises on Papal Primacy, Introduction, Edition, and Translation," *REB* 53 (1995): 41–115 (p. 85). On the date and possible context of the treatise (the debates of 1334/35), see ibid., pp. 61–62.

141. On the Latin view of the Donation as lending support to the Petrine claim, see here pp. 120–21.

142. See appendix 2, part 3, p. 137.

143. August Heisenberg, *Der Bericht des Nikolaos Mesarites*, pp. 20–23.

144. See here p. 103.

145. Humbert de Romans, *Opus Tripartitum*, in Ortuinus Gratius, *Fasciculus rerum expetendarum et fugiendarum*, 2 vols. (London: Chiswell, 1690), 2:212: "Unde Constantinus summe Romanam Ecclesiam sublimavit et ordinavit quod Ecclesiae omnes subessent Ecclesiae Romanae." On Humbert's ideas regarding the union and the crusading movement, see Edward Brett, *Humbert of Romans: His Life and Views in Thirteenth-Century Society* (Toronto: Pontifical Institute of Mediaeval Studies, 1984), pp. 176–94. In his interpolated paraphrase of the *Opus Tripartitum* Bernard Gui (1261/62–1331) kept the reference to the Donation. See Giovanni Domenico Mansi, *Sacrorum conciliorum nova et amplissima collectio*, 54 vols. (Graz: Akademische Druck- und Verlagsanstalt, 1960–62), vol. 24, col. 123D; Fritz Heitke, *Humbert von Romans, der fünfte Ordensmeister der Dominikaner* (Berlin: Ebering, 1933), pp. 138–44.

146. *Tractatus contra Graecos*, PG, vol. 140, col. 537A–B; Buonaccorsi's *Thesaurus veritatis fidei*, in Reusch, *Die Fälschungen*, p. 704, line 31, and p. 705, line 9; the anonymous *Tractatus contra errores Orientalium et Graecorum* of 1305, in Stegmüller,

"Ein lateinischer Kontroverstraktat," p. 145, lines 1–4; Fantinus Vallaresso, *Libellus de ordine Generalium Conciliorum et Unione Florentina*, chap. 68, p. 91, lines 20–23.

147. Stegmüller, "Ein lateinischer Kontroverstraktat," p. 145, lines 7–10.

148. Leo IX's *libellus* states (PL, vol. 143, col. 751A–C) that the First Ecumenical Council confirmed the judicial primacy of the papacy decreed upon earlier by Pope Sylvester (the *Constitutum Silvestri*). This passage of Leo IX's *libellus* is found also in the *Tractatus* of 1305 (Stegmüller, "Ein lateinischer Kontroverstraktat," p. 145, line 16, and p. 146, line 9). The *Constitutum Silvestri* is one of the so-called Symmachian forgeries of the early sixth century. See W. T. Townsend, "The So-Called Symmachian Forgeries," *Journal of Religion* 13 (1933): 165–74; PL, vol. 8, col. 840. Krause, "Das Constitutum Constantini," p. 136 n. 30, shows that the legend of the First Ecumenical Council confirming the judicial primacy of the papacy is found in the Pseudo-Isidorian Decretals of the ninth century.

149. For the plausible attribution of authorship and date to this work, see Dondaine, "Contra Graecos," pp. 409–18. See the relevant text in Stegmüller, "Bonacusius contra Graecos," pp. 68–69.

150. Stegmüller, "Bonacusius contra Graecos," p. 69, lines 10–18, esp. lines 15–18: "quia Roma non est caput ecclesiae propter regalem dignitatem, sed quia beatus Petrus, vicarius Jesu Christi, ibi sedit et ibi vitam finivit et officium suum ibi exercuit, sicut testatur manifeste privilegium Constantini."

151. Raymond-Joseph Loenertz, *Correspondance de Manuel Calécas* (Vatican City: Biblioteca Apostolica Vaticana, 1950), pp. 16, 45–46. Cf. Jean Gouillard, "Manuel Calécas," in *Dictionnaire d'histoire et géographie ecclésiastiques*, 29 vols. to date (Paris: Letouzey et Ané, 1909–), vol. 11, cols. 380–84; "Les influences latines dans l'oeuvre théologique de Manuel Calécas," *Echos d'Orient* 37 (1938): 36–52. Only the Latin translation of the treatise made by the Italian humanist Ambrogio Traversari in 1423–24 has so far been published (PG, vol. 152, cols. 11–258). The Greek text is found in several manuscripts, among which notable are Venice, Bibl. Marc., Fondo antico, Cod. gr. 159 (an autograph copy of Kalekas), Vat. gr. 727 (sixteenth century), Vat. gr. 1112 (fifteenth century); Basel, Universitätsbibliothek, B VI 20 (fifteenth century). I have been able to consult the text in Vat. gr. 727 and Vat. gr. 1112.

152. The section is found in Vat gr. 727, fol. 287r–v. and Vat. gr. 1112, fol. 163r–v. For the Latin translation, see PG, vol. 152, cols. 243C–44A.

153. Thus, Kalekas cites a text allegedly from the Donation where St. Peter is called Christ's vicar (βικάριος), a term used solely in the Kydones version. In addition, Kalekas cites from the *sanctio* of the Donation (that is, the eternal damnation of those who fail to observe it); the *sanctio* is found only in the Chrysoberges and the Kydones versions. However, Kalekas "reports" different phraseology of the *sanctio* than the one found in any known Greek version. One hopes that a critical edition of Kalekas's treatise would illuminate Kalekas's use of his sources and can help to solve the mystery.

154. Christopher Coleman, *Constantine the Great and Christianity* (New York: Columbia University Press, 1914), pp. 185–88; Fuhrmann, *Das Constitutum Constantini*, pp. 11–12. Cf. also Johann Döllinger, *Fables Respecting the Popes in the Middle Ages: A Contribution to Ecclesiastical History*, trans. Alfred Plummer (London: Rivingtons, 1871), pp. 140–42; Zinkeisen, "The Donation of Constantine," pp. 628–30.

155. Rhalles-Potles, 4:553, lines 24–25.

156. Tiftixoglu, "Gruppenbildungen," pp. 71–72, exaggerates, therefore, when crediting Balsamon for being the first medieval thinker to unmask the Donation as a forgery.

157. Pavlov, "Podlozhnaia darstvennaia gramota," p. 37 n. 1, noted Makarios's refutation of the Donation without exploring its context and argumentation. Cf. also Dvornik, *The Idea of Apostolicity*, p. 295 n. 103.

158. On the little that is known about Matthew's biography, see Louis Petit, "Macaire d'Ancyre," in *Dictionnaire de théologie catholique*, 15 vols. (Paris: Letouzey et Ané, 1899–1950), vol. 9, pt. 1, cols. 1441–43; Loenertz, *Correspondance de Manuel Calécas*, p. 94; Vitalien Laurent, "Le trisépiscopat du patriarche Matthieu Ier (1397–1410): Un grand procès canonique à Byzance au début du XVe siècle," *REB* 30 (1972): 9–15; PLP, no. 16254. The full edition of Makarios's canonical works could shed additional light on his life.

159. Laurent, "Le trisépiscopat du patriarche Matthieu Ier (1397–1410)," p. 19, considered it likely that Makarios began the treatise in Paris (which Makarios calls a "famous" city) and assigned the completion of the treatise to the years 1403–4. Dositheos, patriarch of Jerusalem, published the treatise in 1692 in *Tomos katallages*, pp. 1–205, attributing it to an anonymous author. The treatise is currently being re-edited by Christos Triantaphyllopoulos of Royal Holloway, University of London, as a PhD project.

160. Dositheos, *Tomos katallages*, p. 175.

161. See Angelov, *Imperial Ideology and Political Thought*, pp. 372–73.

162. This treatise in 156 chapters explaining the Greek point of view on the Holy Spirit and papal primacy has been edited by Charalambos Dendrinos, "An Annotated Critical Edition (editio princeps) of Emperor Manuel II Palaeologus' Treatise *On the Procession of the Holy Spirit*" (PhD dissertation, Royal Holloway, University of London, 1996) (unavailable to me). Cf. John W. Barker, *Manuel II Palaeologus (1391–1425): A Study in Late Byzantine Statesmanship* (New Brunswick: Rutgers University Press, 1969), pp. 192–93, 437. I inspected the content of the treatise in Vaticanus gr. 1107, fols. 1r–134v, and came across no reference to the Donation.

163. Dositheos, *Tomos katallages*, p. 3.

164. Dositheos, *Tomos katallages*, p. 9, lines 4–12.

165. Dositheos, *Tomos katallages*, p. 9, lines 13–17.

166. Dositheos, *Tomos katallages*, p. 9, lines 17–33.

167. Dositheos, *Tomos katallages*, p. 9, lines 36–40.

168. Dositheos, *Tomos katallages*, p. 9, line 40, and p. 10, line 1. On *Codex Iustinianus*, 1.2.12 (which Makarios of Ankara calls *diataxis* 34 of Justinian), see *Codex Iustinianus*, ed. Paul Krüger, Corpus Iuris Civilis 2 (Berlin: Weidmann, 1929), p. 13 (Latin text), and *Nomokanon in Fourteen Titles*, title 1, chapter 2, in Rhalles-Potles, 1:36 (Greek text). In the eleventh century Niketas of Ankara cited the same wording of the provision as the one cited by Makarios. According to Jean Darrouzès, *Documents inédits d'ecclésiologie byzantine* (Paris: Institut français d'études byzantines, 1966), p. 194, lines 19–20 (see *apparatus*), this wording appears in some yet unknown Byzantine legal compendium.

169. Coleman, *Constantine the Great and Christianity*, pp. 188–91 and 238–42 (appendix 3: "The Text of Nicholas of Cusa's Attack on the Donation").

170. Valla's *Oration on the Falsely-Believed and Forged Donation of Constantine* has been edited by Christopher Coleman, *The Treatise of Lorenzo Valla on the Donation of Constantine* (New Haven: Yale University Press, 1922). Cf. Riccardo Fubini, "Humanism and Truth: Valla Writes against the Donation of Constantine," *Journal of the History of Ideas* 57 (1996): 79–86.

171. Reginald Pecock's refutation has been dated to the years 1449–55, while Aeneas Sylvius Piccolomini composed his *Dialogus pro Donatione Constantini* circa 1453. See Coleman, *Constantine the Great and Christianity*, pp. 199–200; Joseph Levine, "Reginald Pecock and Lorenzo Valla on the Donation of Constantine," *Studies in the Renaissance* 20 (1973): 118–43.

172. Nicholas of Cusa quoted from papal letters to prove his point. See Coleman, *Constantine the Great and Christianity*, pp. 239–30.

173. Coleman, *The Treatise of Lorenzo Valla*, pp. 94–95.

174. See Anthony Grafton, *Defenders of the Text: The Tradition of Scholarship in an Age of Science, 1450–1800* (Cambridge, Mass.: Harvard University Press, 1991), pp. 29–30.

175. See my introduction to this volume, p. 4.

176. See Tiftixoglu, "Zur Genese der Kommentare," p. 484 n. 5, and pp. 489–90. Cf. the discussion of the two different versions by Gilbert Dagron, "Le caractère sacerdotal de la royauté d'après les commentaires canoniques de XIIe siècle," in *Byzantium in the 12th Century* (see n. 38, above), pp. 165–78 (pp. 168–69).

177. According to Tiftixoglu, "Zur Genese der Kommentare," p. 502, the anonymous commentator began his work during the reign of Emperor Alexios II (1180–83).

178. Sinait. gr. 1112, fol. 20r.

179. See Viktor Tiftixoglu and Spyros Troianos, "Unbekannte Kaiserurkunde und Basilikentestimonia aus dem Sinaiticus 1117," *Fontes Minores* 9 (1993): 138–39, with specific examples in n. 4. I am grateful to Dr. Andreas Schminck of the Max

Planck Institute for European Legal History in Frankfurt am Main for his assistance with the title number.

180. Rhalles-Potles, 1:147, line 14 and n. 1, signal the insertion of the word ὀρθόδοξοι before διάδοχοι in a different passage of the Donation, following shortly after the case we noted. Rhalles and Potles mention that their source was Hervet's edition of the *Nomokanon* in 1650 (unavailable to me). The edition by J. P. Migne, PG, vol. 104, cols. 1080D, 1081A, features the adjective *orthodox* in both of the noted cases, even though the 1661 edition by Justel and Voellius (which Migne purports to follow) does not give the variation.

181. Martin West, *Textual Criticism and Editorial Technique Applicable to Greek and Latin Texts* (Stuttgart: Teubner, 1972), p. 24; Elpidio Mioni, *Introduzione alla paleografia greca* (Padua: Liviana, 1973), p. 101.

182. Ms. συνωψισθείσης.

183. Ms. Ἰλλιρικῷ.

184. What follows is the full text of title 8, chapter 1, of the *Nomokanon in Fourteen Titles* along with most of the commentary of Balsamon prior to the citation of the Donation. See Rhalles-Potles, 1:143, line 20–p. 144, line 29.

Emperors, Embassies, and Scholars

Diplomacy and the Transmission of Byzantine Humanism to Renaissance Italy

JOHN W. BARKER

In its two final centuries, under the Palaiologan dynasty, Byzantium was a ruined and increasingly marginalized minor state, caught up in a world of superior powers, in circumstances beyond its own control. As applied mainly to dealings with regimes in the Latin West, Byzantine diplomacy functioned as a fig leaf to cover a government's nakedness in military resources. As such, it did contribute to the empire's survival through almost two centuries of weakness and degradation. With the shrinking of the old bureaucracy, diplomacy depended increasingly upon "the emperor's men of confidence," as Nicolas Oikonomides has put it.[1] Such men were chosen as the sovereign's spokesmen abroad because of their trusted personal ties with the ruler himself, rather than as members of a self-sufficient foreign service.

The character and extent of the late Byzantine diplomatic service is subject to debate.[2] Nevertheless, it involved a significant category of diplomats who were specially qualified for dealing with one area of foreign relations: that is, contacts with Italians, if not with other westerners as well. A core of such diplomats were individuals who were also scholars and intellectuals.[3]

Over the centuries, of course, Byzantine emperors recurrently employed some of its brilliant scholars as diplomats or specialized emissaries. In the ninth century there was the great Photios, before he became patriarch. In the same century there was Constantine the Philosopher, before he became the posthumous St. Cyril, Apostle to the Slavs. In the Palaiologan era itself, we find several striking early cases. Late in 1296, the monk-philologist-teacher Maximos Planoudes was one of two ambassadors sent to Venice to negotiate with its senate. And there were the eminent scholars Theodore Metochites and his student Nikephoros Gregoras, each sent as young men on missions to the Serbian court (1299, 1325). Of course, at the time Metochites already held court posts, on his path to eventual status as Andronikos II's (1282–1328) prime minister. That fact reminds us how closely linked in Byzantium were the careers of professional learning and government service—a link at least as strong in the Palaiologan era as any other time. Thus, the status of distinguished scholar and intellectual could still be in itself an important qualification for diplomatic functions. In the earlier case of Planoudes, we do not know what his diplomatic qualifications were, and we have no other references to his service in this realm. But his appointment that one time most likely had something to do with the fact that, at some time or other, Planoudes had learned Latin. As a consequence, his visit to Venice apparently gave him access to the works of a number of ancient and early Christian Latin authors, of which he and his students back home then made translations into Greek—a rare and isolated cultural bridging that anticipated the later efforts of Demetrios Kydones. [4]

The use of scholars as imperial envoys to the West became particularly noteworthy in the last century of the Byzantine Empire's failing existence. Just how the scholarly and the diplomatic elements did mesh in that period can be illustrated by considering three major personalities who constitute a virtual continuum in the late Byzantine phenomenon of the important scholar-diplomat. That continuum extended over three-quarters of a century, within the long reigns of three Palaiologan emperors: John V (1341–91), Manuel II (1391–1425), and John VIII (1425–48). The three individuals are: Demetrios Kydones; his disciple Manuel Chrysoloras; and the latter's younger-contemporary, George Gemistos Plethon. It is a significant fact that, as they were important ambassadors to the West, all three were simultaneously key figures in the transmission of Byzantine humanism to the Latin scholars of Renaissance Italy.

The most important Byzantine intellectual and scholar of the latter half of the fourteenth century, Demetrios Kydones, was thoroughly grounded in classical Greek literature and was also an accomplished theologian.[5] But he stood apart from most of his Byzantine contemporaries in the attraction he felt to the Latin West. In the early 1350s, during his service at the court of the usurper John VI Kantakouzenos, he acquired a mastery of Latin, a rare feat for a Byzantine scholar of his day. In the process, he became acquainted with the works of St. Thomas Aquinas, and carried out trail-blazing translations of them into Greek—a venture that went far beyond the earlier translating work of Planoudes. Kydones hoped thereby to make his Byzantine brethren discover and catch up with the vast progress of Latin intellectual thought, of which they had been totally unaware.

Unfortunately, beyond a very limited circle, these efforts made little impact on the rigidly traditionalist and closed outlook of Byzantine mentality. Nevertheless, this healthy dose of Western Thomism prompted Kydones to reject what he considered the anti-intellectualism of Hesychasm then prevalent in Byzantium's monastic and theological culture. Above all, it convinced him that, on the controversial issue of the *Filioque* and the Procession of the Holy Spirit, the Latin arguments were superior to those of the Greek church. Accordingly, as his intellectual reorientation progressed in the aftermath of Kantakouzenos's fall from power, Kydones took the decisive step of converting to Latin Christianity, probably in 1357.[6] Indeed, momentarily disillusioned with his homeland, he even considered the idea of moving to Italy or France and becoming an expatriate.[7]

His return to both governmental and intellectual service in the regime of the restored John V Palaiologos, however, gave Kydones new possibilities at home. As teacher to the future emperor Manuel II, as well as to others of that generation, Kydones shaped the continuing tradition of Byzantine classical studies. But, thanks to his knowledge of Latin, together with his bicultural intellect, Kydones could be of special use to John V as that sovereign began to seek military aid for Byzantium, then menaced by mounting Turkish aggression, not from unreliable Orthodox allies but from the Latin West, a policy for which Kydones became a leading advocate. Any such aid would be conditional upon some degree of religious capitulation to the papacy. Kydones logically supported the emperor's unprecedented journey to Rome as a symbolic gesture. Already a Catholic himself, Kydones was a crucial member of the emperor's retinue, and a key figure in the ceremonial procedures when John V made a personal renunciation of Orthodox "errors" and proclaimed a personal conversion to Latin Catholicism in Rome in October of 1369.[8]

Traveling to Italy with John V presumably answered Kydones's personal craving for direct contact with intellectuals in the West. He was delighted by his experiences in Rome and his encounters with both the papal and the cultural circles there. He made important friends and connections among Latin dignitaries and scholars. He apparently won much respect for his bicultural accomplishments, at a time when the classical interests of the new humanistic movement were themselves taking shape. But his stay first in Rome and then in Venice during 1369–71 was focused upon the needs and troubles of his hard-pressed master, and he returned to Constantinople with no opportunity to enlarge his contacts in the West. In the immediately ensuing years, too, John V's policies changed and the emperor became disillusioned with Kydones as an advisor. Seeking release from his court duties, Kydones thought about returning to the Latin West. He even proposed that the emperor appoint him as an ambassador to Avignon, where an old friend of his now reigned as Pope Gregory XI.[9] The proposal was ignored, and during the next two decades Kydones found himself in a constantly shifting position at court, sometimes brought back into service, but more often discredited.

His next sojourn in Latin territory was a stay in 1373–74 on the island of Lesbos where he visited an old friend, its Latin lord Francesco Gattilusio, who was in bad odor with the emperor at the time. Kydones did, however, assist the emperor in dealings with a papal delegation in 1373–74. Then in 1382 he served as interpreter and negotiator, first with the Genoese and then, back in Mitylene on Lesbos, with Gattilusio. Nevertheless, the apparent failure of the pro-Latin policy Kydones had long advocated, plus the hostility his conversion to Catholicism had earned him, led to increasing isolation from John V's court, while the Western crisis of the Great Schism from 1378 onward dashed hopes of meaningful dealings with a divided papacy. His association with Prince Manuel, and with the latter's separatist venture in Thessaloniki at the time, only completed Kydones's exclusion from the emperor's service. The disillusioned old scholar-politician renewed his dreams of withdrawing to the West, finally acting upon them in late 1389. But it was as a private citizen, not as any kind of official, that he made his second journey to Italy. He spent about a year (1390–91) in Venice, where he was formally granted Venetian citizenship on 20 January 1391.[10] He returned to Constantinople, where his former pupil now reigned as Emperor Manuel II.

The restless Kydones made two new journeys to the West: in 1395, or 1394–95, visiting Venice anew but soon returning to Constantinople. He left that city definitively in the autumn of 1396, just about the time of the demoralizing defeat of the Crusade of Nicopolis by the Turks.[11] It has been suggested that on these occasions Kydones had undertaken a mission to plead one last time for Western aid to Byzantium, but there is no concrete evidence to support that claim.[12] In fact, there survive no less than three letters written by Manuel to his old teacher during the latter's final journey:

entirely personal missives, they contain no indication that Kydones was pursuing official business.[13] The second of the three, however, while accompanying a work of his own Manuel sends to his old teacher, ends with a veritable condemnation of Kydones for abandoning his country and meriting the label of deserter.[14] Whether his tone was either bitter or jocular, Manuel was hardly treating Kydones as his official emissary. And we know that it was a completely separate diplomat, our Manuel Philanthropenos, who was the Byzantine negotiator with Hungary and Venice in 1395–96.[15]

During these later visits to Italy, aside from a possible stay in Milan, Kydones seems to have spent most if not all of his time in Venice. We may assume that his pursuits there were largely intellectual, perhaps at least partially related to the activities of his student, Manual Chrysoloras (of which more momentarily). With apparently deteriorating health and well into his middle-seventies, Kydones made the interesting decision to return to Greek lands in 1397. Perhaps the obstacle of the Turkish siege then beleaguering Constantinople prevented him from returning to the capital. On the other hand, his choice of Venetian-held Crete as a destination would make sense for this naturalized Venetian citizen. It was thus on Crete that death came to Demetrios Kydones, the scholar and official, humanist and Roman Catholic, in either late 1397 or early 1398.[16]

Kydones's final sojourns in Venice lead us on in turn to Manuel Chrysoloras, for the two were apparently co-travelers in both 1395 and 1396–97.[17] Modern writers have frequently described these journeys as "embassies." But, again, there is no specific evidence that either Kydones or Chrysoloras were traveling in any explicit governmental service.[18] They may have conveyed pleas for Western aid to Byzantium in purely personal and unofficial capacities, but their operations are more likely to have been intellectual.

By the time of these two journeys, Kydones was well into his seventies, while Chrysoloras would probably have been in his middle forties. The latter was by then rather past his student days as Kydones's pupil, but may still have been regarded as the elder man's continuing protégé. We might speculate that studies with Kydones—a Latin Catholic convert who had translated Aquinas and who had mastered the Latin language—had nudged Chrysoloras in similarly pro-Western directions. Chrysoloras still remained Orthodox in his faith, but it is apparent that he had studied Latin and had attained some command of it before he took up teaching positions in Italy. How much of this, I wonder, might have involved some deliberate plan?

No one so far seems to have considered the possibility that Kydones had in some way been grooming Chrysoloras—openly or unconsciously—for the intermediary role he was to serve, a role no longer feasible for Kydones himself in view of his advanced age and ill health. Could it be that, in his old age, Kydones recalled the stir he had made in 1369 and belatedly conceived the idea of opening the Western humanists to Byzantium's Hellenic legacy? If so, that would mean it was perhaps due to more than just Italian initiatives that Chrysoloras was soon invited to do exactly that. Could it be, then, that the purpose of Kydones's final journeys represent little or nothing diplomatic but were essentially meant to allow the old teacher's introduction of his student to the Italian intellectual scene as his surrogate cultural missionary?

Such thoughts are only speculation. Likewise so the suggestions of Ian Thomson that Chrysoloras's momentous journey to Italy "was politically inspired." Thomson claims that it was Emperor Manuel himself who encouraged, even promoted, the venture as a scheme to cultivate pro-Greek sympathies among influential Italian intellectuals and leaders in the West—a grand diplomatic plan after all![19]

Now, Emperor Manuel II was himself one of the leading Byzantine intellectuals of his day. But he knew no Latin, he seems to have had little interest in or sympathy with Latin learning, and, in his own famous journey to the West, he apparently neither sought nor made any serious contacts with Western intellectuals. Perhaps aware of his own shortcomings, Emperor Manuel might have envisioned a valid intercultural role for Chrysoloras, one that he himself could not pursue. Manuel certainly valued Chrysoloras's linguistic and intellectual talents for their practical diplomatic applications. Nevertheless, there is no explicit evidence whatsoever for Thomson's supposition of consultation and collusion between Chrysoloras and his sovereign. Whatever any undocumented possibilities, we can state with certainty only that the fruits of the two visits by the two scholars in the 1390s were specifically intellectual, and spectacularly so.

We do know that, when Kydones and Chrysoloras arrived in Venice in 1395 (or 1394), they were sought out for instruction in Greek by two enthusiastic Florentines, Roberto Rossi and Jacopo d'Angeli della Scarperia. The latter followed them when they returned to Constantinople and studied there with Chrysoloras and Manuel Kalekas. For his part, Rossi reported to the eminent Florentine humanist, Coluccio Salutati, who then wrote letters to each of the two Byzantine visitors. On 18 February 1396, he wrote to praise Kydones for his unique learning and for inspiring Italians to learn the Greek language and culture. Under the date 8 March 1396, he wrote separately to Chrysoloras, likewise enthusiastic in his praise, but with explicit recruitment in mind. Salutati informed Chrysoloras of an action that had been taken on 23 February by the council of the Florentine Republic, at his initiative, to provide a stipend from public monies as salary for instruction in Greek language and literature that Chrysoloras would give in Florence.[20]

Accordingly, whatever supplemental diplomatic purpose it may have included, the ensuing journey by Kydones and Chrysoloras in autumn 1396 served the purpose specifically of delivering Chrysoloras to his new position. We have no evidence that Kydones went to Florence to witness the epochal initiative of his student's new mission. Still, one cannot help suspecting that he reflected upon it with satisfaction from whatever vantage point.

The illustrious humanistic career of Manuel Chrysoloras in the West is well known. He began his trailblazing program of instruction in Florence from February 1397, completing it by the end of 1399. Indeed, he actually departed before his stipulated time of service was completed, in an arguable breach of contract.[21] He left Florence apparently in response to parallel summonses. One was from the prestige-seeking but influential Duke of Milan, Gian Galeazzo Visconti. The other summons was from his own master and fellow-scholar, Emperor Manuel II himself, who was beginning his personal aid-seeking journey to Western courts. Their meeting in Milan in the spring of 1400 was a grandly festive occasion. While Manuel went on to France, to pursue his own mission in Paris and beyond, Chrysoloras settled down to teaching in Lombardy, apparently in both Pavia and Milan. By that time, however, Chrysoloras may indeed have had his pedagogical and scholarly functions linked by an official diplomatic charge from his sovereign. It is documented that, at least over the winter of 1401/2, Chrysoloras was active in Milan as the collector of monies to be applied to the defense of Constantinople, in accordance with an appeal on Byzantium's behalf almost four years before by Pope Boniface IX.[22] At any rate, when Emperor Manuel began his homeward journey over the winter of 1402/3, he was joined somewhere along the way in Italy by Chrysoloras, who then returned to Constantinople in the emperor's retinue.[23]

Manuel II's journeys in the West may well have marked a shift in Chrysoloras's attitude towards residence and activities in the West. A clue is given in a eulogy of Chrysoloras delivered in Venice in July 1415 by Guarino's student, Andrea Zulian (Giuliano). Zulian noted that Chrysoloras traveled through many courts where he was urged to take up residence but that he returned to Greece "preferring to fulfill his true task, which was to save his country from danger rather than give delight to Italy."[24] From this we might conclude that, at least for the latter portion of his life,

Chrysoloras's scholarly interests were more clearly subordinated to diplomatic obligations.

Chrysoloras did briefly resume residence in the Byzantine capital, where he was joined by a star pupil from his Florence days, Guarino da Verona, who had followed him to pursue further studies directly with him. Nevertheless, Chrysoloras was soon back in Italy, not once, but twice: in 1404 and in 1405–6. Little is known about these two visits, but at least some diplomatic intent is suggested. While in Venice in 1404 he addressed a letter to Pope Innocent VII, and it has been assumed that he did so in the capacity of Manuel II's legate. In the same city in 1406, he appears in a document wherein he is described as "ambassador of the emperor of Constantinople." Earlier that year, on 3 January 1406, he is recorded as participating in the ceremonies in which the city of Padua submitted to the Venetian Republic. That he attended in any official capacity is not clear.[25]

Between these two voyages, Chrysoloras was in Constantinople, from which he addressed another letter, also to Pope Innocent VII, containing a significant request: that he might receive holy orders according to Roman rites. He asked the further concession that, in celebrating the Roman mass, he be allowed to do so in the Greek language. Approval of his request was formally entered in the pope's registers as of 19 February 1406.[26] Word of this action apparently spread among Italy's intellectuals, for we find one of Chrysoloras's former students in Florence, Pier-Paolo Vergerio, writing to a friend soon after that his admired master "longs to be a Latin."[27] Thus did Chrysoloras at last embark upon the path of conversion to Latin Christianity, in the footsteps of his teacher. Embarked, indeed, but how decisively arrived is not clear. While it is likely that from this time Chrysoloras considered himself a Latin Christian, it would nevertheless appear that, down to the end of his life, he had not yet actually taken holy orders.[28]

Setting that question aside, the same double qualification of conversion to Latin faith and of connection with Western intellectual life in which Kydones pioneered now served to win for his pupil and disciple the very diplomatic status that Kydones had proposed for himself back in 1371. Late in the year 1407, Manuel Chrysoloras departed Constantinople for the last time, now holding the unusual position of ambassador-at-large to the courts of western Europe, on behalf of Emperor Manuel II—"une sorte d'agent permanent de son souverain . . . en occident," as Loenertz puts it. As spokesman for his master, Chrysoloras spent the next three years traveling widely, with documented stops in Venice, Genoa, Paris, London, Salisbury, and Barcelona. He conducted negotiations on various matters, attempting

cultivation of friendships through gifts of relics, and generally endeavoring
to renew and extend the contacts that Emperor Manuel had opened up in
his own personal travels of 1400–1403.[29] That little practical result seems to
have come from these exertions is suggested by a frustration-filled letter
written about 1409 or 1410 by Emperor Manuel in response to his ambassador's negative reports.[30]

Whether by design or circumstances, Chrysoloras's efforts shifted from
diplomatic message-carrying to ecclesiastical negotiation. In mid-1410, he
journeyed to Bologna so as to establish contact with Alexander V, a Greek
Cretan by birth, who was the new pope set up by the Council of Pisa the
previous year. By the time he arrived, Alexander had died, and the Pisan
line was now represented by the antipope John XXIII. Was it with Emperor
Manuel's approval, if not instructions, that Chrysoloras remained a part of
Pope John's retinue? We might well assume so, though another explanation
has been suggested for Chrysoloras's willingness to associate himself with a
papal claimant of such shady character. That is the fact that John XXIII had
made his court a center of humanism and humanists. The most notable
among them was the scholar and ecclesiastical statesman Cardinal Francesco
Zabarella, heading a Florentine-focused circle with which Chrysoloras could
happily identify.[31]

That connection took Chrysoloras in turn to Rome, Florence, and Bologna. Along with Zabarella, he became one of the important negotiators
with the German emperor Sigismund, contributing thus to the calling of the
landmark Council of Constance. After rejoining John XXIII in Bologna,
Chrysoloras accompanied that prelate to Constance, arriving 28 October
1414. He was present when that assemblage opened in November 1414, one
of its honored and admired participants; only to die the following 15 April,
mourned as both a great scholar and a revered Christian leader.[32]

It is in connection with another landmark council of the church that we
encounter our third figure, the remarkable George Gemistos Plethon—idio-
syncratic for our purposes as in so much else.[33] Born in Constantinople
about 1360, he was effectively of the generation of Chrysoloras, whom he
must have known well. By age, he could have been a student of Kydones, but
there is no evidence of that, though we do know that he was a teacher of the
eminent Bessarion. A skeptical Christian, a multicultural freethinker by the
standards of his own day, Plethon was already in his fifties when Emperor
Manuel ordered him out of the capital to remoter residence in Mistra
because of his unconventional thinking—even though Manuel and his sons
in the Morea had considerable respect for his intellectual powers. Plethon's

important literary and philosophical work was not to come, however, until the latter part of his long life, and as prompted by his sole experience in a Byzantine diplomatic mission.

That experience resulted from his inclusion in the Byzantine delegation to the church council which opened in Ferrara in 1438 and which reconvened in Florence in 1439 in order to cobble up a Union of the Roman and Greek churches. Along with Emperor John VIII, his younger brother Demetrios, and Patriarch Joseph, the delegates included two Byzantine churchmen who were among Plethon's former students (Mark Eugenikos, metropolitan of Ephesus, and Bessarion of Trebizond, metropolitan of Nicaea) plus a third (Isidore, metropolitan of Kiev) who might also have studied with him. Plethon himself was one of three leading lay scholars of note—the other two being George Scholarios, the future patriarch and enemy of Plethon, and George Amiroutzes, future betrayer of Trebizond, adherent of Mehmed the Conqueror, and possible apostate to Islam.[34] By then in his seventies and of a passing generation, Plethon was respected but relatively irrelevant. His role in the union negotiations was minimal, helping with textual drafting and making only minor contributions to the theological discussions in which he felt little interest, as a philosopher who had all but given up the Christian faith.[35]

As is well known, Plethon's important activity really began when the council was transferred in January 1439 to Florence, and had little to do with the union debates at all. His mission proved, instead, to be the next major contribution of Byzantine humanism to Italian Renaissance humanism: a series of lectures he gave before a circle of enthusiastic Italian Hellenists, lectures he later digested into his treatise entitled *On the Differences of Aristotle from Plato*. Whatever the immediate impact of his performance in Florence, it has long been understood as the inspiration for Cosimo de' Medici's supposed creation of a Platonic Academy, as led by Marsilio Ficino—traditionally identified as one of the important intellectual turning points of the Italian Renaissance.[36] This Florentine adventure was, meanwhile, a turning point for Plethon himself, who was to return to Mistra to write the series of philosophical works on which his reputation was to be based. He died there, more than ninety years of age, in 1452, a year before the fall of Constantinople to the Turks.

In 1464, four years after the fall of Mistra to Mehmed the Conqueror, Sigismondo Malatesta, the bizarre Renaissance ruffian and cultural patron, took the city briefly while commanding a Venetian raiding force. A great admirer of Plethon, Sigismondo had the philosopher's remains exhumed and transferred for reburial in the honor-wall of the Tempio Malatestiano, the pseudo-pagan shrine built for Sigismondo in Rimini by the great Renaissance designer Leon Battista Alberti. Thus did the neo-pagan Platonist find his last repose in a citadel of Italian humanism to which he had made such a crucial contribution.[37]

In the lives of these three great Byzantine scholar-diplomats, we see immediately how much the diplomatic dimensions pale besides the scholarly, almost to an incidental degree. Of our three scholars, Chrysoloras did undertake explicitly diplomatic commissions during his visits to western Europe: to some extent in 1401–2, probably in 1404 and 1405–6, most certainly in 1407–10. His activities from 1410 to his death in 1415 might be seen to some extent as those of a papal diplomat, with barely residual status of a Byzantine emissary. In August of 1413, and described only as "a knight of Constantinople," he was one of the representatives designated to negotiate on behalf of the antipope John XXIII with Emperor Sigismund concerning the location of the council that met the following year in Constance.[38]

It is true that a German chronicler of that council, Ulrich von Richental, identifies "Emanuel von Chrisolena [sic], Ritter" among three "emissaries and councilors of the emperor of Constantinople" (Botten und Raeht des Keysers von Constantinopel), as distinct from those in the service of other lords.[39] Moreover, in the funeral oration given by Andrea Zulian, it is stated that, as an active participant in the council's work, Chrysoloras labored earnestly to effect the reconciliation of the Greeks to Latin doctrine and the re-union of the churches. Of course, such efforts themselves required no official Byzantine credentials. At any rate, Chrysoloras would seem to have had a rather general accreditation as Emperor Manuel's continuing ambassador-at-large in western Europe. It is possible that Chrysoloras was recognized specifically as a Byzantine delegate to the council by its organizer, Emperor Sigismund, especially as a result of Chrysoloras's contact with the latter during the negotiations of 1413–14, when he was officially a spokesman for John XXIII. But for such status there is no explicit evidence. It seems just as likely that Chrysoloras took his place in the council not as Manuel II's official representative but as a part of the retinue of John XXIII.

All in all, Chrysoloras's exact standing is not as clear as glib characterizations have long been making it. On the one hand, he may have had a double status, linked simultaneously to the Byzantine emperor and to the Pisan antipope. On the other hand, his standing may have been ambiguous, at least as we look at it now. That Chrysoloras was Manuel II's official representative at the Council of Constance seems perfectly plausible, if not quite likely, but it is not incontestably documented, and it cannot be stated simply as established fact, as it has so often been.[40]

By contrast, Chrysoloras's earliest visits to Italy are more explicable as scholarly than as diplomatic ventures, as we can also say of the later journeys of Kydones. Kydones's earliest visit to Italy certainly had scholarly impact but was, indeed, made in official capacity—and not so much as a diplomat as in retinue service to John V. Likewise, Plethon's participation in the episode of the Ferrara-Florence Council was not at all diplomatic but simply consultative, with great consequences for the intellectual rather than the diplomatic sphere. After all, Plethon's former pupil and fellow-delegate to the Council of Florence, Bessarion, used his own experience there to win transformation into a cardinal of the Roman church, with even less right to be called a Byzantine diplomat than before.

There is no reason to deny that the respective scholarly operations of Kydones, Chrysoloras, and Plethon could have diplomatic dimensions or impact, even in only broad terms. Nevertheless, our three savants seem only incidentally (or, in Chrysoloras's case, belatedly) to have discharged the full-fledged and formal diplomatic functions that have been adduced to make them into paragons of the Byzantine scholar-emissary. Fascinating footnotes to all this are the religious choices exercised by these three men in connection with their Western dealings. Born Orthodox Christians all, they abandoned the faith of their fathers. Kydones and Chrysoloras were among the most distinguished Byzantine men of learning who converted to Roman Catholicism, as did the Uniate Bessarion. The maverick Plethon scandalized his contemporaries and critics by moving through neo-Hellenic patriotism to neo-paganism.

It is perhaps true that Palaiologan diplomacy lacked solid institutional foundations and relied simply upon the individuals in whom the emperors could repose their personal confidence. If scholars were to be included among such individuals, they were likely to be men with their own, altogether extra-diplomatic agendas, men even quite ready to "jump ship" in religious loyalties. We are left with questions that would more likely to occur to us in our time than to the Byzantines themselves. Such questions hint at the complexities that were altering the world at the end of the Middle Ages. If the Orthodox faith was one of the components of one's identity as a citizen of Byzantium, could these three men be regarded any longer as true "Byzantines" once they had made their divergent choices? Kydones was, after all, in his later years, a citizen of Venice, though this really had more honorary character than present-day legalities of status would involve. Modern dilemmas of "dual citizenship" would probably not have arisen then. But Chrysoloras, even at the time he was Manuel II's official envoy, was apparently a Roman Catholic, a would-be Western monk, and finally an agent of one of the popes. Indeed, as with the later case of Bessarion, he was even considered a possible candidate for the papacy himself—an eventuality that would surely have carried him far from Byzantine diplomatic status![41] Byzantine emperors were not above using foreigners as well as Latinized ex-Byzantines as occasional emissaries, but our examples squarely confront us with sharp paradoxes of identity in the ambassadorial *personae* of Kydones and Chrysoloras, if not also Plethon—not to mention Bessarion.

All the more reason to recognize, then, that diplomatic practices in Palaiologan Byzantium were those of a world very different from ours. We may choose to summon up from our own recollections such American counterparts as a Henry Kissinger or a Robert Reischauer or a Kenneth Galbraith as significant scholar-diplomats; but one could never imagine them shifting allegiances or fundamentals of their identity as did our three Byzantines amid their diplomatic functions. In point of fact, such shifts really do no more than point up the disintegrating state of Byzantine society during its final generations, in an age full of expatriation and intellectual "brain-drain." As our examples illustrate, the diplomatic activities of scholars then were as much a part of their *stepping out* of Byzantium as they were of *serving* it. What Chrysoloras and his two colleagues did or did not do as diplomats remains, then, a matter of scholarly speculation and antiquarian hair-splitting, with perhaps minimal meaning in the end. After all, it is not for their diplomatic activities but for their intellectual legacies that we remember them, and honor them.[42]

NOTES

This paper has undergone a series of transformations. An initial form of it was contributed to a symposium on Manuel Chrysoloras, in November 1997, sponsored by the Hellenic Canadian Association of Constantinople in Toronto. Then a drastically reduced version was presented at a session organized by Dimiter Angelov at the Thirty-ninth International Congress on Medieval Studies in Kalamazoo, Michigan, in May 2004. In present form, the paper is a considerably varied extension of those earlier versions. I must add my specific thanks to Professor Angelov for some useful suggestions in its preparation.

1. Nicolas Oikonomides, "Byzantine Diplomacy, A.D. 1204–1453," in *Byzantine Diplomacy: Papers from the Twenty-fourth Spring Symposium of Byzantine Studies, Cambridge, March 1990*, ed. Jonathan Shepard and Simon Franklin (Aldershot: Variorum, 1992), pp. 73–88. Oikonomides skimmed his information primarily from what Franz Dölger had assembled in the final segments of his monumental *Regesten der Kaiserurkunden des oströmischen Reiches von 565–1453*, vol. 3, *Regesten von 1204–1282*, ed. Paul Wirth, rev. ed. (Munich: Beck, 1977) (first publ. Munich: Oldenbourg, 1932); vol. 4, *Regesten von 1282–1341* (Munich: Beck, 1960); vol. 5, *Regesten von 1341–1453* (Munich: Beck, 1965). Oikonomides reckoned a total of seventy-nine family names of ambassadors over his time period, including some from the most prominent Byzantine families, aristocratic but eventually also mercantile. Oikonomides' study has now been extended by Sophia Mergiali-Sahas in her essay "A Byzantine Ambassador to the West and His Office during the Fourteenth and Fifteenth Centuries: A Profile," *BZ* 94 (2001): 588–604, which surveys thoroughly and identifies carefully the specific individuals who served in varying ambassadorial capacities.

2. Oikonomides, "Byzantine Diplomacy," p. 77: "Byzantium never had a 'foreign service' in the proper sense of the term." However true that statement is up to a point, one may nevertheless discern, here and there through Byzantine history, suggestive instances of diplomats with regional specializations. We might cite the case of Manuel Philanthropenos, who appears as an ambassador twice in the reign of Emperor Manuel II, in widely separated missions of 1396 and 1420. In each case he was negotiator of a treaty with King Sigismund of Hungary, by way of Venice—suggesting his holding of "the Hungarian desk" in the diplomatic corps. See John W. Barker, *Manuel II Palaeologus (1391–1425): A Study in Late Byzantine Statesmanship* (New Brunswick, N.J.: Rutgers University Press, 1969), p. 338 n. 74.

3. Oikonomides, "Byzantine Diplomacy," p. 82, mentions the use of "scholars and humanists" only in a brief and dismissive sentence.

4. For the 1296 embassy, see Dölger, *Regesten*, 4:26, no. 2197. See also Deno John Geanakoplos, *Greek Scholars in Venice: Studies in the Dissemination of Greek Learning from Byzantium to Western Europe* (Cambridge, Mass.: Harvard University Press, 1962), p. 27; Angeliki Laiou, *Constantinople and the Latins: The Foreign Policy of Andronicus II, 1282–1328* (Cambridge, Mass.: Harvard University Press, 1972), p. 106 and n. 84. At least one important translation Planoudes made from Latin was of St. Augustine's *De Trinitate*, and is understood to have been made not after the scholar's visit to Venice, but at the behest of Emperor Michael VIII during the controversy following the Union of Lyons in 1274. (The recent edition of this translation prepared by Manolis Papathomopoulos, Isavella Tsaveri, and Gianpaolo Rigotti [Athens, 1995], is not available to me.) See "Planudes, Maximos," in PLP, no. 23308. For literature on Planoudes in general, the most comprehensive treatment is the article by Carl Wendel, "Maximos Planudes," in *Paulys Real-Encyclopädie der*

Classischen Altertumswissenschaft, ed. G. Wissowa et al., 24 vols. (Stuttgart: Metzler, Druckenmüller, 1894–1978), vol. 20, pt. 2, cols. 2202–53. See also Sophia Mergiali-Sahas, *L'enseignement et les lettrés pendant l'époque des Paléologues (1261–1453)* (Athens: Centre des études byzantines, 1996), pp. 34–42, esp. pp. 36–37 with reference to his embassy; Edmund Fryde, *The Early Palaeologan Renaissance (1261–c.1360)* (Leiden: Brill, 2000), pp. 226–67 (with bibliography), in the wake of Nigel G. Wilson, *Scholars of Byzantium* (Baltimore: Johns Hopkins University Press, 1983), pp. 230–41; and Steven Runciman, *The Last Byzantine Renaissance* (Cambridge: Cambridge University Press, 1970), pp. 59–60. More specifically: Wolfgang O. Schmitt, "Lateinische Literatur in Byzanz: Die Übersetzungen des Maximos Planudes und die moderne Forschung," *JÖB* 17 (1968): 127–47; Elizabeth A. Fisher, *Planudes' Greek Translation of Ovid's Metamorphoses* (New York: Garland, 1990), esp. pp. 29–46, as well as her "Planoudes, Holobolos and the Motivation for Translation," *Greek, Roman and Byzantine Studies* 43 (2002): 77–104, and her unpublished paper "Planudes, Ovid, and the Byzantine Audience for Latin Literature," for the Twenty-fifth Annual Byzantine Studies Conference (abstracts).

5. See "Kydones, Demetrios," in PLP, no. 13876. The best outline of the life and career of Kydones has been given in the essays by Raymond-Joseph Loenertz: "Démétrius Cydonès, I: De la naissance à l'année; II: De 1373 à 1375," *OCP* 36 (1970): 47–72; *OCP* 37 (1971): 5–39; Raymond-Joseph Loenertz, "Essai de chronologie," in his *Recueils des lettres de Démétrius Cydonès*, Studi e testi, 131 (Vatican City: Biblioteca Apostolica Vaticana, 1947), pp. 108–22. See also Kenneth M. Setton, "The Byzantine Background to the Italian Renaissance," *Proceedings of the American Philosophical Society* 100 (1956): 1–76 (pp. 52–57); more recently, the studies by Frances Kianka, "The *Apology* of Demetrius Cydones: A Fourteenth-Century Autobiographical Source," *Byzantine Studies/Études Byzantines* 7 (1980): 57–71, "Byzantine-Papal Diplomacy: The Role of Demetrius Cydones," *International History Review* 7 (1985): 175–213, and "Demetrios Kydones and Italy," *DOP* 49 (1995): 99–110. See now also Mergiali-Sahas, *L'enseignement*, pp. 125–41; and Athanassia Glycofrydi-Leontsini, "Demetrius Cydones as a Translator of Latin Texts," in *Porphyrogenita: Essays on the History and Literature of Byzantium and the Latin East in Honour of Julian Chrysostomides*, ed. Charalambos Dendrinos, Jonathan Harris, Eirene Harvalia-Crook, and Judith Herrin (Aldershot: Ashgate, 2003), pp. 175–85; as well as the shallow survey by Colin Wells in his popular book *Sailing from Byzantium* (New York: Delacorte, 2006), pp. 54–65.

6. Kianka, "Byzantine-Papal Diplomacy," pp. 178–81. For perspective on Kydones's action, see Tia Kolbaba, "Conversion from Greek Orthodoxy to Roman Catholicism in the Fourteenth Century," *Byzantine and Modern Greek Studies* 19 (1995): 120–34, discussing the case of Barlaam of Calabria.

7. Kydones's letter 46, in Raymond-Joseph Loenertz, ed., *Démétrius Cydonius: Correspondance*, 2 vols., Studi e testi 186, 208 (Vatican City: Biblioteca Apostolica Vaticana, 1956–60), 1:79–80; see Kianka, "Byzantine-Papal Diplomacy," pp. 180–81.

8. Kianka, "Byzantine-Papal Diplomacy," pp. 188–96. See also Loenertz, "Démétrius Cydonès," *OCP* 36 (1970): 65–67; older and problematical is Oskar Halecki, *Un empereur de Byzance à Rome: Vingt ans de travail pour l'Union des Églises et pour la défence de l'Empire d'Orient, 1355–1375* (Warsaw: Towarzystwo Naukowe Warszawskie, 1930; repr. London: Variorum Reprints, 1972); but note now Mergiali-Sahas, *L'enseignement*, pp. 131–32.

9. Kydones, *Address to Emperor John*, in Loenertz, *Correspondance*, 1:18–19, 22; see Kianka, "Byzantine-Papal Diplomacy," pp. 205–6; also her "Kydones and Italy," pp. 107–8.

10. Raymond-Joseph Loenertz, "Démétrius Cydonès, citoyen de Venise," *Echos d'Orient* 37 (1938): 125–26; Setton, "Byzantine Background," p. 56; Kianka, "Byzantine-Papal Diplomacy," p. 211; see also Geanakoplos, *Greek Scholars in Venice*, pp. 27–28; and, most recently, and by a distinguished Loenertz student, George T. Dennis, "Demetrios Kydones and Venice," in *Bisanzio, Venezia e il mondo franco-greco (XII–XV secolo)*, ed. Chryssa Maltezou and Peter Schreiner (Venice: Istituto Ellenico & Centro Tedesco, 2002), pp. 495–502.

11. Kianka, "Byzantine-Papal Diplomacy," p. 211, posits only one such journey in that decade, that of 1396; cf. Setton, "The Byzantine Background," p. 57; and Mergiali-Sahas, *L'enseignement*, pp. 233–35.

12. Dionysios Zakythenos, "Démétrius Cydonès et l'entente balkanique au XVIe siècle," in his *La Grèce et les Balkans* (Athens, 1947), pp. 44–56 (p. 47); also Setton, "Byzantine Background," p. 56. Cf. Barker, *Manuel II*, p. 126 n. 4, and p. 419 n. 42.

13. George T. Dennis, ed. and trans., *The Letters of Manuel II Palaeologus* (Washington, D.C.: Dumbarton Oaks, 1977), letter 31, pp. 80–87 (partial translation and comments in Barker, *Manuel II*, pp. 134–37), comments on the disastrous conditions of the moment and essentially congratulates Kydones for having gotten away just before the disaster of the battle. Letter 36, pp. 98–99, makes lighthearted references to Manuel's intellectual debts to Kydones.

14. Dennis, *Letters of Manuel II*, pp. 172–73, no. 62; also translated, with comments, in Barker, *Manuel II*, pp. 417–19.

15. Dölger, *Regesten*, no. 3255; Barker, *Manuel II*, pp. 131–32 and n. 16.

16. Loenertz, *Correspondance de Manuel Calécas*, Studi e testi 152 (Vatican City: Biblioteca Apostolica Vaticana, 1950), pp. 56–57 and 236 (in the letter in which Kalekas reported the death of Kydones to Chrysoloras, the letter's recipient); Setton, "Byzantine Background," p. 57; Kianka, "Byzantine-Papal Diplomacy," p. 211.

17. Giuseppe Cammelli, *I dotti bizantini e le origini dell'umanesimo*, vol. 1, *Manuele Crisolora* (Florence: Vallecchi, 1941), pp. 26–30, 39; Setton, "The Byzantine Background," pp. 56, 57. The first systematic chronology of Chrysoloras's successive sojourns in the West was Remigio Sabbadini, "L'ultimo ventennio della vita di M. Crisolora," *Gornale ligustico* 17 (1890): 321–36. Chrysoloras is no. 31165 in PLP,

fascicule 12, p. 253. There is a thorough study of his career by Mergiali-Sahas, "Manuel Chrysoloras (ca. 1350–1415), an Ideal Model of a Scholar-Ambassador," *Byzantine Studies/Études Byzantines*, n.s. 3 (1998): 1–12. Also, see the article by Antonio Rollo, "Problemi e prospettive della ricerca su Manuele Crisolora," in *Manuele Crisolora e il ritorno del greco in Occidente: Atti del Convegno Internazionale (Napoli, 26–29 giugno 1997)*, ed. Riccardo Maisano and Antonio Rollo (Naples: Istituto universitario orientale, 2002), pp. 31–86. There is a comprehensive if somewhat simplistic survey of Chrysoloras's life in Wells, *Sailing from Byzantium*, pp. 62–88; and, more briefly, the comments of Fryde, *Early Palaeologan Renaissance*, pp. 386, 391.

18. An unnamed Byzantine agent was involved in negotiations with Venice in 1394: if Chrysoloras's earlier journey had begun as early as that, it is not inconceivable that he was the individual; see Barker, *Manuel II*, p. 126 n. 4. But it seems unlikely that such a notable personage would have gone unidentified. This teasing reference is not considered by Mergiali-Sahas, "Manuel Chrysoloras, an Ideal Model."

19. See Ian Thomson, "Manuel Chrysoloras and the Early Italian Renaissance," *Greek, Roman, and Byzantine Studies* 7 (1966): 63–82 (pp. 76–78). Mergiali-Sahas, "Manuel Chrysoloras, an Ideal Model," ventures no comment on this interpretation; but see there pp. 11–12, as well as her broader study, *L'enseignement*, pp. 172–73. Wells, *Sailing from Byzantium*, pp. 83–84, all too casually remarks that Thomson's idea "has been widely accepted by other scholars."

20. Cammelli, *Crisolora*, pp. 29–31. The republic's formal letter of its terms to Chrysoloras, dated 28 March 1396, was drafted by Coluccio himself: Cammelli, *Crisolora*, pp. 33–35 and n. 2.

21. Cammelli, *Crisolora*, pp. 43–104. Thomson, "Manuel Chrysoloras," pp. 79–80, proposes that Chrysoloras "left Florence when he finally realized his failure to arouse the kind of support his country needed." For comments on Chrysoloras's teaching in Florence and his impact upon Italian Humanism, see: Christine Smith, *Architecture in the Culture of Early Humanism* (Oxford: Oxford University Press, 1992), pp. 133–49 (and beyond, for discussion of Chrysoloras's treatise Σύγκρισις τῆς παλαίας καὶ νέας Ῥώμης [Comparison of Old and New Rome]). I have not seen the new edition of this text by Cristina Billò, "Manuele Crisolora, Confronto tra l'Antica e la Nuova Roma," *Medioevo greco* 0 (2000): 1–26, or the Italian translation by Francesaca Niutta, *Manuele Crisolora, Le due Rome: Confronto tra Roma e Costantinopoli; Con la traduzione latina di Francesco Aleardi*, 2000 viaggi a Roma 7 (Bologna: Patron, 2001); on this text there is also now Alessandro Ghisalberti, "Roma antica e la 'nuova Roma' in Manuele Crisolora," *Studi umanistici piceni* 21 (2001): 173–79. More generally, see Nigel G. Wilson, *From Byzantium to Italy: Greek Studies in the Italian Renaissance* (Baltimore: Johns Hopkins University Press, 1992), pp. 8–12; George Holmes, *The Florentine Enlightenment, 1400–50* (London: Weidenfeld & Nicolson, 1969), pp. 8–10; Mergiali-Sahas, "Manuel Chrysoloras, an Ideal Model," pp. 3–6,

and her *L'enseignement*, pp. 137–39; Apostolos E. Vakalopoulos, *Origins of the Greek Nation, 1204–1461*, trans. Ian Moles (New Brunswick, N.J.: Rutgers University Press, 1970), pp. 237–40; Geanakoplos, *Greek Scholars in Venice*, pp. 24–28; John Addington Symonds, *The Renaissance in Italy: The Revival of Learning* (New York: Holt, 1888), pp. 108–13; also, John M. McManamon, *Funeral Oratory and the Cultural Ideals of Italian Humanism* (Chapel Hill: University of North Carolina Press, 1989), pp. 22, 58, 126–27, 129; James Hankins "Chrysoloras and the Greek Studies of Leonardo Bruni," in *Manuele Crisolora* (see above, n. 17), pp. 175–203; and Chryssa Maltezou, "An Enlightened Byzantine Teacher in Florence: Manuel Chrysoloras," in *Orthodoxy and Oecumene: Gratitude Volume in Honour of Ecumenical Patriarch Bartholomaios* (Athens: Harmos, 2001), pp. 443–52.

22. Loenertz, *Correspondance de Manuel Calécas*, p. 68, citing unspecified Milanese archival documents.

23. Cammelli, *Crisolora*, pp. 98–130; however, Loenertz, *Calécas*, p. 68, considers that there is no absolute proof of a return at this time.

24. Cited by Thomson, "Manuel Chrysoloras," p. 81, from the edition by A. Calogerà, not available to me. For a summary of Zulian's eulogy of Chrysoloras, see McManamon, *Funeral Oratory*, pp. 123–26.

25. Cammelli, *Crisolora*, pp. 139–42; also Loenertz, *Calécas*, p. 69; cf. Barker, *Manuel II*, p. 263 and n. 109.

26. The pope's approval of this request was first published by Angelo Mercati, "Una notiziola su Manuele Crisolora," *Stoudion: Bollettino delle Chiese di rito bizantino* 5 (1928): 65–69; see also Cammelli, *Crisolora*, pp. 140–42. Cf. Thomson, "Manuel Chrysoloras," p. 81: "His conversion was perhaps sincere, but it was also possible to see it as yet another conciliatory move to win favor in the West. . . . [His] submission could have been expected to oil the wheels of diplomacy. It need not surprise one that Chrysoloras could have indulged in an act of political expediency."

27. Vergerio, *Epistolario*, ed. Leonardo Smith, Fonti per la storia d'Italia 74 (Rome: Tipografia del Senato, 1934), letter 96, pp. 243–46. Hans Baron, *Humanistic and Political Literature in Florence and Venice at the Beginning of the Quattrocento* (Cambridge, Mass.: Harvard University Press, 1955), pp. 107–13, has explicitly argued that Vergerio's reference was based upon knowledge of Chrysoloras's request; indeed, Baron makes the papal registers' entry (19 February 1406) a decisive point in dating Vergerio's letter 69 (to a friend as yet unidentified) to between late 1406 and late 1407.

28. That Chrysoloras did not go ahead and take Western orders, and that he died a layman, is the emphatic point of Mercati, "Una notiziola," p. 68. That conclusion is echoed by Raymond-Joseph Loenertz, "Les dominicains byzantins Théodore et André Chrysobergès et les négociations pour l'union des églises grecque et latine de 1415 à 1430," *Archivium Fratrum Praedicatorum* 9 (1939): 5–61 (p. 16 and n. 44).

29. Cammelli, *Crisolora*, pp. 143–52; Loenertz, *Correspondance de Manuel Calécas*, p. 70; Barker, *Manuel II*, pp. 154–57 (and notes), 519–24. In his eulogy of Chrysoloras, Andrea Zulian asserts that the ambassador successfully extracted financial contributions from the Western sovereigns he visited and dutifully transmitted them to his master, even while resisting those sovereigns' offers of profitable service with them. See McManamon, *Funeral Oratory*, p.124. On the use of relics in Byzantine diplomatic dealings under Manuel II (and including the missions of Chrysoloras), see pp. 55–59 or Sophia Mergiali-Sahas, "Byzantine Emperors and Holy Relics," *JÖB* 51 (2001): 41–60.

30. See Manuel II's letter 55 in Dennis, *The Letters of Manuel II*, pp. 154–57 and notes; trans. in Barker, *Manuel II*, pp. 266–67, with comments on pp. 519–23; cf. Setton, "Byzantine Background," pp. 57–58. Against its pessimistic picture, contrast the reports of Chrysoloras's success in receiving donations from Western potentates, as mentioned in the preceding note.

31. See Holmes, *Florentine Enlightenment*, pp. 59–63; cf. Mergiali-Sahas, "Manuel Chrysoloras, an Ideal Model," p. 10, and "Byzantine Ambassador to the West," p. 601.

32. Cammelli, *Crisolora*, pp. 153–66; Loenertz, *Calécas*, pp. 70–71; Barker, *Manuel II*, pp. 265–66, 321–22; Joseph Gill, *Council of Florence* (Cambridge: Cambridge University Press, 1959), pp. 20–21; Mergiali-Sahas, "Manuel Chrysoloras, an Ideal Model," p. 11. On a collection of letters and tributes commemorating the great Greek scholar after his death, assembled by Guarino, see Luigi Piacente, "Una miscellanea di epistole in onore di Manuele Crisolora," *Studi umanistici piceni* 19 (1999): 94–103. Chrysoloras was residing during the council at the grand Dominican monastery in Constance, and when he died he was buried in a chapel of its church. The monastery was secularized in 1784 and for a long time has been operated as a hotel. The church itself has been turned into a conference hall, with flooring and wall paneling that now make it very difficult to trace Chrysoloras's grave. Cammelli, *Crisolora*, p. 168 n. 1, quotes Legrand's description of a visit to the grave as it could still be located in the nineteenth century. The tomb inscription is discussed below in n. 41.

33. See "Gemistos, Georgios Plethon," in PLP, no. 3630. For convenience's sake, I have relied here upon Christopher Montague Woodhouse's fundamental book, *George Gemistos Plethon: The Last of the Hellenes* (Oxford: Clarendon Press, 1986); but note also Mergiali-Sathas, *L'enseignement*, pp. 211–12. The prime philosophical study is still François Masai, *Pléthon et le platonisme de Mistra* (Paris: Belles Lettres, 1956); but there is a good sketch of Plethon's career in Steven Runciman's *Mistra, Byzantine Capital of the Peloponnese* (London: Thames & Hudson, 1980), pp. 110–16.

34. Woodhouse, *Plethon*, pp. 128–31; cf. Gill, *Council of Florence*, p. 89 and n. 2.

35. In the collection *Proceedings of the International Congress on Plethon and His Time (Mystras, 26–29 June 2002)*, ed. Linos G. Benakis and Christos P. Baloglou (Athens-Mystras: Société Internationale d'Études Pléthoniennes et Byzantines,

2003), see the articles by Marco Bertozzi, "George Gemistos Plethon and the Myth of Ancient Paganism: From the Council of Ferrara to the Tempio Malatestiano in Rimini," pp. 177–85, and by Andriëtte Stathi-Schoorel, "Plethon the Philosopher of Mystras: Was He Orthodox? Surely Not!" pp. 171–76.

36. The traditional perception is represented by Symonds, *The Renaissance in Italy*, pp. 206–8. But Woodhouse, *Plethon*, esp. pp. 156–70, and 373–74, is rather skeptical as to just how great was the immediate and enduring stimulus Plethon contributed to the intellectual scene in Florence. More conventionally, see Gill, *Council of Florence*, pp. 186–88; Runciman, *Mistra*, p. 116; also Geanakoplos, *Greek Scholars*, pp. 85–86; more superficially, Wells, *Sailing from Byzantium*, pp. 90–103. For all that, the traditional understanding of Ficino and his Academy has been challenged and virtually demolished by the thorough study of James Hankins, "The Myth of the Platonic Academy of Florence," *Renaissance Quarterly* 44 (1991): 429–75.

37. Woodhouse, *Plethon*, pp. 373–75; Symonds, *The Renaissance in Italy*, pp. 34, 209–10; Runciman, *Mistra*, pp. 116–17, 120. Pletho's sarcophagus is in the third from the front of seven arcades on the west (right) side of the building. Its four-line Latin inscription may still be read, and might translate as: "Remains of Iemistius the Byzantine, prince of philosophers of his time, carefully brought here and set herein by Sigismondo Pandolfo Malatesta, son of Pandolfo, commander in the war in Peloponnesus against the king of the Turks, because of the intense love for the learned that inflamed him, in 1465" (IEMISTII · BYZANTII · PHILOSOPHOR · SVA · TEMP · PRINCIPIS · RELIQVVM ·/ SIGISMVNDVS · PANDVLFVS · MAL · PAN · F · BELLI · PELOP · ADVERSVS · TVRCOR ·/ REGEM · IMP · OB · INGENTEM · ERVDITORVM · QVO · FLAGRAT · AMOREM ·/ HVC · AFFERENDVM · INTROQVE · MITTENDVM · CVRAVIT · MCCCCLXV). It may be noted that, of our three scholar-diplomats (four, if we include Bessarion), all but Kydones found their final resting places in European graves—and the Greek Crete where the Latin-Catholic convert Kydones was buried was held then by the Latin Venetians.

38. Documents of 25 August 1413, in Franciscus Palacky, ed., *Documenta Magistri Joannis Hus vitam, doctrinam, causam in Constantiensi Concilio actam et controversias de religione in Bohemia, annis 1403–1418 motas illustrantia* (Prague, 1869; repr. Osnabrück: Biblio-Verlag, 1966), pp. 513–14, no. 56; of 30 August 1413, *Forschungen und Quellen zur Geschichte des konstanzer Konzils*, ed. Heinrich Finke (Paderborn: Ferdinand Schöningh, 1889), p. 243. Cf. Charles-Joseph Hefele, *Histoire des Conciles d'après les documents originaux*, trans. H. Leclercq, 11 vols. (Paris: Letouzey et Áne, 1907–52), vol. 7, pt. 1, p. 101; Cammelli, *Crisolora*, pp. 161–63; Loenertz, "Les dominicains byzantins," p. 12. During early 1414, Chrysoloras remained with Sigismund, and was joined by his nephew, John Chrysoloras, Emperor Manuel's emissary. Sigismund sent John back to Constantinople with a letter (summer, 1414) to Manuel II, inviting him to be represented at the impending council and bestowing German court status upon both nephew and uncle. In his turn, Manuel Chrysoloras himself rejoined John XXIII at Bologna. See Heinrich Finke, ed., *Acta Concilii Constanciensis*, 4 vols.

(Münster: Regensbergsche Buchhandlung, 1896–1928), 1:233–34, and (for the letter) 1:399–401; cf. Loenertz, "Les dominicains byzantins," pp. 12–13.

39. The passage referred to is, unfortunately, not to be found in the modern printed edition by Michael Richard Buck, *Ulrichs von Richental Chronik des Constanzer Concils 1414 bis 1418*, Bibliothek des litterarischen Vereins in Stuttgart 158 (Tübingen: Litterarischer Verein in Stuttgart, 1882). I use it as cited by Loenertz, "Les Dominicains byzantins," p. 14 nn. 36–37.

40. For Zulian's account, see Cammelli, *Crisolora*, pp. 165–66. Citing various sources, Loenertz, "Les dominicains byzantins," pp. 13–14, constructs the hypothesis that Manuel Chrysoloras (together with his nephew, John Chrysoloras) were part of an official Greek delegation at the council. He notes in particular a letter by an unknown Czech writer (Palacky, *Documenta*, p. 538) which speaks of the arrival in Constance on 3 March 1415 (a month and a half before Chrysoloras's death), of "a knight sent by the Greek emperor to deal with the union of the Greeks and the Christians [i.e., Latins]." Loenertz speculates: "Peut-être cet envoyé grec apporta-t-il des lettres de son souverain accréditant Manuel Chrysoloras auprès du concile." He goes on to conclude that "bien qu'il fut venu avec la cour de Jean XXIII, Chrysoloras était consideré à Constance comme chef de l'ambassade grecque." The emissary who arrived on 3 March, according to the Czech source, "marque sans doute la constitution d'une délélgation grecque officiellement accréditée auprès du concile." Loenertz subsequently (*Correspondance de Manuel Calécas*, pp. 70–71) suggests that the Byzantine emissary who arrived on 3 March 1415 was none other than Chrysoloras himself. He also proposed that Chrysoloras did not go to Constance with John XXIII's court in October 1414; rather, Loenertz had Chrysoloras, after a documented (and otherwise unexplained) journey in July 1414 from Bologna to Venice in the company of Guarino, traveling east—for no less a purpose than to meet Emperor Manuel, either on Thasos in late summer of 1410 or at Thessaloniki over the autumn/winter of 1414–15. Loenertz's earlier hypothesis, though not the later one, is followed by Joseph Gill in *The Council of Florence*, pp. 20–21. Dölger, *Regesten*, no. 3329, conflated the sources to designate Chrysoloras as "head" (*Haupt*) of the Byzantine delegation sent to the Council of Constance—two others identified as the Moreote noble Nicholas Eudaimonoioannes and the latter's son Andronikos. But, despite some confusion in the source information, it is clear that the Moreote delegates (now noted as including John Bladynteros) did not arrive at the council at the same time as Chrysoloras, but a good year after his death. They reached Venice in February 1416, where their business was partly to mediate a Dalmatian dispute between Sigismund and Venice, and partly to follow up communications with John XXIII: Dölger, *Regesten*, nos. 3354, 3355; Gill, *Council of Florence*, pp. 21–22; Barker, *Manuel II*, pp. 323–24. Among others, Mergiali-Sahas, "Manuel Chrysoloras, an Ideal Model," p. 11, continues to regard Chrysoloras as "head of an eight-member Byzantine embassy" at the council. Such status is not implausible, but it also remains speculative. There is no clear evidence as to Chrysoloras's movements between July 1414 and March 1415. Nor do we have, in fact, any definitive documentation of

Chrysoloras's formal status at the council vis-à-vis Emperor Manuel II, short of all these inferences and likelihoods. It makes sense to think that Chrysoloras felt capable of speaking for Greek interests, and that he was even informally authorized to do so on a long-standing basis by Manuel; but his attachment to the court of John XXIII must still have been the more immediate basis for his official standing. Still, Mergiali-Sahas, "Byzantine Ambassador to the West," p. 601, offers a compromise classification of Chrysoloras as "a kind of 'double agent'." That might be the simplest resolution of an issue that is perhaps more a modern preoccupation of legalities than would have exercised diplomats of the fifteenth century.

41. Our chief source for the possibility of Chrysoloras's papal candidacy is a flimsy and fulsome one: the epitaph composed by Vergerio for his teacher's tomb. Its final words are: "A man most learned, prudent, and good, who died at the time of the general council of Constance, in such repute that he was held worthy by all of the supreme pontificate" (Vir doctissimus prudentissimus optimus qui tempore generalis concilii constantiensis diem obiit ea estimatione ut ab omnibus summo sacerdotio dignus haberetur). Cf. Cammelli, *Crisolora*, pp. 167–68 and n. 1; Thomson, "Manuel Chrysoloras," pp. 81–82. The inscription's sentiments were echoed in a letter of Guarino and in Zulian's oration. See Cammelli, *Crisolora*, pp. 166–67. How real or widespread this opinion of Chrysoloras might have been is otherwise unattested and quite impossible to judge from these affectionate tributes. Loenertz, "Les dominicains byzantins," pp. 15–16 (extended in his *Correspondance de Manuel Calécas*, pp. 70–71) suggests that Chrysoloras's prospects for achieving the papacy were not so far-fetched, given the symbolism it could have represented in drawing the Greek church to Rome. Loenertz stresses as precedent the recent election of a Greek, Pietro (Petrus) Filargi, as the short-lived Pisan pope Alexander V. But rather than being a "free" Greek of Byzantium, Filargi was a *Cretan* Greek, born a subject of the Venetian Republic, raised a Catholic, and becoming a Franciscan monk who studied at the Universities of Padua, Oxford, and Pavia—a thoroughly Westernized humanist and member of the hierarchical establishment. Thomson, "Manuel Chrysoloras," pp. 81–82, also takes seriously Chrysoloras's papal prospects, even suggesting that the papacy may have been his "eventual aim."

42. As a closing thought, there is an interesting link among three of our four scholar-diplomats, as to their roles in the transmission of ancient Greek texts during the Renaissance. Planoudes was the first to discover the long-neglected text of Ptolemy's *Geography*, drawing it into study and assimilation by Byzantine scholars of the next few generations. Chrysolaras was perhaps the first scholar to bring a copy of its text to Italy, and he helped launch the process of translating into Latin. For his part, Plethon, during his visit to Florence, seems to have given Italian humanists the first stimulation to explore Strabo's *Geography*. Our scholars thus played critical parts in making available to western Europe the geographical knowledge of the ancients that proved so influential at the dawn of the Age of Exploration and Discovery. See Wilson, *Scholars of Byzantium*, pp. 233–34, and *From Byzantium to Italy*, pp. 8–9, 13, 55–56.

THE CHURCH AND THE TURKISH CONQUESTS

The Turkish Conquests and Decline
of the Church Reconsidered

TOM PAPADEMETRIOU

Saintly and ascetic bishops have always existed, as have corrupt and nefarious bishops. During the late Byzantine period, quite a number of bishops under the jurisdiction of the patriarchate of Constantinople were being reprimanded for their lack of discipline and corrupt practices stemming from their dealings with the Turks. The interpretive narrative derived from these cases is that the Turkish conquests were rapacious and "decapitated" the hierarchical leadership in Anatolia. The result of this interpretation is a picture in which the bishops and the church were powerless victims who were cut down by the mighty arm of numberless Turkish hordes. This vision, while capturing a valid aspect of Turkish military campaigns, does not always convey the complexity of the relationships developing between local bishops and the new rulers. Was the local bishop a powerless victim in the face of these enormous social changes?

When considering the many cases in which bishops were accused of being corrupt, of exceeding their jurisdictional authority, and of being disobedient or rebellious against the authority of the holy synod of Constantinople, and ultimately the emperor, the answer is clearly that they were not powerless. Taken at face value, however, the complaints show a declining church with bishops who lacked discipline and were not strong enough to resist the powerful Turkish overlords as they should have. This paper will attempt to re-examine the moments when local bishops in Asia Minor were faced with the reality of often violent change at the hands of the Turks. In an attempt to survive and re-establish their own authority in a new system, bishops appeared open to cooperation with Turkish emirs, in particular, concerning financial arrangements between the local bishop and the emir.

The Church and a Declining State

From the eleventh to the fourteenth century, the Greek Orthodox church gained significant political power just as there was a real decline in Byzantine imperial administration.[1] According to Orthodox ecclesiological terms, each legitimately elected bishop formed the foundation of the local church and was, in a sense, its master. The strict hierarchical structure that developed according to the Justinianic Byzantine imperial model had raised the patriarchate of Constantinople to imperial heights. While Byzantine tradition maintained that the church was under the stewardship and ultimate control of the emperor, it also created significant prestige for the patriarch, who then became a component part of the state structure. In this formulation, church and state had a synergistic relationship, which means that the church shared civil legal principles as well as administrative and judicial duties with the state. The highly centralized church in Constantinople was at times supported by the emperors, who more often than not realized the advantage of working through this institution.[2]

According to historian Michael Angold, the positions of the bishops and metropolitans became increasingly more important to imperial administration during the twelfth century. Relevant developments included the legal reorganization of the twelfth-century canon lawyer Theodore Balsamon, who effectively "enriched [canon law] by annexing much of [civil law]."[3] The jurisdiction of the bishop pertained not only to spiritual matters, but also to civil and judicial matters, particularly in regions outside of the immediate administrative control of Constantinople. For this reason, Byzantine state administration raised the level of the bishop to an important "civil" post, often determining the election of bishops according to political rather than religious priorities.[4]

This interdependence of church and state determined the fate of the church as the state was in the process of contraction. A weakened and decentralized state had grafted much of its civil powers onto the church hierarchy, especially in Anatolia. However, how could the church administration be immune from the very same process of decentralization that the state was experiencing? There is a continued assumption that the church as an institution should have remained hierarchical and centralized while resisting the overall political decentralization and contraction taking place in this later period.[5] In the late Byzantine period, the patriarchate in Constantinople remained the focal point of the Orthodox world, perhaps, more in theory than in fact. Subordinate clergy, including metropolitans and provincial bishops, continued under ecclesiastical jurisdiction of the patriarchate in Constantinople even while their civil authority changed hands. This situation proved difficult for the central authority in Constantinople to accept, and as a result, it resented the activities of accommodation by local hierarchs. It also proved difficult for local hierarchs who were caught between the demands of the synod in Constantinople and the reality they faced on the ground.

In spite of the conflict and difficult balancing act that the provincial clergy faced, the church remained the most widespread and stable Byzantine institution in the Asia Minor provinces.[6] Not only were clergyman responsible for the maintenance of the spiritual life of the empire, but they were charged with specific administrative and judicial functions as well, the mark of a rapidly decentralizing state structure. One example of the church's rising importance in the face of overall Byzantine decline is the prominent role it continued to play in the judicial system, particularly at the beginning of the fourteenth century when there was a general attempt at imperial Byzantine judicial reform. The newly established supreme judicial council of the General Judges of the Romans was made up of four judges, two of whom were ecclesiastics, and two laymen. The judicial reform spawned the proliferation of such courts throughout the provinces of the empire, with clergy taking on the prominent role of judges. Thus, in the late Byzantine period, the clergy played an increasingly important role as judges in the imperial law courts. In addition, an ecclesiastical law court could, when necessary, even replace the imperial courts and authority.[7]

Bishops and Emirs

When imperial control over the church waned, local hierarchs began to disregard the wishes of the central ecclesiastical administration in Constantinople. This was exacerbated under the rule of foreign masters. According to the Byzantine imperial church, however, any adjustments and accommodations made by local bishops to competing political and military power was perceived by the synod of Constantinople as disobedience to the traditional hierarchical order of the holy synod and rebelliousness against the empire. As Theodore Balsamon's balance of power between the church and state had tended towards a type of "caesaropapism," rebellion against the empire and breaking civil law implied breaking canon law as well.[8] With the decline of the state administrative structure in the provinces, however, local hierarchs were left with little choice. Contrary to the theoretical role the hierarchy was supposed to play as representatives of the Byzantine imperial church, the individual hierarchs exercised their privilege of self-determination by making administrative compromises with the new rulers.[9]

Because the ecclesiastical administrative authority of the patriarchate of Constantinople was in the capital city, the Turkish emirates, including the Ottomans, considered local bishops who were elected from the Byzantine center, and who received their episcopal authority from the Byzantine institutional church, as agents of the enemy state. The result was that the bishops would often be forced to flee the provinces to settle in Constantinople, or venture to another Byzantine controlled territory. As individuals, they received stipends for sustenance either from the patriarchal church, or from another revenue producing bishopric assigned by the patriarchal synod. However, some of these local bishops chose to live within the boundaries of a Turkish domain, and as such arranged to coexist with the local emir. In the Ottoman-controlled territory, this was possible largely due to the Ottoman policy of accommodation (*istimalet*) that was the first step in incorporating the entity into the state structure. Going beyond the limits of Islamic law, the Ottomans integrated the church into their administrative system.[10]

How did this integration occur? What elements facilitated this process of integration? The nature of conquests meant that former administrative practices were preserved and absorbed for practical reasons; local populations were thus subdued more easily. The ecclesiastical hierarchy was one such institution that was absorbed by the new masters. From the vantage of the central authority in Constantinople and from the perspective of the local prelates of the provinces, the latter were busy negotiating their existence with their new masters. Considering the situation from the vantage point of the center supposes that theirs was the normative reality, and therefore, one naturally would conclude that any deviations from this normative reality resulted in disobedient bishops.

Examples of interaction between local hierarchy and Turkic emirs are evident in the *Patriarchal Synodal Acta*.[11] The *Acta* give evidence of adjustment to the Turkish conquests and negotiation and collaboration with the new regime. One must interpret local events of resistance as a preservation response, and as part of a longer process of incorporating the Greek Orthodox hierarchy and church into the administrative structure of the conquerors, who, ultimately, were the Ottomans. The church hierarchy and monastic institutions based their relations with Turkish emirs upon shared fiscal interests. Surprisingly, religious and ethnic issues were not of great interest in these negotiations. Understandably, the relations between local emirs and bishops deeply troubled the standing synod in Constantinople. Yet, on the ground, local bishops faced a completely alien ruling regime and had two choices: either flee or capitulate.

It has been argued that the hierarchy was "decapitated" because hierarchs fled their sees for safety.[12] However, evidence from the *Acta* also shows that some bishops chose to stay in their sees and created for themselves a new *modus vivendi*. This new situation spurred cries of injustice from the synod of Constantinople, bemoaning its lack of authority over bishops who chose the latter option of capitulation. The hierarchy and clergy also engaged in disputes among themselves over jurisdiction and property. As will be seen shortly, they chose to solve these disputes by seeking recourse from Turkish authorities, a clear violation of ecclesiastical order. This phenomenon is part of the broader conflict between the centralized, imperial, ecclesiastical bureaucracy and the peripheral tendencies of the provinces. The local hierarchy was still competing with the central administration to see who would play a more significant role. A change in political rule could, thus, be used as an advantage for the local bishop.

In contrast to the Greek Orthodox ecclesiastical structure that had an official political alliance with the Greek Orthodox patriarchate of Constantinople, the non-politically allied Armenian and Syrian patriarchs did not face the same "either/or" choice. By their lack of identification with an enemy state, they were free to pledge loyalty and offer gifts to the new rulers. As a result, they often gained charters of immunity that protected their rights and privileges over their communities.[13] Capitulation was clearly part of their agenda.

The impact of the Turkish invasions on the hierarchy was devastating; some bishops could not report to their proper bishopric and others were forced to flee from their sees because they were violently threatened by the invasions. For assessing the declining number of bishoprics, Speros Vryonis, Jr. relied on the *Notitiae Episcopatuum*, which are lists of the hierarchical sees used by the synods and courts to define seniority and rank that reflected the formal status of the episcopacy.[14] From these lists, he argued, it was possible to measure the contraction of the hierarchy in Asia Minor from the eleventh to the fifteenth century. The presence of a metropolitan see on one list and its disappearance in a subsequent list indicated that there was some type of disruption, namely, either a bishop fled, or was not able to take up his proper appointment. Vryonis argued that one could measure the contraction of ecclesiastical administration by keeping track of what sees were on or off the lists.[15]

From this vantage point, disruption occurred when the metropolitans, archbishops, and bishops were not able to take their places at their own bishopric and were deprived of the ability to be present and to benefit financially from the fiscal holdings. The seizure of their property and income prevented the church from fulfilling important societal duties and functions. Used in this way, the *Notitiae Episcopatuum* argue for a case of massive impoverishment of the church. These lists, however, could also be problematic and certainly require corroborating evidence from other sources to make it convincing.[16] The lists of bishops are known to represent ecclesiastical protocol rather than the actual situation on the ground. For instance, a metropolitan might continue to use the name of his see to identify himself even if he had not been functioning as actual bishop in that place or even if it had become defunct. A corroborating source that does assist in determining whether contraction occurred or not is the collection of synodal decrees from the *Patriarchal Acta* recorded by the patriarchal synod in Constantinople. These *Acta*, however, are uneven as to their content because they record specific ecclesiastical affairs and issues facing the synod of the patriarchate in Constantinople, and they do not reflect the situation in the entire church. The *Patriarchal Acta* show metropolitans that were granted the right to the incomes of other dioceses, "for reasons of sustenance" (kata logon epidoseon).[17] A region that could not sustain a metropolitan or bishop would either be absorbed or absorb another bishopric to make it financially viable. Upheavals caused the phenomenon of absentee metropolitans and bishops. In Vryonis's words, "the victorious *emirs* and *beys* often expelled the hierarchs for extensive periods of time, for as long as 30 years in some cases."[18] Thus, a large number of hierarchs gathered in Constantinople took up temporary postings in other unclaimed bishoprics. But what were the alternatives to flight?

A careful examination of *Patriarchal Acta* reveals that there are twenty-six *Acta* that mention Turks in their text. Often the cases have to do with the local bishop interacting with the local Turkish ruler. These examples can be seen to record discord and oppressive violence, yet they also may represent diverging interests between the hierarchy in the capital and the prelates in the hinterland. Did local bishops resort to accepting the political will of local Turkish emirs because they were forced to, or because they were seeking to escape the centralized control of the Byzantine state? Or were they simply attempting to adjust to the new reality on the ground? Perhaps this is more an issue of the competition of the central authority with the periphery, or even an urban versus rural divide. Most assuredly, however, it was a *Realpolitik* response. Considering this question is helpful because one can begin seeing a different interpretive framework, rather than taking at face value and sympathizing with the testimony of the petitioners and writers of the patriarchal documents. If we consider this aspect of the social transformation taking place in the Byzantine Empire, we may be able to reassess the documents in a slightly different light and offer another dimension to the story of upheaval, impoverishment, lack of discipline among the hierarchy and clergy, and recourse to the Turks.

Cases of Emirs and Bishops

Turning to some examples, we begin with a re-examination of the famous case of Metropolitan Matthew of Ephesos. This is a classic example used by Vryonis for his argument about the Turkish decapitation of the ecclesiastical hierarchy.

In the fourteenth century, the city of Ephesos prospered under the rule of the emirate of Aydin due to good trade relations with the Italian maritime states.[19] General prosperity and thriving city economies in western Asia Minor during the period of the emirates meant that there was a sense of stability with a certain amount of flexibility to allow for commercial cooperation. However, this prosperity contradicts the sorry condition projected by Metropolitan Matthew of Ephesos in his correspondence and in the *Patriarchal Acta*.

As metropolitan of Ephesos, Matthew first appeared in the synodal document of 2 December 1329, and we can trace him in synodal documents at least until June 1339.[20] His main complaint was that he was not allowed to enter into the geographical area in which his see was located. The aforementioned Umur Pasha, the Aydinoglu ruler of Smyrna, was in control of the territory. As a result of his inability to report to his rightful see, Matthew was granted another bishopric's revenue from the area of Thrace which provided his sustenance. Sometime between June 1339 and February 1340

Matthew attempted again to go to Ephesos. He was obliged to offer bribes, so that he was allowed into his bishopric. Although he attempted to gain back the properties and holdings of the church, he was completely unsuccessful in negotiating with Umur Pasha's brother, Khidir. The local church was economically deprived and depended on only six priests to support the work of the entire local community.[21] Matthew says they were not killed or abused because this would have angered the emir, but at the same time, he complains bitterly about the difficulties of not being allowed to take his throne, being deprived of revenues, and about the continued oppression at the hands of the Turkish overlords. If the basic assertions concerning the number of years he was prevented from entering his see, the economic shape of the bishopric, and the small number of priests can be verified, then the situation was, in fact, dismal. However, one must be prepared to look at the matter from an alternative perspective to consider the complexity of the situation and the interests at play.

The first interesting issue to consider is the relationship of the hierarch with the emir of Aydin, Umur Pasha. As mentioned above, many scholars stress the ideological framework of the *ghazi* that would explain an antagonism of the Muslims toward the Christian hierarchs. The *Düstürname* certainly projects Umur Pasha as a *ghazi* even though, clearly, he cooperated fully with both sides of the Byzantine civil conflict.[22] It is, therefore, more useful to frame the question of their relationship in a different way. Moving away from religious or ideological motivations to political and fiscal interests changes the image of their relationship. What reason did Umur Pasha have for allowing the hierarchy of the Orthodox church to re-enter into his territory? Why should a Turkish emir allow a metropolitan, who, in theory, was clearly aligned with the enemy state, to take his place within his own *beylik*? What conditions would the hierarch need to accept to live under Turkish rule? Umur Pasha did not need assistance to subdue the Orthodox population. He was clearly in control of the area. From Matthew's perspective, this meant that most of the Greek Christians were "enslaved."[23] Umur Pasha did not need to elevate or co-opt the local bishop either to claim legitimacy in the eyes of the Orthodox subjects or to gain control of the institutional wealth.

The turning point in Matthew's career came when he decided to follow the advice of an advisor, a man from Chios, who instructed him to offer Umur Pasha a bribe to take his place. He was allowed to take his place in Ephesos only after bribing the emir and giving gifts to the emir's brother. This critical detail is crucial for understanding the relationship of the

Turkish *beylik* vis-à-vis the church hierarchy. The giving of gifts is technically a sign of loyalty and obeisance. In other contexts this may even be a form of *pishkesh,* a type of investiture gift that marks a sign of loyalty to the ruler. There is not much that can be said concerning the gifts to the emir and his brother except to say they were very expensive.[24]

In his correspondence Matthew continued to describe himself nobly as one of the apostles among the non-Greek and non-Orthodox people.[25] Another critical detail to understanding Matthew's position, however, is that he was planning to take over a neighboring metropolis. In this, he opposed the patriarchate in Constantinople. Furthermore, he even became one of the undisciplined metropolitans recorded in a later document because he petitioned the Turkish authorities to support him.

Elizabeth Zachariadou has pointed out the complication in Metropolitan Matthew's case.[26] In 1342, Metropolitan Matthew sought, independently, to ordain one of his own people as bishop to Pyrgion, a nearby city west of Ephesos, and to bring the metropolis under his jurisdiction. In the process, he had accused the current metropolitan of Pyrgion of being a murderer and a perjurer. The synod investigated his charges and found that the metropolitan of Ephesos had manufactured legal charges to subordinate the seat of Pyrgion to the jurisdiction of Ephesos.[27] Matthew went so far as to slander the metropolitan of Pyrgion to Umur Pasha, as well as addressing Umur Pasha as "good son" while he considered himself as the "father."[28] This conflict between Matthew and the metropolitan of Pyrgion, whom Matthew slandered to Umur Pasha to gain Pyrgion's property and revenues, is a situation that was played out many times during Ottoman rule as well.[29]

It is noteworthy that a very common occurrence among the Orthodox hierarchy during the Ottoman period shows up so early. In the Ottoman Empire, one or both ecclesiastical parties were motivated to go to the Ottoman authorities to dispute who controlled the rights to a bishopric's property. In our case, as long as Matthew was identified with the Byzantine state, he could not enter the territory where his episcopal see was located. Yet, when he was able to bribe the emir to pass through his area, and to give gifts to the emir's brother to enter Ephesos, the relationship between the two changed from entirely antagonistic to a somewhat protectionist one based on the dictated terms of the emir, though clearly without the former metropolitan possessions.[30] The attempt to make Metropolitan Matthew of Ephesos a case study of Turkish oppression of the hierarchy raises more questions about the relationship between ruler and ruled than it answers.

From the perspective of Constantinople, it was an example of the lack of ecclesiastical discipline. In the eyes of the patriarchate and the emperor, it is clearly treasonous. However, from the perspective of the local hierarchs who were under the control and power of these local rulers it was expedience, and a new *modus vivendi*. Only by accepting and pledging loyalty to the emirs could they take their proper places. From the perspective of the emirs, these incidents were not calculated and premeditated, but arose out of localized concerns.

Another important pre-Ottoman example was recorded in 1361. The synod complained about having suffered greatly from hierarchs from other jurisdictions encroaching on Constantinopolitan territory. They found the metropolitan of Tyre, who was a suffragan bishop of the patriarchate of Antioch, guilty of encroachment. The complaint was that the metropolitan entered the jurisdiction (*enoria*) of Constantinople, performed priestly functions, ordained clergy, and collected money. These actions were contrary to the canonical order, whereupon a clergyman from outside his jurisdiction must seek permission to enter and act officially. In another case, the metropolitan of Germanoupolis took over two of Constantinople's churches, in Attaleia and Syllaion on the Mediterranean coast near modern-day Antalya. The synod reported that he was able to do this through the authority of the emir in the area. As a result of Germanoupolis's negotiations with the Turkish emir, he held these as his legitimate possession. Constantinople reacted as if it was a case of rebellion. However, the synod could do little more than register the complaint, as they had no real coercive power beyond their verbal condemnation.[31]

Dorotheos, who was the metropolitan of Peritheorion, also sought recourse from the Turks in 1381. Dorotheos had been in prison in Constantinople for an unknown reason. After he escaped, he sought aid from the Turks, and with their backing ruled the church of Peritheorion. Dorotheos refused to return to Constantinople to be judged by the synod. He had made an agreement with the Turks to turn over any prisoners who fled to Peritheorion. The synod was both angry that he honored this apparently dishonorable agreement and that he utilized secular authority, in this case the impious Turks, to take control of the church. The synodal document specifically makes mention of the holy canons and even quotes them as saying "if it happens that any bishop uses lay authority in order to gain control of churches, let him be deposed." The synod recommended that he be removed and exiled not because he "was led astray by the Turks," which they did remark upon, but more so because he had "rejected the authority of this holy synod."[32] As a result the synod deemed that Metropolitan Dorotheos openly rejected Constantinople's imperial and ecclesiastical leadership when in the words of the synodal decree, Dorotheos considered the Turks his "emperors, patriarchs, and protectors."[33]

In another case from 1387, the synod reacted to another situation of direct collaboration between Matthew, the metropolitan of Myra, and an emir who was most likely the Turkish ruler of the Hamid emirate on the Mediterranean coast. The decree claimed that they were both enjoying the spoliation of a metropolitan see belonging to another, namely, Theophilos, metropolitan of Attaleia-Perge. These extra-jurisdictional ecclesiastical properties that were within the emir's territory were granted, by the emir's authority, to the metropolitan of Myra.[34] The patriarchal synod concluded that Metropolitan Matthew of Myra had no right to intervene and take over the prerogatives of the metropolis of Attaleia-Perge. According to the reasoning used by the synod, it was not necessarily unacceptable to receive properties from laypeople or from lay authority, as there was ample precedence for receiving properties from lay benefactors, but rather it was unacceptable because it was a Turkish emir who had made the decision of what should occur with the properties of the church.

The main issue in this incident was that one metropolitan took over the jurisdiction of the other through the designs of the Turkish emir. The issue of taking over abandoned episcopal sees was familiar to the synod, as it was becoming standard practice among provincial bishops. In this case, one solution to this problem might have been to assign the jurisdiction of Attaleia-Perge to the metropolitan Matthew of Myra "for reasons of sustenance" (kata logon epidoseos). It would have been more practical, however, for Attaleia-Perge to have been given over to the needy metropolis of Myra. Metropolitan Theophilos could then have been assigned a bishopric in friendlier territory. The synod, however, did not want to take this approach, because this would appear as if it were condoning the Turkish emir's intervention.

The second important consideration gleaned from this example is that the Turkish emir distributed ecclesiastical jurisdictions and properties to the metropolitan who was cooperative, and was willing to remain under Turkish rule. As a reward for agreeing to stay in his episcopal see, he was granted jurisdiction by the emir that went beyond his enlarged territorial boundaries. The common interest was to use the diocese as an economic revenue source to be exploited jointly. Metropolitan Matthew of Myra was simply shrewd enough to reap the material benefits for having stayed in a

new regime, at the expense, however, of alienating himself from Constantinople.

Another example from the *Patriarchal Acta* of Constantinople concerns
the metropolitan of Chalcedon (Kadiköy) in 1394. When conquering the
regions in Asia Minor across from Constantinople, the Ottomans had taken
over the monastery of Akapnios and its estates, and had granted what would
otherwise be an independent monastery and its properties to the neighboring metropolitan of Chalcedon. Upon learning of this, the patriarchal
synod condemned this transfer.[35] It condemned the metropolitan of Chalcedon for acting as the Ottomans did. The Ottoman intervention irritated
the synod because it was not only a lay authority, but an enemy regime
intervening into ecclesiastical administration. Charging that the metropolitan had violated the holy canons, the synod characterized his sin as greed
and admonished him to read from the work of the third-century writer from
the Pontos, St. Gregory the Wonderworker, on the subject of "greed." The
original context for this "Canonical Epistle" was an unusual incursion by
Goths into Asia Minor to Pontos in AD 257.[36] It is significant that the synod
in 1394 chose this short treatise that details and condemns the sins of
the third-century Christian community of Pontos which collaborated with
Gothic invaders. At the heart of both condemnations were admonishments
of the individuals who out of greed, stole their colleagues' properties.

By focusing on the corrupt and greedy action of an individual, the
synod was responding to a dramatic transition that was taking place threatening the very institution of the church. In this time period, all sorts of
anomalous arrangements were being made that were contrary to the canonical principle of attaching a single bishop to a single see. This would
certainly have caused anxiety among the bishops of the synod in Constantinople, but rather than critique the practice of granting sees "for reasons
of sustenance" (kata logon epidoseon) and, as a result, risk criticizing the
current routine of episcopal appointments, it was easier for the synod to
focus on individuals who clearly were seen as relying for their gain on lay
Turkish authorities. Passing judgment on greedy individuals reflects the fact
that the institution is not being criticized, but it is the corrupt and evil
individuals who deserve stricture. This process of critique might even be
understood to strengthen the power of the synod, which has retained a
moral authority and power of condemnation. In 1394, this meant that the
Ottomans and the metropolitan of Chalcedon had formed a collaborationist
and symbiotic relationship in which the main issue was the collection of
revenues and the administration of property. The synod closed its letter

by warning against the metropolitan being considered a "publican" and "foreigner"—each a terrible characterization.

Another extremely interesting and important example is the accusation levied against Patriarch Matthew I (1397–1410), who was thought to have made secret negotiations with the Ottoman ruler Bayezid in order to preserve his position under the Ottoman regime. At the time of this incident, Bayezid was besieging Constantinople, and things looked rather ominous for the city's inhabitants. While it is unlikely that Patriarch Matthew would have collaborated with the Ottomans, the fact that he felt compelled to respond to this charge in a well-publicized general letter to the faithful in 1401 means that the charge might easily have been believed by his contemporaries. Even if this were a false charge that was motivated by personal envy or political expedience, the fact that his contemporaries were familiar with numerous examples of such collaboration meant that they were conditioned to believe such a charge. The charge had resonance and could be believed even of a patriarch. At any rate, Matthew I felt obliged to dispel any such notions, and he wrote in his defense:

> The claim is that I, having sent a certain person to the emir, arranged for myself to have security from him on my own account in the great city, should indeed it ever be taken. Which act I judge as nothing other than open betrayal of Christ himself.[37]

As patriarch and head of the holy synod, he, of course, denied and even condemned this practice of negotiation with Bayezid.

The Ottomans and the Patriarch

The question remains, however, of what do we make of all the episodes of bishops negotiating with local emirs, and subsequently being condemned by the holy synod. From the standpoint of Constantinople, the story is one of collaboration (in its pejorative sense), greed, betrayal, and corruption. If we take this perspective at face value, surely the situation is bleak and desolate and full of greedy corrupt figures.

The simple counter-response would be to argue that the bishops were simply reacting in a self-preservation mode that would allow them to remain in their churches, and allow for the continuity of their leadership over the Christian population of Asia Minor. Interestingly, we do not find defenses of this nature by any members of this group.

Another way of looking at this situation is to grasp the intentions of the Turkish emirs from their own perspective. While there are no Turkish narrative sources that record these episodes with bishops, there are examples of later Ottoman documents that may reveal how the Turkish emirs considered the bishops and the ecclesiastical institution.

The earliest dated Ottoman document addressed to a Greek Orthodox patriarch of Constantinople (*Istanbul Rum Patrigi*) survives in the monastic archive of Vatopedi on Mount Athos. This document is very explicit in describing the patriarch as a tax farmer and the patriarchate as a tax-farming situation. It is a sultanic decree (*berât*) granted by Bayezid II to Patriarch Symeon sometime between 9 and 18 April 1483 during the latter's third term in office.[38] Patriarch Symeon, who was from Trebizond, was appointed as a tax farmer using the specialized Ottoman term *mültezim*. He was granted the right to travel in person to the sixty-four districts listed in the *berât* to collect taxes in order to submit two thousand gold florins to the imperial treasury (*hazine-i 'amir*). The patriarch was given responsibility over all the metropolitans, bishops, priests, monasteries, and their holdings. These individuals in turn were required to pay to the patriarch the amounts they had collected from their own jurisdictions. The patriarch, thus, was required to submit taxes to the imperial treasury for the entire church.

This document was issued to a sitting patriarch when the Ottomans were firmly in control of Constantinople and beginning their Mediterranean expansion. It is apparent that this is a fiscal document detailing financial responsibilities to the Porte. From this and other Ottoman documents, it appears that the Ottomans were concerned about the fiscal obligations of the church. This is not unusual, because the church was traditionally a tax exempt institution under Islamic law, which the Ottomans could not exploit. However, by treating the patriarch as a tax farmer similar to any other tax farm in the Ottoman realm, the Ottomans could extend their reach into the ecclesiastical economy as well.

For the emirs, the bishops posed a bit of an enigma, a figure of authority that was affiliated with an enemy state. However, just as local Byzantine cities and military leaders capitulated to Turkish rule by various means, the bishops were often faced with the choice of fleeing or capitulating, and often chose to stay. This, of course, is registered in the patriarchal documents with deep shock and disappointment. If we settle for Constantinople's assessment, then we may miss a more complex and interesting reality of the relationships between the emirs and the bishops.

NOTES

1. For a comprehensive discussion of this development see, Michael Angold, *Church and Society in Byzantium under the Comneni, 1081–1261* (Cambridge: Cambridge University Press, 1995).

2. Speros Vryonis, Jr., *The Decline of Medieval Hellenism in Asia Minor and the Process of Islamization from the Eleventh through the Fifteenth Century* (Berkeley and Los Angeles: University of California Press, 1971), p. 198. The issue of a centralized church based in Constantinople contrasts with the highly decentralized church which is the picture that we get in the Ottoman situation.

3. Angold, *Church and Society*, p. 8.

4. Helen Saradi, "Imperial Jurisdiction over Ecclesiastical Provinces: The Ranking of New Cities as Seats of Bishops or Metropolitans," in *Byzantium in the 12th Century*, ed. Nicolas Oikonomides (Athens: Hetaireia Byzantinon kai Metabyzantinon Meleton, 1991), pp. 150–51 nn. 6, 8.

5. Vryonis, *Decline*, pp. 76–77.

6. George Ostrogorsky, *History of the Byzantine State*, trans. Joan Hussey (Oxford: Blackwell, 1956), p. 487.

7. Ostrogorsky, *History of the Byzantine State*, p. 504. For more on the General Judges see, Paul Lemerle, "Documents et problèmes nouveaux concernant les Juges généraux," Δελτίον τῆς Χριστιανικῆς Ἀρχαιολογικῆς Ἑταιρείας, 4, no. 4 (1966): 29–44; Paul Lemerle, "Le juge général des Grecs et la réforme judiciaire d'Andronic III," in *Mémorial Louis Petit* (Bucharest: Institute français d'études byzantines, 1948), pp. 292–316; Paul Lemerle, "Recherches sur les institutions judiciaires à l'époque des Paléologues. I: Le tribunal impérial," in *Mélanges Henri Grégoire*, 4 vols., Annuaire de l'Institut de philologie et d'histoire orientales et slaves 9–12 (Brussels: Secretariat des editions de l'Institut de philologie et d'histoire orientales et slaves, Université Libre de Bruxelles, 1949–53), 1:369–384; Paul Lemerle, "Recherches sur les institutions judiciaires à l'époque des Paléologues. II. Le tribunal du patriarchat ou tribunal synodal," *Mélanges Paul Peeters*, 2 vols., Analecta Bollandiana 67–68 (Brussels: Société des Bollandistes, 1949–50), 2:318–33. In his discussion of legal issues during the Ottoman period Nikolaos Pantazopoulos argued that the dispensation of justice fell into the hands of the church during the late Byzantine period, and in particular, because the hierarchs became the leaders in each of the councils of general judges. More importantly, he argued that because the military and political authorities fell under the court's judicial jurisdiction, therefore, the church was the real head of the court and ultimate authority in charge. This can be debated, however, in cases where decentralization is already in effect, and the bishop represents just one among many competing interests. See Nikolaos Pantazopoulos, *Church and Law in the Balkan Peninsula during the Ottoman Rule* (Thessaloniki: Institute for Balkans Studies, 1967), pp. 39–43.

8. Angold, *Church and Society*, pp. 102–3.

9. Speros Vryonis argues that the dissolution of state control, and the subsequent weakening of the official church hierarchy in Asia Minor by the repeated and violent Turkish invasions, led to large-scale conversions and the Turkification of Asia Minor; see Vryonis, *Decline*, p. 500. Vryonis attempts to show both the Byzantine and Turko-Islamic factors producing the vast cultural transformation in Asia Minor. In doing so, he focuses extensively on Byzantine political and cultural decline, and Turko-Islamic political and cultural ascendance.

10. Halil Inalcik, "The Status of the Greek Orthodox Patriarch under the Ottomans," *Turcica* 21–23 (1991): 407–37 (p. 409).

11. Miklosich-Müller, vols 1 and 2. Some of the documents of the patriarchal register have been re-edited by Herbert Hunger and Otto Kresten, *Das Register des Patriarchats von Konstantinopel*, 3 vols., Corpus Fontium Historiae Byzantinae 19 (Vienna: Österreichische Akademie der Wissenschaften, 1981–2001). See also Jean Darrouzès, *Les regestes des actes du patriarcat de Constantinople*, vol. 1, *Les actes des patriarches*, fasc. 5–7 (Paris: Institut français d'études byzantines, 1977–91) (detailed survey of patriarchal documents from 1310 to 1453)

12. Speros Vryonis, Jr., "Decisions of the Patriarchal Synod in Constantinople as a Source for Ottoman Religious Policy in the Balkans prior to 1402," *ZRVI* 19 (1980): 283–97.

13. Vryonis, *Decline*, p. 199. Vryonis offers a lengthy example of the Armenian patriarch Basil (ca.1090–91) who appealed to the sultan Malik Shah for lenient treatment. After offering many gifts of gold, silver, and cloths, he received exemption for the churches, monasteries, and priests of all payments, and received honors as well.

14. Vryonis, *Decline*, p. 302. See *Notitiae episcopatuum ecclesiae constantinopolitanae*, ed. Jean Darrouzès, Géographie ecclésiastique de l'Empire byzantin 1 (Paris: Institut français d'études byzantines, 1981) Also see Joan M. Hussey, *The Orthodox Church in the Byzantine Empire*, Oxford History of the Christian Church (Oxford: Clarendon Press, 1986), who echoes this.

15. Vryonis, *Decline*, pp. 302–10, esp. p. 311, where he explains: "The *Patriarchal Acta* therefore furnish further striking confirmation of the highly disruptive character of the Turkish conquest, a characteristic already established from chroniclers and other contemporary literature."

16. Michael Hendy warns against the unreliable nature of the *notitiae* and argues that because of their deceptive nature they require corroborating evidence, which is almost impossible to come by. See Michael Hendy, *Studies in the Byzantine Monetary Economy, C. 300–1450* (Cambridge: Cambridge University Press, 1985) pp. 68–145. Also see Michael Angold, *Church and Society*, p. 140 n. 4.

17. Vryonis, *Decline*, pp. 288–302, offers analysis of this phenomenon when he examines 140 *Acta*.

18. Speros Vryonis, Jr., "The Byzantine Patriarchate and Turkish Islam," *Byzantinoslavica* 57 (1996): 68–111 (p. 75).

19. Clive Foss, *Ephesos after Antiquity: A Late Antique, Byzantine and Turkish City* (Cambridge: Cambridge University Press, 1979), p. 158; Paul Lemerle, ed., *L'émirat d'Aydin, Byzance et l'Occident: Recherches sur "La Geste d'Umur Pacha"*, Bibliothèque byzantine, Études 2 (Paris: Presses universitaires de France, 1957).

20. Miklosich-Müller, 1:149–51; Hunger and Kresten, *Das Register,* vol. 1, no. 100; Darrouzès. *Les regestes des actes,* no. 2153 (December 1329).

21. Max Treu, *Matthaios Metropolit von Ephesos: Über sein Leben und seine Schriften* (Potsdam: Programm des Victoria-Gymnasiums zu Potsdam, 1901); for extensive excerpts of Matthew of Ephesos's correspondence see Vryonis, *Decline,* pp. 345–46.

22. Irène Mélikoff-Sayar, ed., *Le Destan d'Umur Pacha,* Bibliothèque byzantine, Documents 2 (Paris: Presses universitaires de France, 1954); Elizabeth Zachariadou, "Holy War in the Aegean," in *Latins and Greeks in the Eastern Mediterranean after 1204,* ed. Bernard Hamilton, Benjamin Arbel, and David Jacoby (London: Cass, 1989), pp. 212–25.

23. Vryonis, *Decline,* p. 348.

24. Vryonis, *Decline,* p. 347.

25. Vryonis, *Decline,* p. 345.

26. Elizabeth Zachariadou, *Deka Tourkika engrapha gia ten Megale Ekklesia: 1483–1567* (Athens: Ethniko Hidryma Ereunon, Institouto Byzantinon Ereunon, 1996), p. 96 n. 21, suggests that Vryonis took only Matthew's side and did not consider that Matthew was also in conflict with the patriarchate over the metropolis of Pyrgion.

27. Vryonis, *Decline,* p. 328.

28. Miklosich-Müller, 1:237. Also see Vryonis, *Decline,* p. 332 n. 220.

29. Miklosich-Müller, 1:236. Also see Vryonis, *Decline,* pp. 326–27 and 332. See also Zachariadou, *Deka Tourkika engrapha,* p. 96 n.21.

30. Miklosich-Müller, 1:235–37.

31. Miklosich-Müller, 1:412, 511–12

32. Miklosich-Müller, 2:38. Also see Vryonis, *Decline,* p. 332. The document's reference to the holy canons is unavailable to the present author.

33. Miklosich-Müller, 2:38. Also see Vryonis, *Decline,* p. 332.

34. Miklosich-Müller, 2:92–95. Also see Vryonis, *Decline,* p. 333.

35. Miklosich-Müller, 2:200–201. Also see Vryonis, *Decline,* p. 333.

36. Michael Slusser, ed., *St. Gregory Thaumaturgus: Life and Works,* The Fathers of the Church 98 (Washington, D.C.: Catholic University of America Press, 1998), p. 2 n. 8. For this passage see "Canonical Epistle," pp. 147–51.

37. Miklosich-Müller, 2:626. See the translation in John W. Barker, *Manuel II Palaeologus (1391–1425): A Study in Late Byzantine Statesmanship* (New Brunswick: Rutgers University Press, 1969), pp. 208–11.

38. Zachariadou, *Deka Tourkika engrapha*, p. 157, plate 1a.

From Constantinople to Moscow

The Fourteenth-Century Liturgical Response to the Muslim Incursions in Byzantium and Russia

PHILIP SLAVIN

Magistro meo Amnon Linder

The Western liturgy of war has long been a subject of scholarly in-vestigation.[1] Intensive research has been carried out particularly in recent years. One has to mention the studies undertaken by Penny Cole,[2] Christoph Maier,[3] Alison McHardy,[4] Michael McCormick,[5] and especially Amnon Linder,[6] who edited over one hundred liturgical texts in his recent monumental study *Raising Arms: Liturgy in the Struggle to Liberate Jerusalem in the Late Middle Ages*.[7] However, the issue has been studied from the Western perspective only, while its Byzantine counterpart has been nearly entirely neglected. The purpose of the present paper is to examine a liturgical cor-pus produced in Byzantium around the middle of the fourteenth century in a response to a sociopolitical crisis created by civil wars, the outburst of the Black Death, the Zealot movement of Thessaloniki, and continuous Turkish invasions.[8] At least twenty-two new prayers were composed between ca. 1336 and ca. 1360, and there are more scattered around in various manuscripts.[9] Those known have been published in 1730 in Jacques Goar's *Euchologion*[10] as well as in 1901 in Dmitrievskii's description of liturgical manuscripts kept in the libraries of the Christian East.[11] In order to bring the unknown prayers to light, I have started compiling a catalogue of un-published prayers.[12]

When reading and analyzing these prayers one has to pose several questions. What do they reflect? What information can we glean from them?

What is their broader historical significance? In the course of the discussion, I shall attempt to answer these questions. The discussion will be built in the following four stages: first, identifying, classifying, locating, and dating the prayers; second, analyzing the prayers in terms of theme and structure; third, comparing the prayers to their Western counterpart; and fourth, showing their importation into fourteenth-century Russia, itself attacked by a Muslim foe, the Tatars.

Classification and Identification

One can divide our prayers into thematic subcategories, an approach used by Miguel Arranz in his editions of prayers and other liturgical texts:[13] first, prayers against heathens (MIL 1); second, prayers against civil enemies (MIL 2); third, prayers against heathens and civil enemies together (MIL 3); fourth, prayers against wars and mortality (MIL 4).

MIL 1

[1:1]. *Office against the advance of barbarians and heathen invasions* (GOA, p. 641=ZER, p. 561)

It is impossible to identify the office, but it was probably compiled sometime in the course of the fourteenth century.

[1:2–9]. *Canon of supplication to the Most Holy Mother of God in the expectation of war* (GOA, pp. 642–44=ZER, pp. 562–67=MOG, pp. 159–67)

The canon is entitled *Ōda Iōannou*, but it does not provide any further information about the author, John. It is clear that he was not a leading ecclesiastical figure, for otherwise he would be referred to by his official title like the authors of other prayers. So one might hypothesize that he was a priest or a monk. The text of the canon reveals its provenance and suggests an approximate date of the composition. A continuous appeal to the Virgin and a plea for the salvation of her city reveals that it was composed in Constantinople, whose saintly patron was the Virgin. The reference to fear and a feeling of captivity of the citizens of Constantinople might suggest that it was written in or shortly after 1354 under the immediate impact of the fall of the strategic fort of Gallipoli on the Hellespont. Demetrios Kydones, a contemporary of the events, notes that after the news of the fall of Gallipoli had reached Constantinople, its population was stricken with fear. "Are we surrounded by the walls of the city or captivated by the armies of the heathen?" the citizens asked themselves.[14] If this interpretation is correct, then the author of the canon was an anonymous priest or monk, whose *floruit* can be located in Constantinople around the year 1354/55. The prosopographical guide to the Palaiologan period lists at least four possible candidates for the identification,[15] but it would be rash to prefer any of them unless further information on our John emerges.

The shadowy John was certainly not the first one to appeal to the Mother of God in times of troubles. There was a long hymnographic and homiletic tradition centered on the Virgin. While its roots can be traced back to late antiquity,[16] the hymnographic and homiletic development becomes especially evident during the iconoclast period (726–843), when the Virgin became increasingly associated with the material world and humanity.[17] The Virgin's human nature enabled her to become the protector, defender, and intercessor in all things worldly and terrestrial. War was certainly one of them. In his famous third homily on the attack on Constantinople by the Rus in June 860, Patriarch Photios beseeches the Mother of God to save the city and deliver its faithful from the wrath of the invaders.[18] Similarly, the anonymous sixth-century *Akathistos Hymn*, which served as a source of inspiration for Photios's homily, depicts the Virgin as victorious in the battle against the barbarian invaders.[19] When Dorotheos, metropolitan of Mitylene, delivered his homily on the siege of Constantinople by the Turks in 1422, he borrowed large pieces from Photios's homily.[20]

The perception of the Mother of God as a victorious intercessor was not confined to homiletic and liturgical texts. Iconography was yet another expression of this role of the Virgin. Marian icons were protective symbols for cities and armies in times of war, and they served as visual objects of veneration before battles and after victories.[21]

> [1:10]. *Prayer of Makarios Chrysokephalos of Philadelphia against heathen invasions* (GOA, pp. 645–46=ZER, pp. 567–69=PG 150, cols. 237–40=MOG, pp. 167–70)

The content of the prayer suggests that it was written during a siege. Makarios's long term in office as metropolitan bishop of Philadelphia (1336–82) knew at least one siege laid by the Turks between the fall of 1335 and the spring or summer of 1336.[22] The prayer might have been composed in the spring or summer of 1336, namely, shortly after Makarios's consecration, or later during his episcopate.

[1:11]. *Another prayer against heathen invasions* (GOA, pp. 646–47=ZER, pp. 569–72=MOG, pp. 171–74)

The author, provenance and exact date of the prayer are unknown, although it is likely to have been written somewhere between ca. 1340 and ca. 1360, if we judge from its structure and contents, which are similar to those of other newly composed prayers.

[1:12]. *Another prayer of Kallistos for similar circumstances* (GOA, pp. 649–50=ZER, pp. 575–76)

The author in question is the patriarch of Constantinople, Kallistos I (1350–53, 1355–63). This prayer conveys an image of captivity already described above in MIL 1:2–9. This could imply that the prayer was also composed shortly after 1354/55 under the immediate impact of the fall of Gallipoli and after Kallistos was reappointed to his office.

[1:13]. *Another prayer of Kallistos for the Christian people* (GOA, pp. 650–51= ZER, pp. 577–78=MOG, pp. 178–80)

Again, the image of captivity could mean it was composed in or shortly after 1354.

[1:14]. *Prayer of Gregory Palamas of Thessaloniki against heathen invasions* (PAL, pp. 311–12)

Robert Sinkewicz dated this prayer to ca. 1350, and there is no way to offer a more precise date.[23]

[1:15]. *Prayer of the most holy patriarch Lord Philotheos against enemies* (DMI, p. 290)

It is unclear what enemies of the emperor are mentioned here, civil or foreign. At any rate, it was composed during the first brief term in office of Patriarch Philotheos Kokkinos in 1353–54 (patriarch again in 1364–76).

[1:16]. *Order of chanting during an assault of barbarians and heathen invasions* (MOG, pp. 157–59)

Unfortunately, I have not seen the prayer in its genuine Greek version, but only in its Church Slavonic translation found in the *Potrebnik* of Petro Mogila (1646). The prayer concentrates on the war against the Turks. Neither author, nor provenance or date, can be established.

MIL 2

[2:1]. *A prayer of Kallistos for the emperor and his army* (GOA, pp. 651–52= ZER, pp. 578–79)

The prayer does not speak of a Turkish invasion, but only of sedition and rebels. The civil war in question is that between John V Palaiologos and John VI Kantakouzenos, which resumed in the summer of 1352 and continued until the end of 1354. Hence, the prayer must have been composed between the summer of 1352 and the end of 1354. In fact, I would prefer to date it between the summer of 1352 and August of 1353, namely, before Kallistos resigned from his office and retired to the Iviron monastery until he was called back in the beginning of 1355. During his retirement, Kallistos was politically inactive, and, therefore, it would be unjustified to suppose that he continued writing military prayers, being remote from the main events.

[2:2]. *Another prayer of Kallistos on the feast of the Elevation of the most honorable and life-giving Cross* (GOA, pp. 652–53)

Just like the previous prayer, this one says nothing about the Turks and beseeches God to assist the emperor in the civil strife. The most probable date for it would be 14 September 1352, the feast of the Elevation of the Cross.

MIL 3

[3:1]. *Prayer of the most holy patriarch Kallistos in people's calamity. Can be also said during deadly pestilence* (GOA, p. 648=ZER, pp. 572–73= MOG, pp. 175–77)

The prayer speaks both of Turkish invasions and a civil war. During the second stage of the civil war (1352–54), Kantakouzenos used Turkish mercenaries twice: in the summer and winter of 1352.[24] Hence, it is possible that it was then that the prayer was composed.

[3:2]. *Philotheos's prayer to the most holy Mother of God* (DMI, pp. 288–89=MOG, pp. 179–82).

This prayer conveys the image of "captivity" and therefore is dateable to the year of 1354 during the first term in office of Patriarch Philotheos.

MIL 4

[4:1–2]. *Two prayers of Kallistos for people in calamity. Can be also said during deadly pestilence* (GOA, pp. 648–49=ZER, p. 574=MOG, pp. 177–78)

Kallistos mentions here a terrible mortality, by which he, probably, means the Black Death. Hence, these prayers could have been composed either during the disastrous year of 1347 (before Kallistos was appointed as a patriarch) or during the renewed outbreak of the plague in 1361/62.[25]

So, out of twenty-two votive prayers, sixteen are dedicated to the war with the Turks, two to a civil strife, two more to the war against the Turks and a civil war simultaneously, and another two to a plague and a war together. In other words, the exceeding majority of the prayers have the war conflict with the Turks as their main subject. This circumstance itself shows that the Turkish incursions were the main liturgical concern in the years of the mid-fourteenth century crisis.

Prayers against Heathens: Biblical and Hellenic Dimensions (MIL 1, MIL 3, and MIL 4)

Prayers against heathens are characterized by a dichotomy between two dimensions. One is biblical, with Judeo-Christian motives and ideals, while the other is purely Hellenic, classical, and patriotic in its character. The two dimensions coexist and complement rather than contradict each other. This should not be a surprise, for Byzantine civilization grew out of these two cultures, adopting and preserving their values.

Let us turn first to the biblical dimension of the prayers. The ideological core here is the war between Christianity and Islam, between light and darkness, between God and Satan. The Turks are never referred to by their proper name, but are rather called ungodly ones, heathens,[26] Ishmaelites, and Hagarenes.[27] They are described as ferocious lions, dogs, bulls, and wolves desiring to devour lambs, namely Christians, who are butchered mercilessly.[28] The infidel armies are penetrating into God's inheritance and vineyards in order to pollute them.[29] The frequent motif of pollution of the inheritance is taken from the Psalm 78 (79): "Lord, the heathen are come to Thy inheritance."[30] Most of the prayers use and quote the verses of the Psalm in order to underline the biblical dimension of the war with heathens. The latter plunder God's temples, altars, and property of the church, threatening the Holy City itself.[31] Constantinople (in fact, any Byzantine city attacked by the Turks) is depicted here as Jerusalem, the Holy City, which the infidel are trying to conquer.[32] The Christians living there feel surrounded not by the mighty walls of the city, but by wicked armies of the infidels, which keep them as though in captivity. This serves as a mirror to the contemporary mood and reflects well the feeling of the captivity discussed above.[33] Fearing destruction, the Byzantines plead God and the Virgin Mary to release them and their city from the heathen hordes.[34] Besides the fear of perdition, there is also a fear of exile. Hence, there is repetitive supplication to God not to let the infidel force the Christian people into a faraway land, where the true God is unknown. There, far from the divine temples, one will not be able to praise God.[35] The idea of exile and destruction of the temples seems to derive from the Babylonian captivity, which occurred after the destruction of the First Temple by the hordes of Nebuchadnezzar.

However, the Christian people are to be saved by God. With the help of God, the Virgin Mary, and the military angels, the Christian army shall rise and slay the heathens who do not acknowledge the Word of God.[36] Here the Christians are identified with different biblical figures, like Moses, Joshua Ben Nun, Gideon, and David, who fought and conquered their pagan enemies.[37] The Turks are compared to Pharaoh, Sennacherib, Adad, the king of Edom, Madianites, and Amalecites.[38] After the heathen armies have been crushed, they shall acknowledge the True God, namely, convert to Christianity.[39] In other words, the ultimate purpose of the war against the infidel is his conversion.

The Christians are not flawless: the invasion of the Turks is understood here as divine punishment for multiple sins, blasphemies, and impiety.[40] So the calamities are not coming from nowhere, and the immoral behavior of the contemporary Christians is the first and foremost cause of their misfortunes. Hence the prayers implore God to forgive their sins and to avert his anger from the wicked and perverse generation (again, the motif is taken from Psalm 78).[41] The Christians are aware of their multiple sins, and they repent like the repenting Publican and Ninevites.[42] God cannot forsake his children in the darkest hour of need and, therefore, one prays for salvation from the heathen yoke.

So far we have seen the biblical dimension of the prayers. Let us now turn to the classical level, which reveals a Hellenic, ethnic, and patriotic character. The war with the Turks is not only the confrontation of Christianity with Islam, but also of the Hellenes with the barbarians. Here the Turks are called "barbarians," while their rulers (emirs) are referred to as "satraps," "kings," "tyrants," and "princes of barbarian lands."[43] The terms satraps and kings (*basileis*) are used in their negative sense, implying the leaders and rulers of Persia, namely, Turkish rulers (unlike the *basileis* used in reference to the Christian emperors, or the *basileus*, in reference to God). This goes back to Herodotus, who referred to the Persian rulers as *basileis* and their governors as *satrapai*.[44] What is striking, though, is that in the Herodotean vocabulary the term *tyrannoi* signified actually local Hellenic

rulers, not the Persian ones.[45] In the classical sense, the Persians were always
seen as ruthless barbarians, invading territories of free Greece. They also
were perceived as culturally inferior to the Greeks. Contemporary authors,
such as John Kantakouzenos and Nikephoros Gregoras, called the Turks
"Persians," while their leaders were referred to as "satraps."[46] The war between Byzantium and the Turks was understood, therefore, as a renewed
struggle between the ancient Greeks and Persians. No doubt, the frequent
reference to the Persians in liturgy, historiography, and rhetoric of the mid-
fourteenth century reflects the Hellenic revival under the Palaiologoi.[47]
Having lost much of its territories between the eleventh and the fourteenth
century, Byzantium progressively became a homogeneous Greek state. Permanent confrontations with foreign enemies, like the Turks and Latins,
contributed increasingly to the formation of what can be called in modern
terms "Hellenic national consciousness." One prayer (composed in the fifteenth century and still unedited) begins with the appeal "Kyrie, ho theos
hēmōn, ho tous basileis tōn Helēnōn phēmōsas."[48] Some late intellectuals,
such as John Argyropoulos (1415–87), native of Constantinople, who ended
his days in Italy, certainly considered themselves and their rulers Hellenes,
not Romans.[49] It should be noted, however, that the official imperial ideology of Byzantium as successor of the Roman Empire persisted well until
1453.[50]

As we have stated above, the ethnic element of the prayers goes hand
in hand with their biblical dimension. Sometimes, the two dimensions are
interwoven. An excellent example of it might be the incipit of the fifth *Ode
of John*: "Satrapai, tyrannoi, basileis archontes chōrōn barbarikōn epi kakō
symphronēsantes kata tautēs sou tēs poi mnēs."[51] Clearly enough, it is a
paraphrase of Psalm 2:2: "parestēsan hoi basileis tēs gēs kai hoi archontes
synēchthēsan epi to kata tou kyriou kai kata christou autou." The classical
terminology is mixed here with biblical Hebrew idioms, emphasizing how
deeply the two dimensions are mixed with each other.

Prayers against Civil Wars (MIL 2 and MIL 3)

Let us turn now to the prayers aimed against civil wars. The late Byzantine
prayers against civil strife plead God to be a firm shield of the emperor
and his loyal subjects and to strengthen his armies in the struggle with his
enemies.[52] They distinguish between two kinds of enemies: visible and invis-
ible.[53] They bid God to let the Christ-loving emperor emerge victorious and
subdue all his enemies beneath his feet.[54] Again, the emperor is identified

here with various biblical figures, such as Abraham, Moses, Joshua Ben Nun, Gideon, and David, who overcame their enemies (note that all these figures represent leaders of the ancient Hebrews).[55] However, victory is not the ultimate goal here, but a condition for the continuation of the emperor's reign. The prayers beseech God to help the emperor to expand the limits of his empire and to bestow peaceful times upon his reign, both over land and sea.[56] There is an imploration that the emperor be preserved from civil strife, rebellion, and opponents.[57] The key terms used here are *stasis* (sedition, rebellion) and *emphylioi polemoi* (internecine or civil wars): none shall ever rise against his authority given to him by God—a reference both to the invading Turks and civil opponents. After their defeat, his opponents must learn that there is only one true *basileus*, namely Christ.[58] Since the terrestrial emperor symbolizes the heavenly one, there cannot be more than one earthly ruler, and the legitimate *basileus* is to subdue the rival *basileus*. Once the order and unification of the empire is restored, the subjects of the emperor shall glorify God's name "with one piety and with one heart."[59] Again, the prayers call upon the Virgin Mary, the guardian angels, and the saints for intercession. Interestingly enough, one prayer speaks of emperors in the plural (*hoi basileis*). This could imply that its compiler must have referred not only to the current emperor, under whom the prayer was composed, but to the following emperors to come. In other words, the authors intended that their prayers would serve not only their generation, but also generations to come.

Evolution and Polysemy of the Prayers

Although the prayers in question were composed during the disastrous years of the mid-fourteenth century, they have old roots. In fact, they evolved out of other cognate and kindred rites. One such rite was the imperial liturgy, namely, prayers said for the emperor on different occasions, such as coronation and war.[60] As we have said above, this liturgy was born probably in the late Roman Empire. The earliest surviving example is the famous Euchologion Barberini gr. 336, dated to the second half of the eighth century.[61] In fact, these prayers are found in most of the extant *euchologia*. The imperial prayers beseech God to keep the emperor alive;[62] to subdue all the barbarian nations under his feet;[63] to bestow peace upon his reign.[64] Similarly, they call the emperor "the most pious"[65] and the heathens "warlusting";[66] speak of the emperor in plural;[67] and ask for the intercession of the Virgin Mary and all the saints.[68]

Another liturgical rite serving as a source for our prayers is earlier votive prayers against different calamities, such as drought, earthquake, bad harvest, and pestilence.[69] Rites devoted to most of these calamities include a nine-ode canon dedicated to the Virgin Mary (a standard liturgical form), which corresponds structurally and ideologically with the nine-ode canon of MIL 1:2 (the *Ode of John*).[70] Furthermore, the votive prayers present disasters as a divine punishment.[71] Hence the prayers call for penance and forgiveness of sins.[72] Nearly every prayer begs God to avert his anger from the suffering Christians and to set them free from calamity.[73] Again, the Virgin, martyrs and saints play here the role of intercessors.[74] Often enough there is a plea to save a city from a number of disasters, which might include ones which are not the prayer's immediate aim.[75] For example, the *Nine Odes against Drought* bid the Virgin Mary to release her "city and people from barbarian assault, famine, pestilence, earthquake and from any sinister disaster."[76] The *Nine Odes against Earthquake* implore God to save the city from "quake, sword, severe captivity, incursion and attack of heathens, famine and from any other calamity."[77] One can notice the use of well-known Psalm 78 (79).[78] For instance, the *Nine Odes against Earthquake* beseech God to not let his inheritance perish.[79] Another prayer against earthquakes implores God to keep his people from the hands of barbarians, so that the latter would not ask "where is your God?"[80] One can infer that odes dedicated to the Virgin Mary were a normal liturgical practice during disastrous times and assaults of heathens or civil foes.

It is quite clear that John, the phantom author of the late Byzantine odes, had earlier votive prayers as a model for his composition. First, he composed his prayer in the form of the Nine Odes canon. Second, the prayers were centered on the Virgin Mary as the main intercessor. Third, although their main intention was to protect the faithful from warfare and chaos, the prayers contained more pleas, such as protection from famine, pestilence, earthquake, and various other calamities.

This brings us to another aspect of military prayers: their polysemy, namely, multitude of meanings and goals.[81] They should not be seen as an independent liturgical genre, standing alone. They constitute an entity, a mosaic, which was constructed from different pieces of a puzzle taken from other, earlier kindred rites. These rites are votive prayers on liberation from natural disasters such as drought, earthquake, famine, pestilence and others. Therefore, our military prayers must be understood and studied in the wider context of cognate votive prayers. The *Nine Odes against Earthquake* do not only beseech God to save his people from earthquake, which is the subject of the *Odes*, but they also beg him to spare them from other disasters, which are subjects of other votive prayers. Similarly, the prayer MIL 3:2 implores God to save his beloved city not only from wars, but also from famine, death, earthquake, drought, flood, and fire. In other words, our military prayers aim at more than one target, and they are ready to answer more than one challenge. This was dictated by the harsh reality of the day. For example, the year 1347 saw continuing Turkish incursions, the Zealot riot in Thessaloniki, and an outburst of the Black Death. The year of 1354 witnessed assaults of the Turks, a severe earthquake which devastated the coast of Thrace, and a civil strife between John V Palaiologos and John VI Kantakouzenos. Hence, the polysemous dimension of the military prayers answered well the needs of late Byzantine society, which experienced more than one crisis at the same time. However, the prayers attempted to achieve yet another goal: forgiveness of sins through penance. Often enough, one encounters elements and motives of the penitential liturgy, which served as an additional source of evolution and borrowing for our prayers.[82] As we have seen above, our prayers identify the contemporary generation with the Ninevites, the praying Publican and the repenting thief, crucified alongside with Christ; most of the prayers implore God to receive the penance.[83] These and other motives are found in various penitential prayers. In other words, in studying the military prayers one always needs to take into account the penitential liturgy.

To conclude, the military prayers are a complex phenomenon. They should by no means be seen as a separate rite which developed independently of other cognate rites. In fact, they evolved out of earlier liturgical rites, borrowing their structures, ideas, and motifs. Those liturgical rites were prayers for the emperor, votive prayers against various calamities, and, finally, penitential prayers. The reason for this complexity is clear: our prayers intended to achieve more than one goal.

Byzantine Military Prayers and Their Western Counterpart

The Byzantine prayers find an interesting parallel in the late medieval West where votive masses against the infidel were composed between the fourteenth and the sixteenth century. A comparison between the Byzantine military prayers and their Western counterpart can provide some historically illuminating insights. The Latin votive masses pursued a twofold purpose: to liberate Jerusalem from Muslim hands and to protect the Christian communities of the West from the Turkish threat. The difference between the "Saracens," "Turks," "pagans," and "infidel" is very blurred, and the terms seem to have been virtually interchangeable in Latin liturgy. Some manuscripts carry the rubric *Contra Turcos*, while some others have the headings *Contra Sarracenos, Contra Paganos*, and *Contra Infideles*.[84] Hence, it becomes evident that the Latin prayers aimed not only against the most immediate threat, that is, the Turks threatening the Catholic world, but also against any Muslim infidel in general.

The comparison between the two liturgies reveals a certain similarity. For example, both liturgies use the same comparative figures from the Old Testament.[85] Both liturgies use Psalm 78 (79);[86] both traditions speak of the intercession of the Blessed Virgin Mary and the saints,[87] use Jerusalem as a point of reference,[88] compare the Turks to dogs and wolves, on the one hand, and the Christians to lambs, on the other;[89] speak of devastated temples, vessels, and vineyards;[90] perceive the invasions as a divine punishment for temporary sins.[91] In both instances, there is no uniformity as to the name of the enemy: the Latin sources do not distinguish between the *Turci, Sarraceni, gentes, infideles*, and *pagani*, while the Byzantine prayers identify the Turks with the *hoi barbaroi, Hagarēnoi*, and *ethnē*. Both traditions value the victory of the Christian emperor or king and the ultimate restoration of peace.[92] Like the Byzantine prayers, the Latin masses evolved from other, earlier liturgical prayers and are largely based on them.[93] Finally, the Western masses also include the polysemous dimension, focusing on more than one target.

All this brings us to the theme of holy war in the two traditions. While none is likely to deny that the notion of holy war, that is, Crusade, existed in the late medieval West, there is a lively debate about the situation in Byzantium. Some scholars have argued that the Byzantines had no such notion at all,[94] and that Byzantine war ideology was that of the *bellum justum*, not *bellum sacrum (hieros polemos)*.[95] Other scholars contend, each to different degree, that Holy War ideology indeed existed in Byzantium.[96] Neither group of scholars concentrated on the later period, nor did they use the military prayers in order to gain a wider comparative perspective on the issue. In my view, the prayers should be considered in discussions of Byzantine military ideology. The prayers indeed reveal elements of an ideology of holy warfare, although the ideas in question do not fully correspond to those embodied in the Western crusading liturgy during the late Middle Ages. Let us focus first on the similarities. The Byzantine prayers perceive the struggle between the Christian Greeks and Muslim Turks as a struggle between light and darkness, God and Antichrist. This notion was quite a widespread one in crusade propaganda in the West. The biblical imagery within the prayers represents yet another element of *sacred* war. The identification of Constantinople with Jerusalem and its church (Hagia Sophia?) with the Temple can be compared to the Western idea of liberation of Jerusalem and purification of its temple (the church of the Holy Sepulchre) from the infidel. And finally, the very use of the Psalm 78 (79) and wish to protect God's vineyards point to the idea of the war in the name of God. Hence, the sacral dimension of the war against the infidel.

Apart from the obvious similarities, one notices elements that are peculiar and unique to the Byzantine liturgical tradition. First, the classical dimension of Greeks versus Persians is missing from the Western prayers, and this is hardly surprising. Medieval Western Christendom was a multiethnic entity and furthermore lacked the historical example of the Greco-Persian wars, since its historico-cultural ties with the Hellenic past were loose, to say the least. Its historical consciousness was that of one, united entity, namely, the Christian Empire (=Church), which is a direct heir of the Roman Empire. That is why it saw the struggle between Christian states and the Turks only as a religious one. By contrast, late Byzantine society became increasingly conscious of its Hellenic roots and history. It is no wonder, then, that it attempted to bestow an ethnic character upon the wars with the Turks.

Second, the Byzantine prayers were said in the very "war zones," under immediate and direct threat by the Turks. The Byzantine prayers urged God and the Virgin Mary to hurry and protect the faithful and to slay their foes as soon as possible.[97] In other words, the two traditions involved different temporal and geographic notions. The Turks threatened the Byzantines at a time and geographic area that were immediate. The Western prayers, on the other hand, were said in most cases in geographic locations remote from the war. It is clear that when Pope Clement V issued the Holy Land Mass in 1309, he knew that the Holy Land was ruled by the Mamlukes.[98] But the Holy Land and the Mamluk territories were located far enough from Catholic states, so that the latter were not under direct threat of the infidel. Failed expeditions, such as the one undertaken by Marshall Boucicaut in 1396 or the Varna crusade of 1444, still could not mean any real menace to the French kingdom. However, the situation changed rapidly after 1453, under the direct impact of the fall of Constantinople. The Turks started to advance further into central and southern Europe. The conquest of Otranto in August 1480 and fall of Hungary in 1526 have certainly added the geographic dimension to the Western anti-Turkish liturgy.

Third, although both liturgies reflect holy war ideas, there is one significant difference between them. The Western prayers implore God to destroy
the infidel and liberate the Holy Land, thus tacitly indicating the wish to
send the Christian army beyond the sea to reconquer Jerusalem from Muslim hands. The Byzantine litanies, on the other hand, ask God, the Virgin
Mary, and the saints to defend their own people from the heathen threat,
thus implying a mere desire for a victory at home, without pursuing the war
to the Holy Land. Hence, the Western military liturgy had a more offensive
character than the Byzantine ones.

Another significant difference between the two liturgies lies in their
overall structure. Western anti-Turkish liturgy is either part of a mass or
an entire mass. In 1309 Pope Clement V established a triple set of *Collecta—
Secreta—Postcommunio* as the structural base for the Holy Land Mass.[99] There
were several textual varieties in this triple set, but as a rule, the *Collecta* part
implored God to behold the tribulations of the faithful and come to their
help, while the *Secreta* and *Postcommunio* prayers beseeched God to defend
the Christians and free them from the heathens. In other words, the triple
set was interwoven into the very fabric of mass and constituted a part of it.
From ca. 1453 onwards, we see entire masses dedicated to the war against
the Turks, the Dedicated War Mass.[100] In other words, the Western anti-
Turkish liturgy had a constant, standardized structure, whether as a mass or
as a part of it. This set structure prevented the Western liturgy from developing various new forms and practices. By contrast, the Byzantine war
prayers were separate litanies, neither a part of a mass, nor a mass in its
entity. Every prayer varied in its size, structure and meaning.

Finally, another difference between the Byzantine and Western prayers
is in their appeal. Some Byzantine prayers appeal directly to God, while
some others to the Virgin Savior and Protector. The Western prayers, on the
other hand, always appeal to God, while the name of the Blessed Virgin
Mary as an intercessor is mentioned rarely and in third person only. This is
hardly surprising, since the Western tradition lacked the same image of the
victorious Virgin, the intercessor of besieged citizens and fighting soldiers.

To conclude, the Western and the Eastern anti-Turkish prayers share
common thematic elements and motifs. However, there are important differences. The Byzantine prayers were more ethnic in character, conscious
of the immediate danger, free in form, separated from mass and more
Mary-centered. The Western prayers (at least, most of them) were said from
a safe distance from the threat; they possessed constant forms and formulas;
they were interwoven into the mass and were always addressed God.

The Man of His Time: Kiprian of Kiev and His Translations

The Greek prayers did not limit themselves to Byzantium; neither was Byzantium the only Orthodox power experiencing a Muslim threat at the time. From the second half of the fourteenth century, the Ottoman Turks advanced into the Balkan Peninsula. In 1389 the Serbs suffered heavy losses at the Battle of Kossovo. In 1393 the Turks subdued Bulgaria after capturing its capital, Turnovo. Russia had its own infidel: the Tatars of the Golden Horde. The Russian armies under the command of the Grand Prince of Moscow Dmitrii Donskoi overcame the Tatar forces in the famous Battle of Kulikovo in 1380. Wars with the Tatars did not end until the year 1480. The principality of Wallachia was also involved in a military conflict with the Turks. In 1461 and 1462, the famous Vlad III Țepeș, otherwise known as Vlad Dracul, succeeded in beating off the Turkish invasion. However, in December 1476, Vlad Dracul was killed in a battle and Wallachia surrendered to the Turks.

Permanent conflicts with Muslim foes created an increasing demand for the war liturgy against the infidel among the Orthodox population. This liturgy was thus translated into Old Church Slavonic, the liturgical language of the Slavs and Wallachians. Cyprian, or Kiprian Tsamblak, metropolitan of Kiev (1375, 1381–82, 1390–1406), played the main role in the translation and transmittance of these prayers. Born in Bulgaria around 1330 where he was educated and had assumed the monastic habit, Kirpian came to Constantinople sometime in the late 1360s or early 1370s and became attached to the retinue of Patriarch Philotheos Kokkinos (1353–54, 1364–76). He had also spent time as a monk on Mount Athos. During his long sojourn in the Greek-speaking lands, Kiprian acquired mastery of the Greek language. In 1373 he was sent by Philotheos as *apokrisiarios* to Russia and pagan Lithuania on a mission of reconciliation between the two principalities. Here Kiprian was backed by the Lithuanian nobility, which asked the patriarch of Constantinople to appoint him metropolitan bishop over their country. Their plea was satisfied, and in 1375 he was made metropolitan over Lithuania, Kiev, and Russia. His appointment was not recognized by the Russian authorities, and in 1378 Kiprian was forced to return to Constantinople. A compromise was reached in June 1380, when a new patriarch, Neilos, appointed Kiprian metropolitan over Lithuania and Little Russia, while the title of the metropolitan of Kiev was given to Pimen. In 1381 Kiprian came to Moscow, where he joined the Grand Prince Dmitrii Donskoi, with whose help he expected to depose his rival. Pimen was captured and exiled, while Kiprian moved to his see, without the approval from Constantinople. A year later, however, Pimen was set free and Kiprian was forced into exile. In 1386 Kirpian returned to Constantinople once more, hoping to have the patriarch intervene on his behalf. This did not happen until late 1389, when the new patriarch Anthony IV deposed Pimen and restored Kiprian to the office of "Metropolitan of all Rus." He remained in this office until his death in 1406.[101]

Both in Byzantium and Russia, Kiprian devoted much energy to composing, copying and translating books. According to Russian sources, he "transcribed many holy books from Greek into Russian."[102] His most significant translations into Church Slavonic were a series of liturgical books, namely the *Sluzhebnik* and *Trebnik* (two parts of the *Euchologion*, the former covering the Liturgies of St. Basil and St. John Chrysostom, as well as the liturgy of the pre-sanctified, while the later containing various prayers for special occasions, such as our military prayers), *Ustav* (=*Typikon*) and *Psaltyr'* (=*Psalterion*), as well as some minor liturgical works.[103] It is unknown when and where were these books translated. It is highly unlikely that Kiprian translated them before he came to Russia in 1373: his ecclesiastical status was not high enough to permit him to make an authoritative and compelling translation to be accepted by the Russian church. It is more likely that the translations were made during his term in office as metropolitan, although it is unclear when exactly. Our only indication is *Gosudarstvennyi Istoricheskii Muzei* (State History Museum, Moscow, henceforth *GIM*), *Sinodal'noe Sobranie* (Synodal Collection, henceforth *Syn.*) MS 601 (344).[104] The manuscript in question is a *Sluzhebnik*, compiled in 1397, which reads on folios 72v and 132v that "Kiprian, the humble metropolitan of all Rus, had copied this *Sluzhebnik* from Greek books into Russian language by his own hand" (sii sluzhebnik prepisan ot Gretskikh knig na Russkyi iazyk rukoiu svoeiu Kiprian smirenye mitropolit Kyevskyi vseia Rusi).[105] The next sentence reads: "Shall you copy or study from these books . . . remember our humility, so that also you shall be honored with the same remembrance" (elitsy zhe prepisuete i pouchavaetesia simi knigami . . . pominaite nashe smirenie, iako da i vy tomu zhe pominaniiu spodobleny budete).[106] This address in the first person indicates that Kiprian's liturgical *floruit* must have been in 1397, or even before. It is likely that the codex in question is not Kiprian's autograph, as it differs in palaeography from his autograph translation of John Klimax's *Heavenly Ladder* in 1387.[107]

Unlike the *Sluzhebnik* compiled in 1397, there is no indication when Kiprian might have translated the *Trebnik*. The earliest Russian *Trebnik* to mention Kiprian as its author is *GIM, Syn.* MS 375 (*olim* 326), compiled in 1481. The codex has a colophon stating that it has been "copied from the translation of the metropolitan Kipria word by word" (pisan s mitropolicha s Kiprianova perevodu slovo v slovo).[108] To make things even more obscure, the 1481 *Trebnik* does not feature *any* anti-heathen prayers. This is rather surprising, since Kiprian could not have been indifferent toward the Muslim threat of the Orthodox world. He himself witnessed the Turkish incursions of the 1350s and 1360s, and sojourned in Moscow while Donskoi's troops fought at Kulikovo on 8 September 1380. The Russian chronicles narrate how Kiprian blessed and absolved Dmitrii before the battle, pouring holy water upon him and sending priests and deacons to various parts of the city to bless Dmitrii's warriors.[109] Kiprian himself was in Moscow on 26 August 1382 when the Tatar leader Tochtamysh plundered the city; he was injured and robbed, along with Grand Princess Evdokiia, by the Tatar soldiers. After humiliations and implorations, Kiprian and Evdokiia were allowed to leave Moscow.[110] These are just a few examples proving that Kiprian was emotionally involved in the Orthodox struggle against the Muslim invaders. Hence, it is striking that the *Trebnik* of 1481 neglects the anti-heathen prayers.

Fortunately, the 1481 *Trebnik* is not our only evidence. A late fifteenth-century manuscript, *Moskovskaia Dukhovnaia Akademiia* (Moscow Theological Academy), MS 77 serves as our earliest textual witness to the anti-Turkish prayers in Russia and contains, inter alia, the canon of Philotheos against the heathens and a subsequent prayer, which is *not* found in Goar's *Euchologia*.[111] By the end of the canon there is a colophon saying "[this is] the creation of the Most Holy and Ecumenical Patriarch Philotheos and translation of Kiprian, the humble metropolitan of all Rus" (tvorenie sviateishego i vselenskago patriarkha Filofeia i potruzhenie zhe Kipriana smerennago mitropolita vseia Rusi).[112] Philotheos's canon and the anti-heathen prayer are found also in a later, sixteenth-century codex, *GIM*, MS 618 (354).[113] In other words, these two manuscripts establish an obvious connection between Philotheos's authorship and Kiprian's translation. What they do not establish, however, is whether the remaining prayers found in the Constantinoplitan *Euchologia* were indeed translated by Kiprian. The earliest compilation to include most of the Byzantine military prayers in their Slavonic version is the so-called *Trebnik* of Petro Mogila, printed in Kiev (1646).

It has, inter alia, the prayers MIL 1:2–11, 13, MIL 3:1–2, and MIL 4:1, as found in the fourteenth-century *Euchologia* from Constantinople, as well as some similar and obviously later prayers for the Russian emperor in his struggle against the infidel and for peace in the Russian realm.[114]

The above discussion can be summed up as follows. Several liturgical books were translated by Kiprian in the end of the fourteenth century from the Constantinopolitan *Euchologion*, among them *Sluzhebnik* and *Trebnik*. Unfortunately, neither book has come down to us in its original form, as compiled and written by Kiprian himself. The earliest codex to contain an anti-Turkish prayer which is known to have been composed by Philotheos and translated by Kiprian is dated to the late fifteenth century, that is, almost a hundred years after Kiprian's death. The earliest compilation of most translated military prayers is the much later *Trebnik* of Mogila. Can we use this as an *argumentum ex silentio* and question Kiprian's authority as the translator? Or was it merely an unfortunate coincidence that no early codex containing his translations is extant?

Four circumstances support the hypothesis that our anti-Turkish prayers were translated by Kiprian. First, the *Sluzhebnik* of 1397 corresponds, more or less, to the surviving fourteenth-century Greek *Euchologion* in its structure and content. Second, the anti-Turkish prayers were especially important in Kiprian's time, given the political and military situation, both in Byzantium and Russia. It is nonetheless striking that the 1481 *Trebnik*, allegedly copied from an earlier Kiprian codex, neglects the anti-heathen prayers. Third, the very career of Kiprian suggests that he was the translator of these prayers. As a member of the highest orders of Byzantine and Muscovite society, serving as patriarchal *apokrisiarios* and Metropolitan of All Russia and being a close associate of the Grand Princes Dmitrii Donskoi and his son, Vasilii Dmitrievich, Kiprian should have been closely involved in contemporary politics. The Islamic threat, whether posed by the Ottoman Turks or the Tatars, stood at the center of the political and military life in Byzantium and Muscovite Russia. Liturgy, as we have seen, was considered a powerful weapon in the war against the infidel, which Kiprian, the head of the Russian church, must have realized. Kiprian himself watched the Turkish and Tartar incursions from a close distance and even was found in a life-threatening situation in 1380. These are just a few examples proving that Kiprian *could not have been* indifferent toward the situation in Russia. A more profound study of Kiprian's involvement in secular politics is yet to be done.

Fourth and finally, the issue of literacy in Muscovite Rus makes a compelling argument in favor of Kiprian's authorship of the translations. Few people knew Greek in that time, and a large degree of linguistic ignorance continued well until the times of Peter the Great. As Francis J. Thomson has stated, the Greek (Byzantine) works in their Slavonic translations reached Muscovy largely from Bulgaria and Serbia, where they were translated by local literati.[115] While this view might be somewhat exaggerated, as some scholars have noted,[116] there is no doubt that few Russians had a good command of Greek compared to their southern Slav brothers. A Bulgarian by birth with excellent Greek, Kirprian was, in fact, one of these few people living in Russia who knew Greek.

Taken together, these four circumstances enable us to arrive at the conclusion that it was unlikely for anyone else but Kiprian to translate the military prayers. He was the right man to come in the right time.

Conclusions

Military liturgy played an important role in the attempt to overcome the crisis of the mid-fourteenth century. The different aspects of the crisis—Turkish incursions, losses on the battlefield, the outburst of the Black Death, and civil strife—gave birth to more than twenty new liturgical works composed within a short period of time. This is a significantly large number, which points to how seriously the crisis was perceived by the Byzantine church.

The prayers against the Turks express a synthesis between biblical and classical values in the Byzantine mind during the fourteenth century. The biblical and the classical levels of the prayers were interwoven and in no way contradicted each other. They depict the emperor as a sole ruler over the Christian nation. His exclusiveness derives from God, and it is from him that the emperor receives his authority to rule over his people. Hence, his victories and defeats derive, too, from God's will. Any domestic war against the emperor is considered to be a rebellion (*stasis*) against him, as specified in some prayers. In other words, the military prayers underline the sacral character of the Byzantine monarch.

The military prayers composed in the period do not constitute a separate genre. They evolved out of earlier kindred rites, such as coronation prayers and votive prayers said in times of disasters, and are a piece in a larger liturgical mosaic devoted to calamities. Therefore, they are to be studied and understood in a wider context.

The comparison of the prayers with their Western counterpart furnishes illuminating insights. The Eastern prayers are conscious of the Turkish threat both on a temporal and geographical level, unlike the Western ones. For example, when the MIL 1:12 prayer was uttered by the people of Philadelphia, the Turkish armies camped right before the city's walls and were ready to storm them. Byzantine war liturgy was more independent in form and content than its Western counterpart; it was also more Mary-centered, because the image of the ever-victorious Virgin played an important part in Byzantine war ideology. The comparison shows that the Byzantine church dressed the military confrontation with the Turks in the fourteenth century with the language of sacred warfare.

The military prayers were not limited to Byzantium only. Quite soon after their composition they were translated into Church Slavonic by Kiprian of Kiev. The arrival of Kiprian at Moscow happened at a significant historical moment, when the Russians faced their own infidel and needed the military prayers to be translated into Church Slavonic.

The prayers are an excellent source for understanding the spiritual reaction to, and perception of, the crisis of the mid-fourteenth century both in Byzantium and in Russia. Naturally, sources belonging to other literary genres should be taken into account if we are to gain fuller picture of ecclesiastical perceptions of warfare in this period. The sources in need of study include contemporary homilies by theologians and preachers such as Makarios Chrysokephalos and Gregory Palamas, who were also authors of military prayers. One should, further, not overlook cases of visual representation of praying at times of war and should draw a distinction between personal and collective liturgical rites. These matters, not covered by the limited scope of this paper, remain a task for future investigation.

Appendix

Manuscripts Containing Military Prayers[117]

I. GREEK CODICES

1. Jerusalem, Library of the Greek Orthodox Patriarchate

Collection of the monastery of the Holy Cross, Cod. 67 (14th or 15th c.), fols. 272r–79r (a prayer against a barbarian assault)[118]

2. Moscow, State History Museum (Gosudarstvennyi Istoricheskii Muzei)

Synodal Collection (ex-Sinodal'naia Biblioteka), Cod. gr. 454 (*olim* 47) (*anno* 1607), fols. 446r–77r: fol. 446r (an office against a barbarian assault), fols. 447v–52r (a *Kanōn paraklētikos* to Theotokos), fols. 452v–59r (two prayers of Makarios Chrysokephalos against the assault of barbarians), fols. 459r–70r (eight prayers of Patriarch Kallistos against calamities, assaults of Hagarenes and brigands), fols. 470r–77r (An *akolouthia tēs koinēs paraklēseōs*)[119]

Synodal Collection (ex-Sinodal'naia Biblioteka), Cod. gr. 349 (*olim* 336) (15th or 16th c.), fols. 32v–33r, 49v–57r (?): fols. 32v–33r (a prayer *kata polemiōn*); fols. 49v–57r (prayers for various occasions)[120]

3. Vatican Library

Cod. Barberini gr. 410 (15th c.), fols. 168v–72v, 173v–75v, 181v–82r: fols.168v–70v (a prayer of Patriarch Philotheos against plague=GOA, pp. 630–31); fols. 170v–72v (a prayer of Philotheos against enemies= DMI, p. 290=MIL 1:15); fols. 173v–75v (a supplicant prayer to Theotokos, by Philotheos= DMI, pp. 288–89=MOH, pp. 180–82, MIL 3:2); fols.181v–82r (a prayer for the emperor=GOA, p. 733, lines 7–19)[121]

Cod. Barberini gr. 459 (16th c.), fol. 2v (a prayer for King Philip II of Spain, ranslated into Greek from Latin; for the occasion of the Battle of Lepanto, 1571?)[122]

Cod. Palat. gr. 364 (14th c.), fol. 27v (a prayer for averting enemies)[123]

Cod. Vat. gr. 344 (*olim* 15, *deinde* 898) (14th c.), fol. 241v (a prayer for emperors = GOA, pp. 733–34)[124]

Cod. Vat. gr. 847 (*olim* 575) (15th c.), fols. 272v–73r (prayers for emperors)[125]

Cod. Vat. gr. 1538 (*olim* 1554) (15th c.), fols. 199r–203v (a protective prayer against personal enemies written by a certain *fra* Jacob)[126]

II. SLAVIC CODICES

1. Moscow, State History Museum (Gosudarstvennyi Istoricheskii Muzei)

Synodal Collection (ex-Sinodal'naia Biblioteka), Cod. slav. 307 (374) (Serbian, first half of the 15th c.), fols. 250v–54r (an indigenous Serbian supplication to BVM against the Ishmaelites)[127]

Synodal Collection (ex-Sinodal'naia Biblioteka), Cod. slav. 618 (354) (Russian, 16th c.), fols. 265v–70r (Kiprian's translation of Philotheos's prayer against the heathen incursions, *not* printed in Goar)[128]

NOTES

I am grateful to Dimiter Angelov of the University of Birmingham, Anne-Laurence Caudano of the Pontifical Institute for Medieval Studies, Toronto, and Amnon Linder of Hebrew University, Jerusalem, for their most generous and helpful suggestions. All errors are, of course, mine.

1. The pioneering studies were Carl Erdmann, "Der Heidenkrieg in der Liturgie und die Kaiserkrönnung Ottos I.," *Mitteilungen des Instituts für Österreichische Geschichtsforschung* 46 (1932): 123–42, and L. Brou, "L'oraison 'Deus Qui Conteris Bella' de la messe votive 'Tempore Belli,'" *Ephemerides Liturgicae* 60 (1946): 293–307.

2. Penny J. Cole, *The Preaching of the Crusades to the Holy Land, 1095–1270* (Cambridge, Mass.: Medieval Academy of America, 1991); Penny J. Cole, "Purgatory and Crusade in St. Gregory's Trental," *International History Review* 17 (1995): 713–25; Penny J. Cole, "Cambridge, Fitzwilliam Museum, MS McClean 51, Pope Sixtus IV and the Fall of Otranto (August 1480)," in *A Distinct Voice: Medieval Studies in Honor of Leonard E. Boyle*, ed. Jacqueline Brown and William P. Stoneman (Notre Dame: University of Notre Dame Press, 1997), pp. 103–20.

3. Christoph. T. Maier, *Preaching the Crusades: Mendicant Friars and the Cross in the Thirteenth Century* (Cambridge: Cambridge University Press, 1994); Christoph T. Maier, "Crisis, Liturgy and the Crusade in the Twelfth and Thirteen Centuries," *Journal of Ecclesiastical History* 48 (1997): 628–57.

4. Alison K. McHardy, "Liturgy and Propaganda in the Diocese of Lincoln during the Hundred Years War," *Studies in Church History* 18 (1982): 215–27; Alison

K. McHardy, "The English Clergy and the Hundred Years War," *Studies in Church History* 20 (1983): 171–78.

5. Michael McCormick, "The Liturgy of War in the Early Middle Ages: Crisis, Litanies and the Carolingian Monarchy," *Viator* 15 (1984): 1–23; Michael McCormick, "A New Ninth-Century Witness to the Carolingian Mass against the Pagans (Paris B.N. lat. 2812)," *Revue Bénédictine* 97 (1987): 42–86; Michael McCormick, "Liturgie et guerre des Carolingiens à la première croisade," in *Militia Christi e crociata nei secoli XI–XII, Atti della undecima settimana internazionale di studio* (Milan: Vita e pensiero, 1992), pp. 209–40.

6. Amnon Linder, "The Liturgy of the Liberation of Jerusalem," *Mediaeval Studies* 55 (1990): 110–31; Amnon Linder, "'Deus Venerunt Gentes': Psalm 78 (79) in the Liturgical Commemoration of the Latin Destruction of Jerusalem," in *Medieval Studies in Honour of Avrom Saltman*, ed. Bat-Sheva Albert, Yvonne Friedman, and Simon Schwarzfuchs (Ramat Gan: Bar Ilan University Press, 1995), pp. 145–71; Amnon Linder, "Individual and Community of the Liturgy of the Liberation of Christian Jerusalem," in *Information, Kommunikation und Selbstdarstellung in mittelalterlichen Gemeinden*, ed. Alfred Haverkamp, Schriften des historischen Kollegs, Kolloquien 40 (Munich: Oldenbourg, 1998), pp. 25–40; Amnon Linder, "The Loss of Christian Jerusalem in Late Medieval Liturgy," in *The Real and Ideal Jerusalem in Jewish, Christian and Islamic Art*, ed. Bianca Kühnel (Jerusalem: Center of Jewish Art of the Hebrew University, 1999), pp. 165–78; Amnon Linder, "The Liturgy of the Liberation of Jerusalem," in *Verso Gerusalemme: Il Convegno Internazionale nel IX Centenario della I Crociata, Bari, 1999*, ed. Franco Cardini (Lecce: Congedo, 1999), pp. 57–66; Amnon Linder, "The Liturgy of the Latin Kingdom of Jerusalem," in *Knights of the Holy Land: The Crusader Kingdom of Jerusalem*, ed. Silvia Rozenberg (Jerusalem: Israel Museum, 1999), pp. 95–99; Amnon Linder "Ha-liturgiya be-maāvaq neged ha-turkim be-shalhei yemei ha-beinaiyim" (The Liturgy in the Struggle against the Turks in the Late Middle Ages), *Historiya* 8 (2000): 73–105 (in Hebrew).

7. See LIN. There is another forthcoming publication by Amnon Linder, *Speculum Subversionis Hierusalem*, Corpus Christianorum, Continuatio Mediaevalis (Turnhout: Brepols).

8. For a survey of the history of this period, see, inter alia, Donald Nicol, *The Last Centuries of Byzantium, 1261–1453* (Cambridge: Cambridge University Press, 1993), pp. 141–250.

9. See the appendix.

10. See GOA.

11. See DMI.

12. See the appendix.

13. Here I follow the example of Miguel Arranz, who assigned specific *sigla* to prayers he studied and edited. I propose here the *siglum* MIL (*militares preces*) for our

military prayers. For the *sigla* used by Arranz, consult Miguel Arranz, "Les sacraments de l'ancien Euchologe constantinopolitain," *OCP* 49 (1983): 42–90, 284–302; Miguel Arranz, "Les prières pénitentielles de la tradition byzantine," *OCP* 57 (1991): 87–143, 309–29; 58 (1992): 23–82; Miguel Arranz, "Couronnement royal et autres promotions de cour: Les sacrements de l'Institution de l'ancien Euchologe constantinopolitain III–1," *OCP* 56 (1990): 83–113.

14. *Demetrii Cydonis Oratio de non reddenda Callipoli*, PG, vol. 154, col. 1013A–C.

15. PLP, 8700, 8579, 95132, and 92166–92179 (which is one and the same person).

16. Averil Cameron, "The Cult of the Virgin in Late Antiquity: Religious Development and Myth-Making," in *The Church and Mary*, ed. Robert N. Swanson, Studies in Church History 39 (Woodbridge: Boydell, 2004), pp. 1–21.

17. Mary B. Cunningham, "The Meeting of the Old and New: The Typology of Mary the Theotokos in Byzantine Homilies and Hymns," in *The Church and Mary* (see n. 16, above), pp. 52–62. On Mary's humanity, see Jane Baun, "Discussing Mary's Humanity in Medieval Byzantium," ibid., pp. 63–72.

18. *The Homilies of Photius, Patriarch of Constantinople*, trans. Cyril Mango (Cambridge, Mass.: Harvard University Press), p. 95.

19. Athanasios Papadopulos-Kerameus, "Akafist Bozh'ei Materi," *VV* 10 (1904): 375–401. The author wrongly credited Photios with the composition of the hymn.

20. *The Homilies of Photius*, p. 82.

21. On the iconographic tradition of victorious Mary in Byzantium, see Bissera V. Pentcheva, *Icons and Power: The Mother of God in Byzantium* (University Park: Philadelphia State University Press, 2006).

22. Peter Schreiner, "Zur Geschichte Philadelphias im 14. Jahrhundert (1293–1390), *OCP* 35 (1969): 375–431, esp. pp. 396–401.

23. Robert Edward Sinkewicz, "Gregory Palamas," in *La théologie byzantine et sa tradition*, ed. Carmelo Giuseppe Conticello and Vassa Conticello, 2 vols. (Turnhout: Brepols, 2002), 2:152.

24. Nicol, *Last Centuries of Byzantium*, pp. 237–38.

25. Nicol, *Last Centuries of Byzantium*, pp. 216–18.

26. MIL 1:3, 1:5, 1:7.

27. MIL 1:8.

28. MIL 1:7, 1:8, 1:14.

29. MIL 1:10.

30. The use of this psalm in the Western sources has been studied by Penny J. Cole, "O God, The Heathen Have Come into Your Inheritance (Psalm 78:1): The Theme of Religious Pollution in Crusade Documents, 1095–1188," in *Crusaders and*

Muslims in Twelfth-Century Syria, ed. Maya Schatzmiller (Leiden: Brill, 1993), pp. 84–111; Linder, "Deus Venerunt Gentes," pp. 145–71.

31. MIL 1:6.

32. MIL 1:10.

33. See above, pp. 202–3.

34. MIL 1:7, 1:10,1:11, 1:12, 1:13, 3:2.

35. MIL 1:12 .

36. MIL 1:9, 1:10.

37. MIL 1:3 , 1:9, 1:11.

38. MIL 1:2, 1:3, 1:8, 1:9.

39. MIL 1:10 .

40. MIL 1:7, 1:10, 1:11, 1:12, 1:13, 1:14, 1:15, 1:16, 3:1, 4:1, 4:2.

41. MIL 1:12, 1:13, 1:16, 3:2.

42. MIL 4:1, 4:2.

43. *Satrapai, tyrannoi, basileis, archontes chōrōn barbarikōn* (MIL 1:5).

44. For example, Herodotus, *Historiae*, 3.21, 3.63, 3.122, 4.197 (*basileus*); 1.192, 3.89 (*satrapai*).

45. For example, Herodotus, *Historiae*, 1.6–7, 3.125, 5.92, 7.10, 9.90, and passim.

46. See Ludwig Schopen, ed., *Ioannis Cantacuzeni eximperatoris historiarum libri IV*, 3 vols. (Bonn: Weber, 1828–31), 1:151–52, 492, 499, 506; 2:56, 70, 77, 82, 181, 257, 392, 396, 467, 482, 492, 530, 532, 550–51, 555, 583, 593–95; 3:37, 65–66, 85, 87, 114–16, 147, 162, 242, 248–49, 348.

47. On the Hellenic revival, see, inter alia, Steven Runciman, *The Last Byzantine Renaissance* (Cambridge: Cambridge University Press, 1970), pp. 1–23; Alexander Vasiliev, *History of the Byzantine Empire* (Madison: University of Wisconsin Press, 1952), pp. 582, 687.

48. Codex Vat. gr. 1538 (*olim* 1554), fols. 199r–203v (see the appendix, p. 222).

49. For example, in a letter of John Argyropoulos to John VIII (1440), the latter was called by this title. See Runciman, *The Last Byzantine Renaissance*, pp. 21–22. The most important study on Hellenic nationalism in late Byzantium is Paul Magdalino, "Hellenism and Nationalism in Byzantium," in *Neohellenism*, ed. John Burke and Stathis Gauntlett (Canberra: Australian National University, 1992), pp. 1–29 (repr. in Paul Magdalino, *Tradition and Transformation in Byzantium* [Aldershot: Variorum Reprints, 1991], study 14).

50. The most important studies on official imperial ideology in the later Palaiologan period are Hans-Georg Beck, "Reichsidee und nationale Politik im

spätbyzantinischen Staat," *BZ* 53 (1960): 86–94; Jan-Louis van Dieten, "Politische Ideologie und Niedergang im Byzanz der Palaiologen," *Zeitschrift für Historische Forschung* 6 (1979): 1–35.

51. MIL 1:5.

52. MIL 3:2.

53. MIL 2:1, 2:2, 3:1, 3:2.

54. MIL 2:2.

55. MIL 2:1.

56. MIL 2:1. Perhaps this is a carryover from the ancient Roman formula of the imperial peace "Pax terra marique."

57. MIL 3:1.

58. MIL 3:2.

59. MIL 2:2.

60. The coronation prayers were assembled and edited in Arranz, "Couronnement royal."

61. The manuscript partially printed by Goar has been studied by A. Strittmatter, "The *Barberinum Sancti Marci* of Jacques Goar," *Ephemerides Liturgicae* 47 (1933): 329–67. It has been edited in BAR.

62. BAR, p. 197.

63. BAR, pp. 195, 197.

64. BAR, pp. 196, 197, 199, 200.

65. BAR, pp. 199–200.

66. BAR, p. 199.

67. BAR, pp. 199–200.

68. BAR, pp. 199–200.

69. So far there is no critical edition of these votive prayers. I have used the edition of Goar. See, GOA, pp. 610–41.

70. GOA, pp. 610–12, 620–22, 627–29.

71. GOA, pp. 611, 613, 621, 622, 624, and passim.

72. GOA, pp. 612, 622, 623, 624, 638, and passim.

73. GOA, pp. 611, 613, 621, 622, 636, and passim.

74. GOA, pp. 612, 625, 637, and passim.

75. GOA, pp. 611, 612, 613, 617, 618, 620, 622, 623, 632, 635.

76. GOA, p. 612.

77. GOA, p. 622.

78. GOA, pp. 618, 625, 630, 638, and passim.

79. GOA, p. 620.

80. GOA, p. 623.

81. The idea of liturgical polysemy is discussed in LIN, p. 364.

82. A vast corpus of penitential prayers was edited by Arranz, "Les prières pénitentielles."

83. See n. 42, above.

84. LIN, p. 124.

85. LIN, p. 197.

86. LIN, pp. 2, 4, 6, 10, 11, 22, 26, 27, 32, 38–40, 42, 44–48, 50, 52, 54–56, 58, 60, 62–64, 68–70, 72, 81, 91–92, 100, 118, 172, 181–83, 185, 188.

87. LIN, pp. 197, 256, 269, 271.

88. LIN, pp. 196, 265.

89. LIN, pp. 197, 264.

90. LIN, pp. 197, 264.

91. LIN, pp. 257,258, 260, 268.

92. LIN, pp. 200, 202, 269, 272.

93. LIN, p. 364 and passim.

94. Vitalien Laurent, "L'idée de guerre sainte et la tradition byzantine," *Revue historique du sud-est européen* 23 (1946): 71–98; Paul Lemerle, "Byzance et la croisade," in *Relazioni del X Congresso internazionale di scienze storiche*, vol. 3, *Storia del medioevo* (Florence: Sansoni, 1955), p. 617.

95. Angeliki Laiou, "On Just War in Byzantium," in *To Hellenikon: Studies in Honor of Speros Vryonis, Jr.*, ed. John Langdon et al., 2 vols. (New Rochelle, N.Y.: Caratzas 1993), 1:153–77; George T. Dennis, "Defenders of the Christian People: Holy War in Byzantium," in *The Crusades from the Perspective of Byzantium and the Muslim World*, ed. Angeliki Laiou and Roy Parviz Mottahedeh (Washington, D.C.: Dumbarton Oaks, 2001), pp. 31–39.

96. René Grousset, *Histoire des Croisades et du royaume franc de Jérusalem*, 3 vols. (Paris: Plon, 1934),1:15; Tia Kolbaba, "Fighting for Christianity: Holy War in the Byzantine Empire," *Byzantion* 68 (1998): 194–221.

97. The prayers frequently repeat the word *nyn* (now) (GOA, pp. 642–51) and such words as *prophthason* (=hurry up) (GOA, pp. 643–44); *tachinon* (=quickly) (GOA, p. 643).

98. Regarding the mass, see Linder, *Ha-liturgiya*, p. 79 and LIN, pp.120–22.

99. LIN, pp. 118–50.

100. Linder, *Ha-liturgiya*, pp. 83–87, and LIN, pp. 175–273.

101. On Kiprian, see, inter alia, Ivan D. Mansvetov, *Mitropolit Kiprian v ego litugicheskoi deiatel'nosti* (Moscow: Tip. M. N. Lavrova, 1882); Mikhail N. Tikhomirov, *Istoricheskie sviazi Rossii so slavianskimi stranami i Vizantiei* (Moscow: Nauka, 1969), p. 44; Anton V. Kartashev, *Ocherki po istorii russkoi tserkvi*, 2 vols. (Moscow: Nauka, 1991), 1:321–23, 333–38; Lev A. Dmitriev, "Literaturno-knizhnaia deiatel'nost' mitropolita Kipriana i traditsiia Velikotyrnovskoi knizhnoi shkoly," in *Uchenitsi i posledovateli na Evtimii Tŭrnovski: Vtori Mezhdunaroden Simpozium Veliko Tŭrnovo, 20–23 Mai 1976* (Sofia: Izdatelstvo na Bŭlgarskata Akademiia na Naukite, 1980), pp. 64–70; Dmitrii S. Likhachev, "Kiprian," in *Slovar' knizhnikov i knizhnosti drevnei Rusi*, vol. 2, *Vtoraia polovina XIV–XVI v.* (Leningrad: Nauka, 1988), pp. 464–75; Gerhard Podskalsky, *Theologische Literatur des Mittelalters in Bulgarien und Serbien* (Munich: Beck, 2000), pp. 212–19, 324–29, 499–507.

102. The quotation is taken from Dmitrii S. Likhachev, "Literatura vremeni natsional'nogo pod'ioma," in *Pamiatniki literatury drevnei Rusi, XIV-seredina XV veka*, ed. Lev A. Dmitriev and Dmitrii S. Likhachev, 4 vols. (Moscow: Khudozh. Liter., 1981), 4:6. See also Feodor Buslaev, *Istoricheskaia khrestomatiia tserkovnoslavianskogo i drevne-russkogo iazykov* (Moscow: Univ. tip., 1861), pp. 138–39.

103. The best introduction to Kiprian's liturgical translations is Mansvetov, *Mitropolit Kiprian*. See also Evgenii Golubinskii, *Istoriia russkoi tserkvi*, 4 vols. (Moscow: Universitetskaia tipografia 1883–1916), vol. 2, pt. 2, pp. 406–10.

104. Described in great detail in Aleksandr Gorskii and Kapton Nevostruev, *Opisanie slavianskikh rukopisei Moskovskoi sinodal'noi biblioteki: Otdel tretii: knigi bogosluzhebnye* (Moscow: Sinodal'naia tipografia, 1869), pp. 11–20.

105. Printed in Buslaev, *Istoricheskaia khrestomatiia*, pp. 135–36.

106. Buslaev, *Istoricheskaia khrestomatiia*, pp. 135–36.

107. O. A. Kniazevskaia and E. V. Cheshko, "Rukopisi Mitropolita Kipriana i otrazhenie v nikh orfograficheskoi reformy Evfimiia Tyrnovskogo," in *Uchenitsi i posledovateli na Evtimii Tŭrnovski* (see n. 101, above), pp. 282–92; Likhachev, "Kiprian," p. 471.

108. Noted in Mansvetov, *Mitropolit Kiprian*, p. 46.

109. "Patriarshaia ili Nikonovskaia Letopis" (Patriarchal or Nikon's Chronicle), *sub anno* 6890 (=1382), in *Polnoe sobranie russkikh letopisei*, ed. Mikhail N. Tikhomirov, 14 vols. (Moscow: Nauka, 1962–2000), 11:53.

110. "Patriarshaia ili Nikonovskaia Letopis," p. 73.

111. I could not consult the manuscript in either original or descriptive form.

112. Gorskii and Nevostruev, *Opisanie slavianskikh rukopisei*, pp. 55–56.

113. Gorskii and Nevostruev, *Opisanie slavianskikh rukopisei*, pp. 55–56.

114. MOG, pp. 157–82.

115. Consult Thomson's essays collected in his *The Reception of Byzantine Culture in Mediaeval Russia* (Aldershot: Ashgate, 1999): "The Nature of the Reception of Christian Byzantine Culture in Russia in the Tenth to the Thirteenth Centuries and its Implications for Russian Culture" (study 1); "Quotations of Patristic and Byzantine Works by Early Russian Authors as an Indication of the Cultural Level of Kievan Russia" (study 2); "The Implications of the Absence of Quotations of Untranslated Greek Works in Original Russian Literature, together with a Critique of a Distorted Picture of Early Bulgarian Culture" (study 3); "The Bulgarian Contribution of the Reception of Byzantine Culture in Kievan Rus': The Myths and the Enigma" (study 4); "'Made in Russia': A Survey of the Translations Allegedly Made in Kievan Russia" (study 5): "The Corpus of Slavonic Translations Available in Muscovy: The Cause of Old Russia's Intellectual Silence and a Contributory Factor to Muscovite Cultural Autarky" (study 6); "The Distorted Mediaeval Russian Perception of Classical Antiquity: the Causes and the Consequences" (study 7).

116. Simon Franklin, "Po povodu 'Intellektual'nogo molchaniia' drevnei Rusi (o sbornike trudov F. Dzh. Tomsona), *Russia Mediaevalis* 10 (2001): 262–70.

117. This is a very preliminary catalogue, which I have just started to compile and I hope to expand in the future.

118. Athanasios Papadopoulos-Kerameus, *Hierosolymitikē Bibliothēkē*, 5 vols. (Saint Petersburg, 1897; repr. Brussels: Culture et Civilisation, 1963), 3:125.

119. Arkhimandrit Vladimir, *Sistematicheskoe opisanie rukopisei Moskovskoi sinodal'noi biblioteki* (Moscow: Sinodal'naia tipografia, 1894), p. 383.

120. Vladimir, *Sistematicheskoe opisanie*, p. 651.

121. André Jacob, "Les Euchologues du fonds Barberini grec de la Bibliothèque Vaticane," *Didascalia* 4 (1974): 131–222 (p. 180).

122. Jacob, "Les Euchologues," p. 193.

123. Henry Stevenson, *Codices manuscripti Palatini Graeci Bibliothecae Vaticanae* (Rome: Ex Typographeo Vaticano, 1895), p. 223.

124. Robert Devreesse, *Codices Vaticani Graeci*, vol. 2, *Codices 330–603* (Vatican City: Biblioteca Apostolica Vaticana, 1937), p. 21.

125. Robert Devreesse, *Codices Vaticani Graeci*, vol. 3, *Codices 604–833* (Vatican City: Biblioteca Apostolica Vaticana, 1950), p. 406.

126. Cyrus Giannelli, *Codices Vaticani Graeci*, vol. 4, *Codices 1485–1683* (Vatican City: Biblioteca Apostolica Vaticana, 1950), p. 106.

127. Printed partially in Gorskii and Nevostruev, *Opisanie slavianskikh rukopisei*, pp. 181–84.

128. Gorskii and Nevostruev, *Opisanie slavianskikh rukopisei*, pp. 55–56.

Contributors

Dimiter G. Angelov is University Research Fellow and Lecturer of Byzantine History at the University of Birmingham.

John W. Barker is Professor Emeritus of History at the University of Wisconsin-Madison.

Angeliki E. Laiou was Dumbarton Oaks Professor of Byzantine History at Harvard University.

Tom Papademetriou is Assistant Professor of History at The Richard Stockton College of New Jersey.

Günter Prinzing is Professor of Byzantine History at Johannes Gutenberg-Universität, Mainz.

Philip Slavin is Postdoctoral Associate at the Economic Growth Center, Yale University.

Kostis Smyrlis is Assistant Professor of History at New York University.

Alkmini Stavridou-Zafraka is Professor of Byzantine History at the Aristotelian University of Thessaloniki.

Index

Typeset in 10/13 New Baskerville
Designed and composed by Heather M. Padgen
Manufactured by Sheridan Books, Inc.

Medieval Institute Publications
College of Arts and Sciences
Western Michigan University
1903 W. Michigan Avenue
Kalamazoo, MI 49008-5432
http://www.wmich.edu/medieval/mip

 Western Michigan University